CHARLEY'S WAR

17 October 1916 – 21 February 1917

Llyfrgelloedd Caerdydd
www.caerdydd.gov.uk/llyfrgelloedd
Cardiff Libraries
www.cardiff.gov.uk/libraries

D1420836

CHARLEY'S WAR: 17 October 1916 – 21 February 1917
ISBN 1 84576 270 3
ISBN-13 9781845762704

Published by
Titan Books
A division of Titan Publishing Group Ltd
144 Southwark Street
London SE1 0UP

Charley's War is © 2006 Egmont Magazines Ltd. All rights reserved. No portion of this book may be reproduced or transmitted, in any form or by any means, without the express written permission of the publisher.

A CIP catalogue record for this title is available from the British Library.

This edition first published: October 2006
2 4 6 8 10 9 7 5 3 1

Printed in Italy.

Also available from Titan Books:
Charley's War: 2 June 1916 – 1 August 1916 (ISBN: 1 84023 627 2)
Charley's War: 1 August 1916 – 17 October 1916 (ISBN: 1 84023 929 8)

Grateful thanks to Pat Mills, Matt Smith and Jon Oliver at *2000 AD*, Trucie Henderson, Neil Emery and Yvonne Oliver for their help and support in the production of this book.

Cover photo used by permission of the Imperial War Museum, London (Q-771).
Poppy artwork © 2005 Trucie Henderson.
Photo credits: Page 4: Joe Colquhoun photograph © IPC.
Page 6: *The Nations at War* (New York, 1917).
Pages 7 & 9: *The Great World War: A History* (Gresham Publishing Company, five volumes 1915-1917).
Pages 7-8: *Collier's New Photographic History of the World's War* (New York, 1918).

Strip commentary © 2006 Pat Mills.
'Shock and Awe' © 2006 Steve White.
Joe Colquhoun interview © 1982 Lew Stringer/*Fantasy Express*.

What did you think of this book? We love to hear from our readers.
Please email us at: readerfeedback@titanemail.com, or write to us
at the above address.

Much of the comic strip material used by Titan in this edition is exceedingly rare.
As such, we hope that readers appreciate that the quality of the materials can be variable.

www.titanbooks.com

CHARLEY'S WAR

17 October 1916 – 21 February 1917

PAT MILLS
JOE COLQUHOUN

JOE COLQUHOUN IN CONVERSATION

by Stephen Oldman

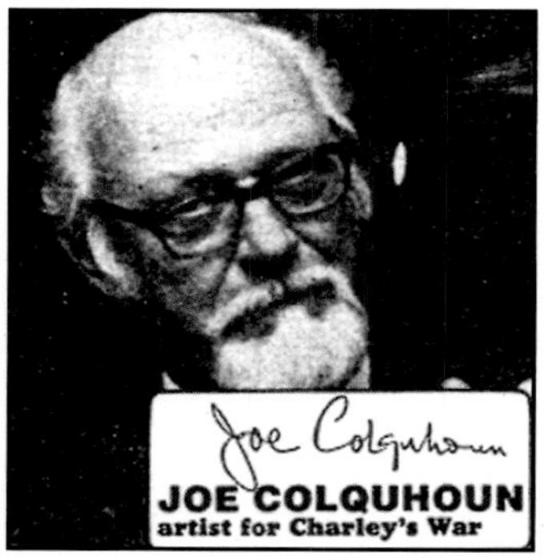
Joe Colquhoun
JOE COLQUHOUN
artist for Charley's War

The *Charley's War* artist was notoriously retiring, to the extent that it is believed that only one interview with him exists, conducted by Stephen Oldman in 1982 for the fanzine *Fantasy Express*. The following excerpt is drawn from that interview, with the kind permission of Lew Stringer.

How did you enter the comics field?

I'd always wanted to draw; even as a kid, I'd always wanted to be a comic artist – ever since I was old enough to pick up a pencil – so of course, I spent a lot of my early life drawing alone. I drew in an old ledger book; I would draw stories, just make them up, mainly in the adventure line – desert island stuff, war… I suppose it's stood me in good stead for what was to come! I was brought up on the usual diet – most kids were then: *Comic Cuts*; The 'Tu'penny Bloods'; *Magnet*; *Champion*; *Triumph*; *Wizard* and *Hotspur*, which were all prose stories – and well-written, for what you paid – with one-off illustrations. I always remember a chap called Simmons in *Champion* and *Triumph*, and a chap called Chapman, who stood out to me as very good artists.

Kids who could draw were often lionised at school and one got a false sense of one's capabilities at the time, because there was no competition. Though I was into comic strip in a minor form, it was never really my intention to be an artist. The war was on the horizon anyway, and we didn't think much about the future, to be honest. I got a place at Kingston-upon-Thames art school about halfway through the war; I did a stint there and then joined the navy, which I was in until 1947, when I went back to Kingston and did a more prolonged course in book illustration: this knocked the rough edges off my work.

I still had a hankering to work in the comic strip field, but it was very limited at the time. *Eagle* had just started publication, but at my present stage of development I knew I hadn't a hope of getting in there… then, suddenly, I saw an advert in a trade magazine, asking for samples for a new independent comics publishing project, and I jumped at this with alacrity! I met with a couple of ex-GIs who seemed pleased with the samples I had from art school though, as I later found out from the fees they paid, they'd be lucky to get anybody. They paid the princely sum of £1.50 per page!

Our work was crude and rushed – it had to be; the printing was atrocious and although we had a foothold in the market, we'd rarely see our work in print. The very first publication I saw my own work in gave me the most euphoric feeling I ever had: it's like riding a bike, or having your first woman, I guess – never to be repeated. We were doing just one-off stories, covering war, space, sport – very American-orientated, very well written, and all done by the Yanks. I was there for seven or eight months and certainly never earned a fortune, though I did learn speed and a certain amount of slickness. However, the general consensus was that this outfit wasn't going anywhere, and I hadn't been paid for ages. I'd just got married and things were pretty grim.

I managed to get an interview with the editor of *Eagle*, and showed him what I could salvage from the Americans… and although he was very compassionate, it obviously wasn't quite what they were looking for. He said, "Why don't you go across to Amalgamated Press? They've just started a comic called *Lion*." *Lion* was a little more downmarket than *Eagle* but I saw a nice chap there, called Stan Boddington.

He mentioned something about artists writing scripts, and I said, "Of course I do that as well," (though, in truth, I'd never done any in my life). His ears pricked up and he sent me away to write an adventure strip. Unfortunately – with me being influenced by the American writers I'd worked with – I wrote a story set in the Pacific, which had a very illogical beginning, rambling on and on into a very chaotic climax. AP were unimpressed, but we thrashed it out and they condensed it down to a half-decent four-page story.

AP then promptly relegated me to working on *Champion*, which still consisted mainly of illustrated prose stories, though they did have a two-page centre-spread. They got me to write and draw this two-pages-per-episode epic, called *Legionnaire Terry's Desert Quest*, which was all very much my own work, with very little interference from anyone. It became very much the basis for my scriptwriting experience.

Who were your artistic influences in those days?

The artist who most influenced me in those days was good old Alex Raymond, of *Rip Kirby* fame. His distinctive style; his ratio of black to white; his economy; his minimal use of cross-hatching – he was the quintessence of what I would be happy to emulate, and his influence stayed with me for a very long time, until I eventually developed my own style. If his influence is still visible in my work, I'll be bloody happy!

Have the weekly schedules caused you many problems?

From the beginning, yes; serialisation is one of the world's worst ways to make a living. Deadlines and pressure can become pretty punitive from time to time. The worst is trying to get ahead for a holiday, and up comes bloody Easter, and the office are on the phone saying, "You have to gain four days." When you're working six to seven days a week, its nearly impossible, but you do it somehow. There were periods when I was a bit more ambitious, or needed to earn a bit more money, so I took on the Annual jobs as well, and even though you could be more slapdash, it was still very much a dash. I now try to take on as little work as possible and still remain solvent! I try to work Monday to

Friday, 9am to 6pm, but it all depends. If there's a cast of thousands in Charley, or the 15th Ablutions are going over the top, it can take a hell of a lot longer.

Does your attitude to the work change with each job you do?

I can say – with a certain amount of satisfaction – that I've done my very best in every job I've done. You know there's a readership out there somewhere. so you want to do the best you can for your own personal pride, as well as to justify your wages. Of course, bad scripts have a very depressing effect; I feel happier if I know I have a rapport with the author, even if I have never met the guy. I was least interested in my own work when I was on *Buster*. I enjoyed 'Zarga' very much but it was relatively short-lived, and I was then relegated to childish material such as 'The Ski-Board Squad' and 'The Runaway Robinsons' – a *Little Orphan Annie*-type story which wasn't my thing. It wasn't the author's fault; it just wasn't my scene at all.

I think I've always put more into my work than my colleagues; they are wise, and have learnt the economy of line. Omission is always more difficult than overworking. I think my main failing is that I put in everything AND the kitchen sink. Most of it gets lost in the printing as well, so in effect it's a waste of time, and as time is money in this game, I'm a bit of a mug, really… but the leopard cannot change his spots.

In the '60s, your work was published alongside the greats – Eric Bradbury, Mike Western and Geoff Campion; were you aware of them?

No, because until very recently, IPC insisted on absolute anonymity – I mean even if you signed at the bottom of the page because of sheer pride in your work, they whited it out. We were anonymous until recently, when *Battle* put the credits up; I gradually got to know who the various artists were, if only by reputation, and formed a few opinions. I wasn't familiar with Western's work in the '60s, but I thought Bradbury, Lawrence and Campion were excellent.

You've worked on many scripts, but are there any you would have liked to have done more on?

That's easy – 'Football Family Robinson' was cut off in its prime; even though it was football, it was done with tongue-in-cheek, ribald humour, and offered some good characterisations of the whole family. The saneness of it, really – plus it had a good author: Tom Tully. Another was 'Cap'n Codsmouth', my first ever slapstick comedy strip… that I was quite pleased with, actually. I also wrote the script, which was the first I'd done since I packed in *Roy of the Rovers*. Again, it was cut off in its prime, I think. The only other one is 'Zarga', and the rest, I think, had reached saturation point where I was happy to move on.

Obviously, you have a leaning toward humour. Do you have a favourite humour artist?

Yes – Nobby Clark, who drew in *Tiger*. I also believe he did 'Butlers Diary'. He had a smooth, clean, flowing line and drew amiable little characters – but also drew stunning little dolly-birds when they were allowed! The other characters he did were 'Wild Bill Hiccup', and a WW2 pilot in the Luftwaffe called 'Messy Schmidt' – I thought he was an absolute scream! I would like to do more humour work; I like *Charley's War*, but it can be a sombre subject and doing it seven days a week can be a little depressing. It would be nice if I could find the time to do another 'Cap'n Codsmouth', or 'The Goodies', to relieve the tension once in a while.

Charley's War is considered by its fans – and professionals in the business – to be the best strip in Britain at the moment; how do you feel about that?

First of all, let me say how flattered and surprised I am that its been talked about like that by so many upmarket intellectuals; I was astounded when one learned professor said, "It stands equal with *All Quiet on the Western Front* as a social document." That seems a bit high-flying for me, to be honest, but I'm beginning to understand it, in a way. I think that's due to the inspiration and dedication of Pat Mills, which I think has really rubbed off on me. I don't want to let him down and again, I'm very interested in the subject, even though it can depress me and is very emotive. In particular – though you will find it hard to believe – re-reading the sequence at the end of the Somme left me almost in tears.

When I was first asked to take on *Charley's War*, I said, "My God, how can you take as something as static and non-moving as trench warfare and make any kind of subject matter for a script?" Dave Hunt, the editor at the time, said, "Don't worry – we've got a great author! He'll pull it off!" I'd never met or even heard of Pat, so I was still very sceptical, but as the strip developed, I began to realise that we were really on to something – and it seemed to catch on. I've been very dedicated to the detail in the trenches and most of the stories are drawn from factual history, which leads to a certain amount of authenticity that's lacking in the more 'blood-and-guts' World War Two stories.

Finally – and this is only my own opinion – *Charley's War* illustrates a period that was already dying when we began the strip; a time when words like 'honour', 'duty' and 'patriotism' actually meant something. I believe that when reading this epic, kids today will have a sneaking – almost atavistic – feeling that in this sick and rather selfish world, where violence and amorality seem to pay dividends, they might actually be missing out on something. It sounds very pretentious… but just think about it. ✢

CHARLEY BOURNE, RETURNING HOME FROM FRANCE ON CONVALESCENT LEAVE, WAS AMONG THE SURVIVORS AND GAVE A HELPING HAND TO OTHERS IN NEED.

WE'VE GOT YOU, CHUM! WELCOME ABOARD!

WRITER: P. MILLS
ARTIST: J. COLQUHOUN
LETTERER: M. PETERS

SHOCK & AWE

The Bombing of Britain in the Great War

by Steve White

ABOVE: A zeppelin overflies its battleship group.

People tend to think of zeppelins in one of two ways: as great airborne luxury liners of the sky… or dark, menacing, droning monsters spilling death from above. In Britain between 1914 and 1918, the latter was definitely the more prevalent preconception.

Germany had become synonymous with the building of airships prior to the outbreak of war, particularly under the auspices of Ferdinand von Zeppelin – the man whose name became forever associated with these vessels.

The strategic value of the airship had already been considered even before fighting had begun. It was well known that the UK was in range of the German airships, as they had been used as passenger carriers by what could be considered the world's first commercial airline: Deutsche Luftschifffahrts-AG (DELAG). However, the Germans were keen exponents of developing the military potential of zeppelins as well. The army, having six airships at its disposal, was soon pressing them into action following the invasion of Belgium in 1914, bombing Liège and Antwerp. But the raids took place in daylight and the zeppelins suffered accordingly: two were shot down, another so badly damaged it had to make a forced landing near Cologne, and another captured by the French. Hardly the most auspicious start to operations.

Meanwhile, the German Navy remained keen on the use of airships, even though, in 1914, it only had a single zeppelin. However, the Navy saw the airship as an excellent scouting and reconnaissance platform, which could replace the far more expensive and complicated light cruiser warships generally employed in the task. In this mission, it succeeded admirably, conducting approximately 1,200 flights over the North and Baltic Seas, many of which served to direct German warships against their British counterparts.

The German Naval Air Service were also keen on the use of zeppelins as bombers. However, the German Kaiser, Wilhelm II, was only convinced to use them in this capacity after attacks on Germany by French bombers. Permission was given for attacks on Britain to start in January 1915, with the first raid getting underway on the 19th. Two zeppelins targeted Great Yarmouth, Kings Lynn, Sheringham and their surrounding towns, dropping twenty-four high explosive and incendiary bombs. Four people were killed and sixteen injured in what is considered to be the first ever aerial bombardment of civilians, but material damage was light. However, media reaction and public fear – as is so often the case – proved a far more potent weapon for the Germans.

The raids continued, with a further nineteen sorties

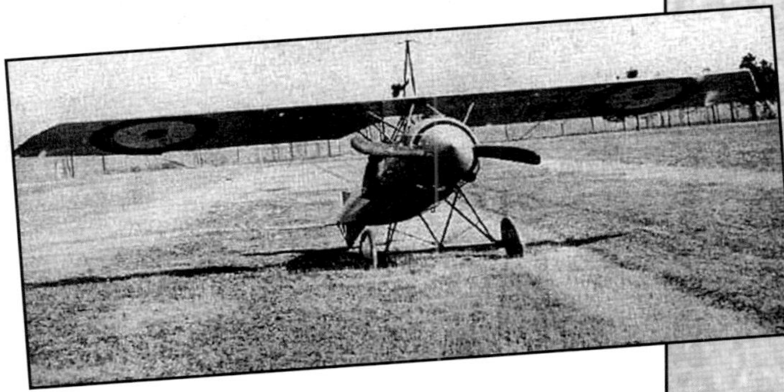

throughout the year including, on 8 September, the first raid on London, during which one zeppelin, *L.13*, penetrated to the very centre of the city. By the end of the year, the thirty-seven tons of bombs dropped in the raids had left 181 people dead and 455 injured. *L.13*'s raid alone had caused half a million pounds' worth of damage to London.

But the raiders didn't have it all their own way. On the night of 6 June, Flight Sub-Lieutenant Rex Warneford of the Royal Naval Air Service was flying a stripped-down version of the French Morane-Saulnier 'Parasol' aircraft from Furnes, in France. His intended mission was an attack on the zeppelin sheds at Evere, just north of Brussels, in German-occupied Belgium. However, as he passed Bruges, he spotted zeppelin *LZ.37*, returning from a bombing attack on London. As he approached it, machine-gun fire from the airship drove Warneford away, but he manoeuvred into position and opened fire with his hand-held .303 rifle. Achieving no visible results, Warneford was now fighting to keep up with the far more powerful airship. Finally, after a pursuit lasting two hours, he nursed and bullied the 'Parasol' into a position only 150 feet above the zeppelin and proceeded to drop the six firebombs the aircraft was carrying.

One of the bombs ignited the volatile hydrogen gas inside the airship, causing a violent explosion that flipped the little 'Parasol' onto its back. As Warneford regained control, the burning remains of *LZ.37* crashed onto the convent of Saint Elizabeth outside of Ghent. All but one of the twenty-eight crewmen were killed whilst, on the ground, one nun was killed and several others badly burnt.

Meanwhile, a ruptured fuel line had forced Warneford to land his 'Parasol' in an open field in German-held territory – still in complete darkness. Using a handkerchief and a cigarette holder, he managed to repair the damaged pipe and restart the engine. By 10.30am he was back in Furnes and being fêted as a hero. King George V immediately awarded him a Victoria Cross, whilst the French bestowed upon him the Knight's Cross of the Legion d'Honneur. Sadly, however, Warneford died ten days later in a flying accident.

Warneford's efforts were the exception that tended to prove the rule in 1915. Britain remained without any effective countermeasures to the zeppelin menace. Their operating height put them beyond the effective reach of most aircraft, whose ammunition remained inadequate for destroying the airships anyway. Initially, air defence was split between both the Army and the Royal Navy, but, in February 1916, sole command was given to the Army, who began increasing the number of guns and searchlights in use. Many of the cannons were artillery pieces converted for anti-aircraft roles whilst the police had first manned the searchlights. However, the army took control after nervous policemen had triggered alerts when they mistook low clouds for airships.

The zeppelins conducted twenty-three raids throughout 1916, during which 125 tons of bombs were dropped, killing 293 people and injuring 691. Despite the increase in casualties, the damage remained relatively light. The British were helped by the relatively primitive state of the equipment on the zeppelins, which made accurate navigation and bombing difficult, and the airships were further hampered by the imposition of a blackout in London. Only ten percent of the bombs dropped are believed to have hit their intended target. The improvement in anti-aircraft defences also forced the airships to operate at higher altitudes – from 6,000 feet to over 12,000 feet.

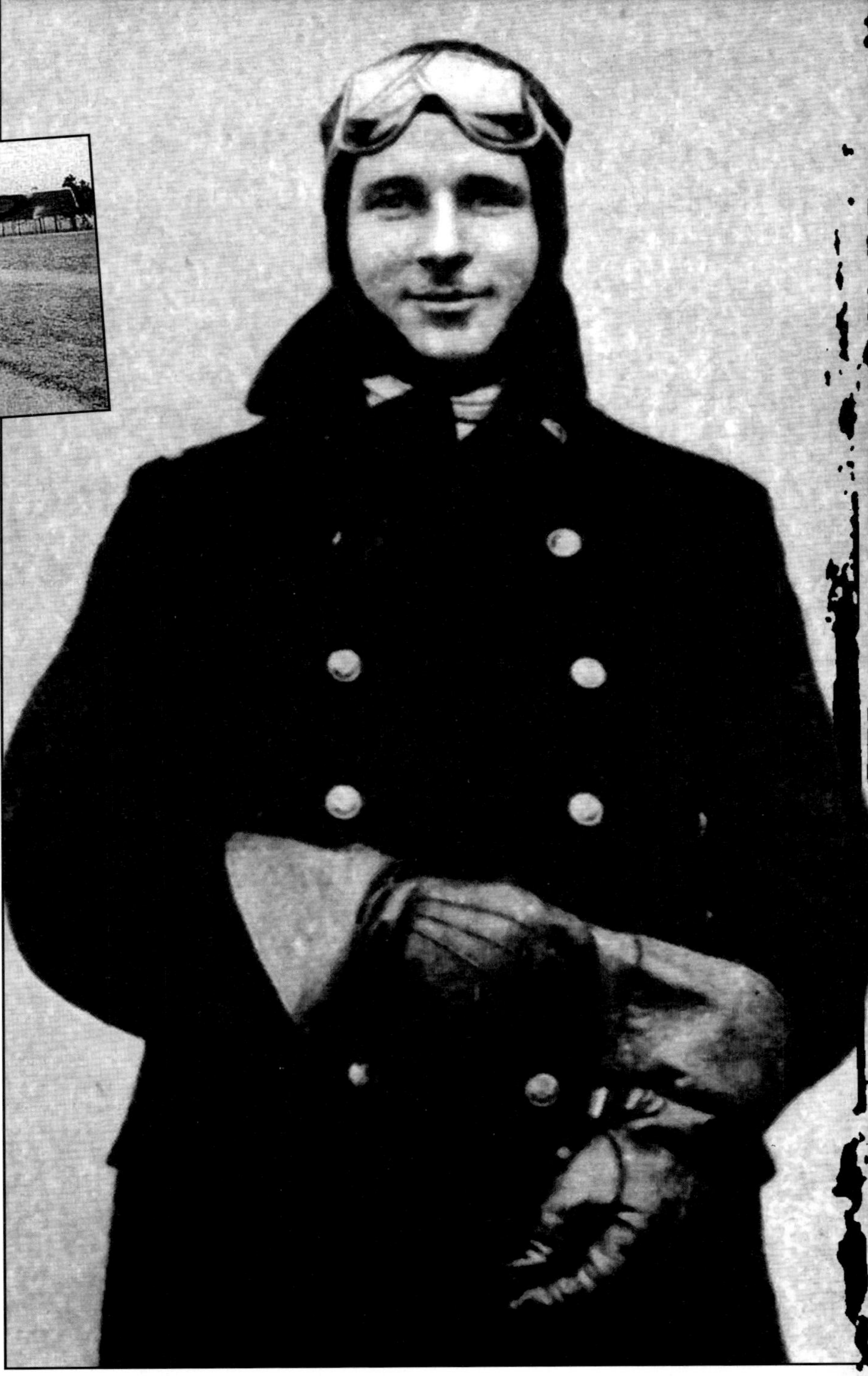

ABOVE LEFT: The Morane-Saulnier 'Parasol' aircraft.

ABOVE: Flight Sub-Lieutenant Rex Warneford, VC.

This did nothing to improve crew comfort in the freezing, thinner air. To avoid observers on the ground, the airships also favoured operating above the clouds; again, this did little to aid accurate bombing.

1916 had got off to a bad start for the airships, with four being lost whilst conducting bombing raids on the Western Front during the Battle of Verdun. However, by now, the Germans had two generations of airships in service. Von Zeppelin's newest versions were far larger and more powerful than before. However, they were only slightly faster and could not operate any higher.

But any improvements were countered by British advances. In the middle of the year, RFC (Royal Flying Corps) aircraft were carrying a mix of three new types of ammunition, all named after their inventors; the 'Pomeroy' and the 'Brock' high-explosive types, and the 'Buckingham' incendiary round. Individually, these rounds were ineffective but combined, they were lethal; the explosive rounds punctured the skin of the airship, allowing the incendiary rounds to blast through, ignite the gas inside the zeppelin and set fire to it – the German crews' worst nightmare.

As late summer gave way to autumn there was a surge in the tempo of the raids, with attacks on 31 July, then 2 and 8 August, then 24 August. 2 September then saw the largest zeppelin raid of the war, with twelve German Navy and four Army airships crossing into England, packing a total bomb load of thirty-two tons.

Zeppelin *SL.11*, an older, wooden model, was bombing the suburbs of North London when, just after 1.10am, she was illuminated by searchlights and spotted by 2nd Lieutenant William Leefe-Robinson flying an RFC BE2C scout aircraft. His aircraft's machine-guns were using the new Brock-Pomeroy ammunition mix. He was at 12,000 feet, above the airship, and dived towards it, picking up speed, passing through ineffectual friendly anti-aircraft fire from the ground and pulling up beneath the belly of the airship. He fired a full drum of ammunition into the zeppelin, but without effect. He repositioned himself and unleashed a second drum into one side but, again, without effect. Finally, he moved behind *SL.11* and from a range of as little as 500 feet opened fire again. This time, he saw a glow appear on the rear of the airship, which in seconds became a raging inferno, clearly visible across London and to the other airships in the raiding party. It crashed in Cuffley with the loss of sixteen crewmen. Leefe-Robinson became another recipient of the Victoria Cross.

The evening of September 23 saw another massed raid as a dozen Navy airships crossed the Essex coast; some bound for London, others for targets in the Midlands. *L.33* was bombing targets around Stratford and Bow, in London's East End, but was meeting stiff resistance. She was quickly illuminated by searchlights, then an anti-aircraft shell exploded inside the airship, causing severe structural damage but no fires. The loss of *SL.11* had been a blow to the morale of the zeppelin crews, but it was an old, wooden vessel – not like the more advanced metal airships used by the Navy. One of her engines was damaged and she was forced to dump much of the water ballast she carried as she began to drop at 800 feet a minute. However, *L.33* then came under attack by RFC pilot Lieutenant A.G. Brandon, who in a twenty-minute attack poured Brock-Pomeroy ammunition into the zeppelin. Damage was minimal but by then *L.33* was already heading earthwards, finally crash-landing at Little Wigborough, near Colchester in Essex. The crew jumped clear, then tried to destroy the vessel by firing flares into it. Although the zeppelin caught fire, much of it remained intact and was used by the British to improve their own relatively poor designs.

The German woes weren't over yet. *L.32*'s timid Captain, nervous about the heavy defences around London, spent his time circling to the east of the city before pressing towards his target. Suffering apparent engine trouble, the airship emerged from cloud and was immediately illuminated by searchlights. Disgorging its bombs, it turned back towards the sea in an effort to escape. However, it had been spotted by 1st Lieutenant Frederick Sowery, in a BE2C, who fired two drums of Brock-Pomeroy into the zeppelin's flank. Sowery had more success with his machine-gun fire than Brandon and *L.32*'s hydrogen ignited, the airship bursting into flames. The wreckage came down near Billericay, in Essex, with the loss of the entire crew. However, officers from the Naval Intelligence Division quickly arrived at the crash site and were able to find a copy of the German Navy's cipher book, which the Captain had taken aboard against orders – an extraordinary bit of luck for British code-breakers.

The loss of two airships left the Germans disconsolate. A raid two nights later was a much more cautious affair. However, on 1 October, another eleven-ship raid was mounted.

BELOW: The framework of a zeppelin shot down over England.

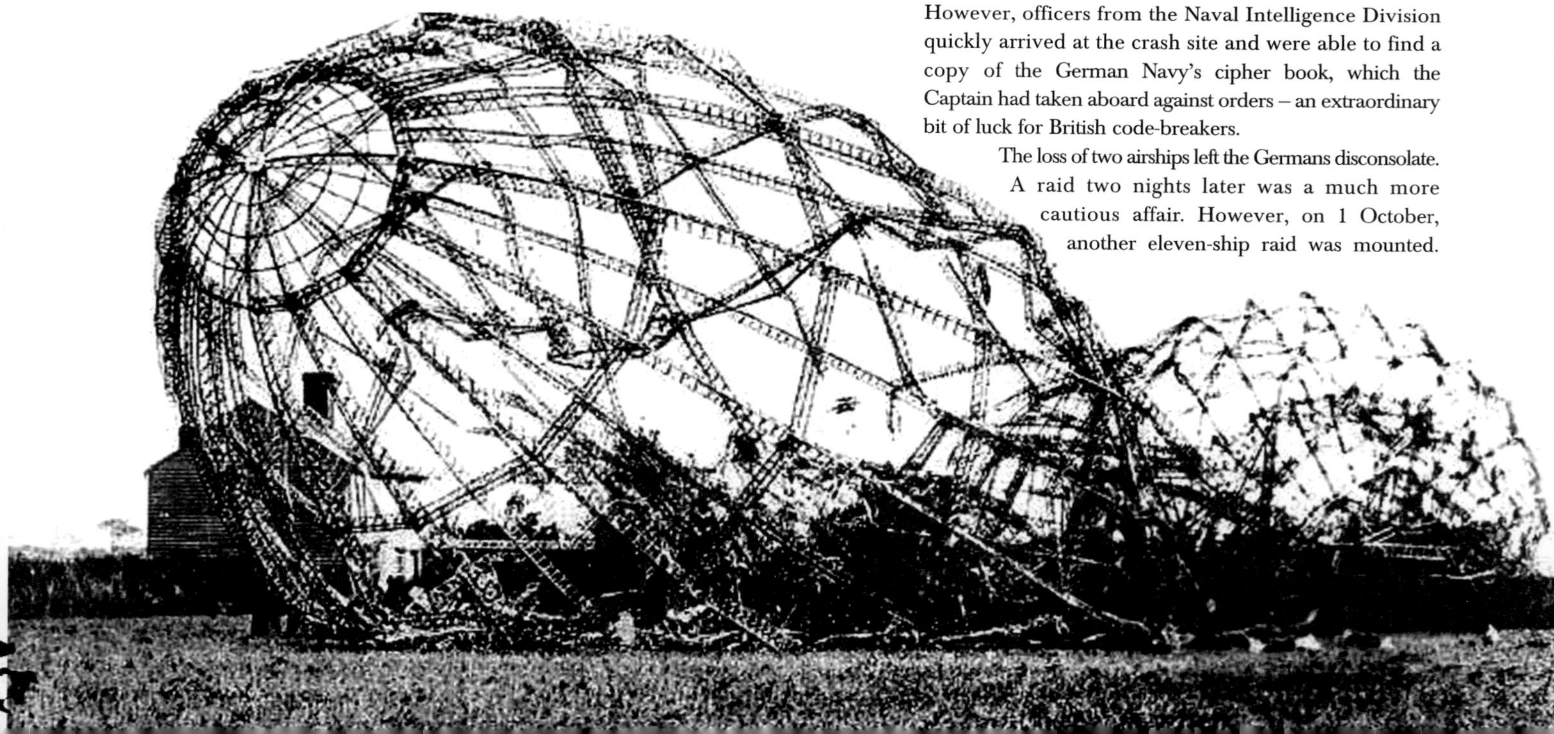

ABOVE: Two zeppelins in their hangar.

This last raid of 1916 was led by Commander Heinrich Mathy, one of the zeppelin fleet's veteran captains, and a survivor of the previous attacks. However, only two airships were given permission to attack London, including Mathy's *L.31*, but as he passed over Chelmsford, he realised the defences had already been alerted to his presence and were waiting for the Germans. *L.31* turned away, switching his engines off in the hope of fooling the gunners and searchlight operators on the ground. But as he fired up the propellers and turned back towards the city, the anti-aircraft guns opened up. Mathy dumped his bombs and turned away once again, but unbeknownst to him, 2nd Lieutenant W. J. Tempest had been closing on the airship and launched an attack against the belly of the zeppelin, despite heavy defensive fire from the Germans. A drum of Brock-Pomeroy ammunition started a fire, causing a gout of red flame to burst from *L.31*'s nose. The burning zeppelin crashed quickly to earth outside Potters Bar. Locals found Mathy lying still alive on the ground, badly burned, but he died shortly afterwards. This was the last time a German airship attacked London.

1916 was the main focus of the zeppelins' bombing efforts. Raids continued against industrial targets in Northern England, but the Germans began to rely more and more on the Gotha strategic bomber. Things reached their nadir on the night of 19 October 1917. Eleven zeppelins, a third generation of airships, conducted a 'silent raid'. These ships had been stripped of much of their defensive armament and, wherever possible, their internal structure. This meant the zeppelins could operate as high as 20,000 feet. Heading into the Midlands, the raid took the British by surprise, but things quickly started to go wrong. The extreme operating height caused altitude sickness amongst the crews – who were also freezing cold – whilst engine troubles caused by the thin air plagued

the airships. The zeppelins also found themselves at the mercy of gusting winds which blew the fleet southwards. One found itself over London where it dropped a bomb on Piccadilly, but ground mist and the blackout left the Germans milling helplessly over enemy territory.

However, the real disaster came as the Germans tried to make their way home. Lost, and fighting both the enemy and the elements, six had to take an arduous, dangerous route home across neutral Holland and not so neutral – in fact, downright aggressive – France. Amongst them was *L.55*, which set an altitude record of 24,000 feet as it attempted to clear the Western Front. When the airship finally crash-landed in Germany, many of the crew were stricken with altitude sickness and oxygen deprivation. By the morning, four others had failed to make it to safety and were still over enemy territory. As the British and French listened to radio intercepts of desperate pleas for help by the German crews, the four zeppelins were shot down one after another.

From 1917 to the end of the war in November 1918, only eleven more raids were conducted, the last on 5 August, when five zeppelins arrived over Norfolk, but failed to drop any bombs. However, one, *L.70*, was shot down by ground fire. Amongst those who were killed in the resulting crash was Commander Peter Strasser, commandant of the German Naval Airship Department. *L.70* was the last of over sixty zeppelins lost to varying causes throughout the First World War. During the fifty-one raids conducted, 557 people were killed and 1,358 injured by the 5,806 bombs dropped. The raids themselves did little to halt Britain's industrial war efforts but it has been argued that the zeppelin's effectiveness lay in their psychological impact and the diversion of aircraft and men probably better used on the Western Front. ✛

PREVIOUSLY IN *CHARLEY'S WAR*

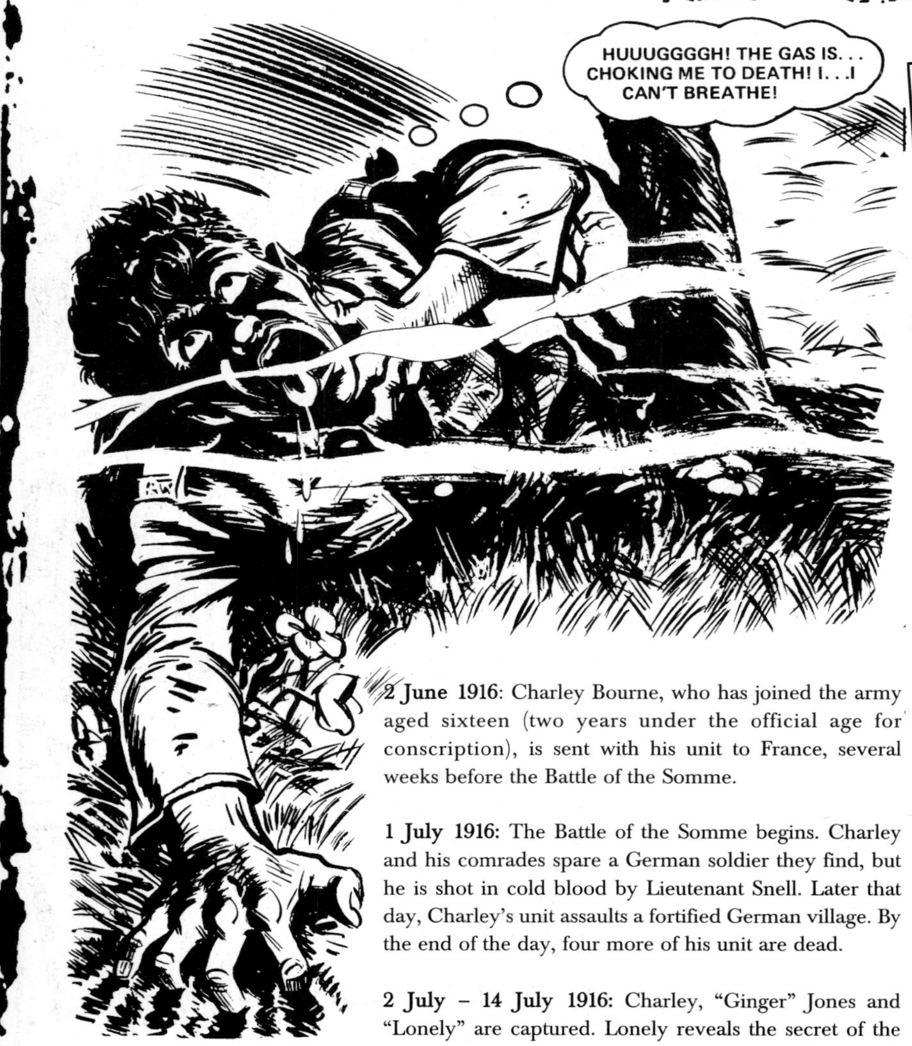
HUUUGGGGH! THE GAS IS... CHOKING ME TO DEATH! I...I CAN'T BREATHE!

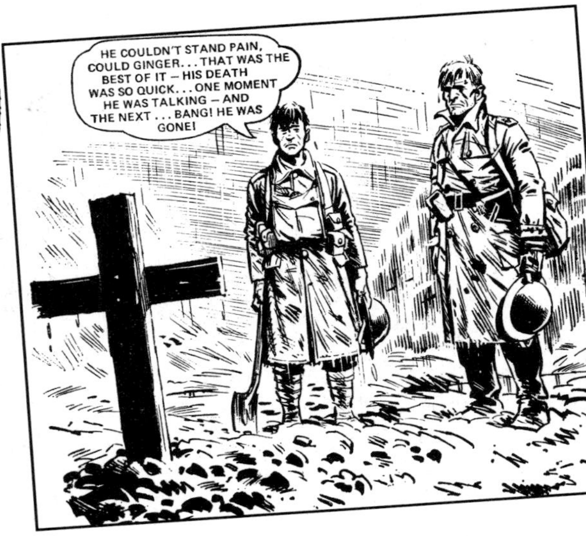
HE COULDN'T STAND PAIN, COULD GINGER... THAT WAS THE BEST OF IT – HIS DEATH WAS SO QUICK... ONE MOMENT HE WAS TALKING – AND THE NEXT... BANG! HE WAS GONE!

2 June 1916: Charley Bourne, who has joined the army aged sixteen (two years under the official age for conscription), is sent with his unit to France, several weeks before the Battle of the Somme.

1 July 1916: The Battle of the Somme begins. Charley and his comrades spare a German soldier they find, but he is shot in cold blood by Lieutenant Snell. Later that day, Charley's unit assaults a fortified German village. By the end of the day, four more of his unit are dead.

2 July – 14 July 1916: Charley, "Ginger" Jones and "Lonely" are captured. Lonely reveals the secret of the "lost platoon", his old unit. During the escape, Charley inhales poison gas and becomes gravely ill.

14 July 1916: Charley, Ginger and Lonely meet a group of British cavalrymen. Lonely bravely sacrifices himself during a German attack. Eventually Charley and Ginger find their way back to their Sergeant, Tozer, who punches them both for temporarily going absent without leave.

1 August 1916: On Charley's seventeenth birthday, the British forces accidentally begin shelling their own side. Charley volunteers to be a communications runner in the hope that he can end the bombardment, but is delayed by Snell. Lieutenant Thomas orders Charley's unit to retreat, and is later arrested for cowardice.

August 1916: After a run-in with "The Beast", a vicious military policeman, Charley refuses his order to execute Lieutenant Thomas (who is killed in any case, aged twenty-two). Charley and his comrade "Weeper" are sentenced to fourteen days' punishment, strapped to the wheel of a field gun. During an air raid, The Beast attempts to leave Charley to die, but is killed himself.

September 1916: Ginger is killed by a stray shell, causing Charley to temporarily break down. Charley's unit is reinforced by tanks, and on 15 September Charley is joined by his cowardly brother-in-law, "Oiley". With the help of the tanks, Charley's unit progresses into the village of Flers. Oiley deliberately injures himself to be sent home, and Charley covers for him.

17 October, 1916: Colonel Zeiss, a new German commandant, unleashes the "Judgement Troopers". Breaking the established regulations of war, these 'dirty tricks' soldiers advance on the British lines unarmed before picking up previously concealed weapons. A vicious, frantic battle begins… ✛

ABOVE RIGHT: A devastated Charley takes his friend Ginger's remains for burial.

ABOVE LEFT: Charley feels the effects of a poison gas attack.

RIGHT: Charley is bloodied but unbowed after his punishment at the hands of "The Beast".

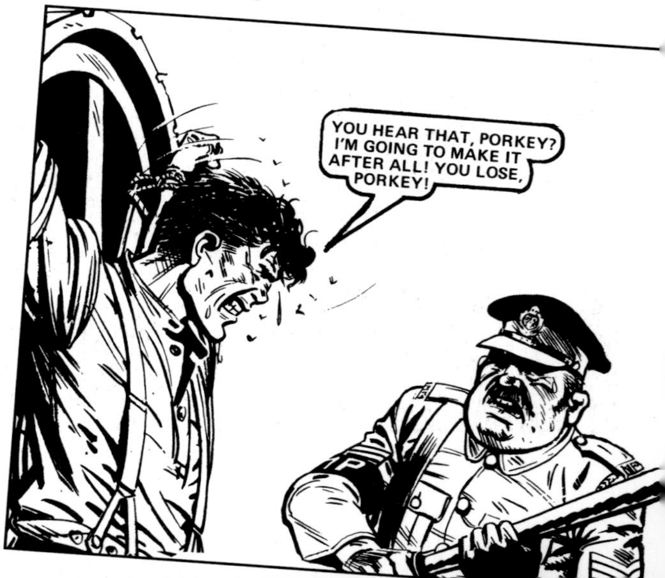
YOU HEAR THAT, PORKEY? I'M GOING TO MAKE IT AFTER ALL! YOU LOSE, PORKEY!

CHARLEY'S WAR

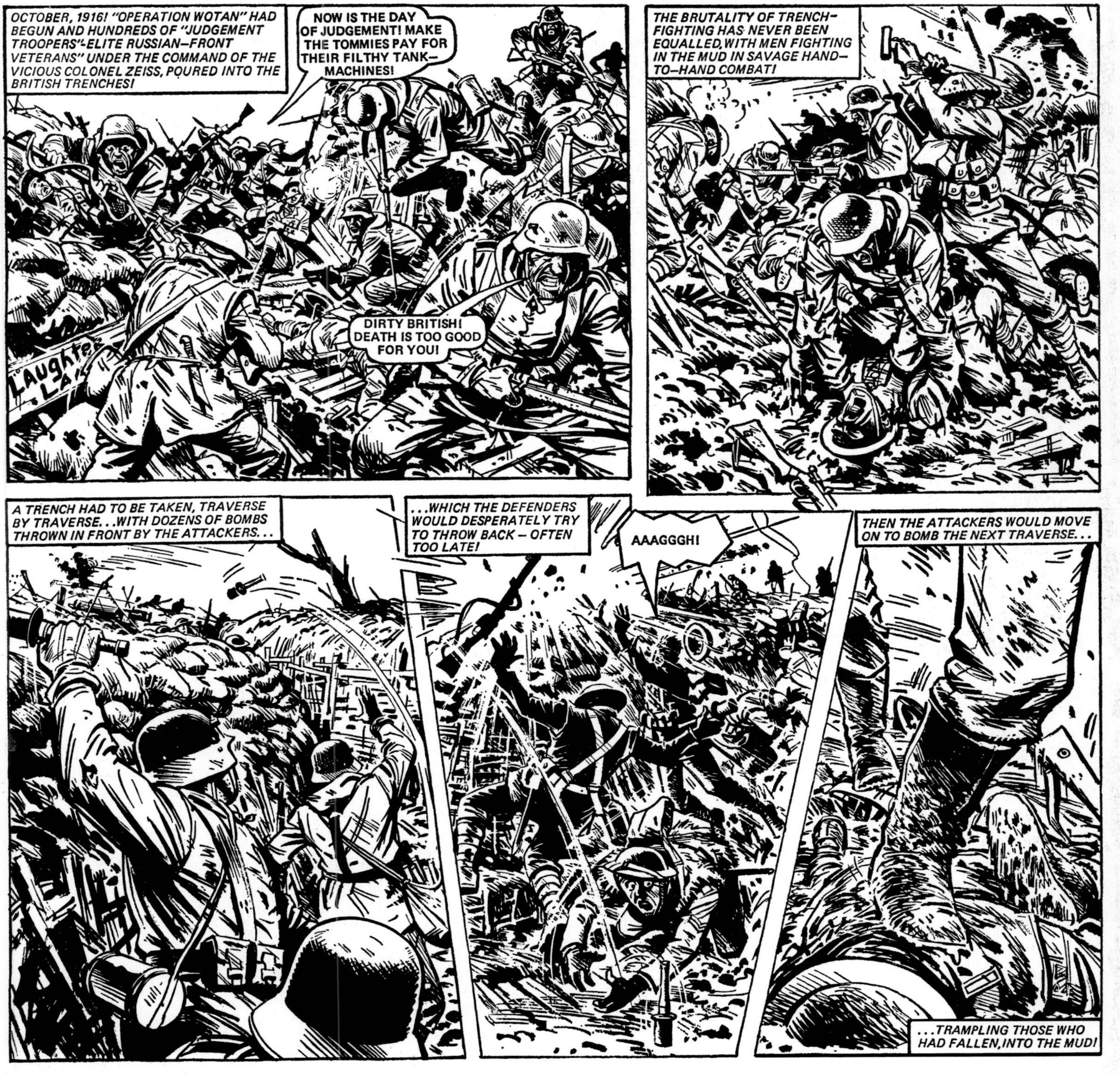
OCTOBER, 1916! "OPERATION WOTAN" HAD BEGUN AND HUNDREDS OF "JUDGEMENT TROOPERS"-ELITE RUSSIAN-FRONT VETERANS" UNDER THE COMMAND OF THE VICIOUS COLONEL ZEISS, POURED INTO THE BRITISH TRENCHES!
NOW IS THE DAY OF JUDGEMENT! MAKE THE TOMMIES PAY FOR THEIR FILTHY TANK-MACHINES!
DIRTY BRITISH! DEATH IS TOO GOOD FOR YOU!
THE BRUTALITY OF TRENCH-FIGHTING HAS NEVER BEEN EQUALLED, WITH MEN FIGHTING IN THE MUD IN SAVAGE HAND-TO-HAND COMBAT!
A TRENCH HAD TO BE TAKEN, TRAVERSE BY TRAVERSE. . .WITH DOZENS OF BOMBS THROWN IN FRONT BY THE ATTACKERS. . .
. . .WHICH THE DEFENDERS WOULD DESPERATELY TRY TO THROW BACK – OFTEN TOO LATE!
AAAGGGH!
THEN THE ATTACKERS WOULD MOVE ON TO BOMB THE NEXT TRAVERSE. . .
. . .TRAMPLING THOSE WHO HAD FALLEN, INTO THE MUD!

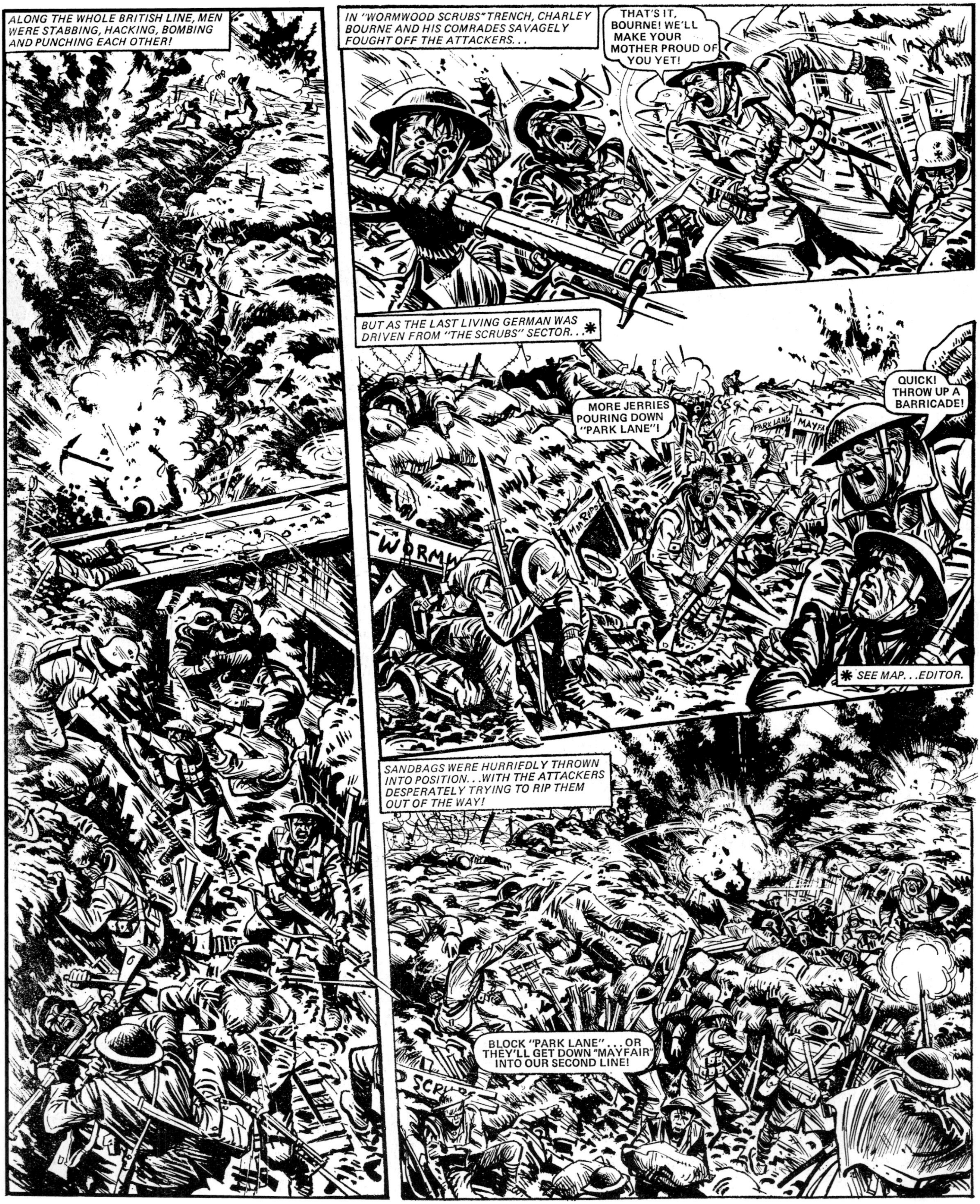

ALONG THE WHOLE BRITISH LINE, MEN WERE STABBING, HACKING, BOMBING AND PUNCHING EACH OTHER!
IN "WORMWOOD SCRUBS" TRENCH, CHARLEY BOURNE AND HIS COMRADES SAVAGELY FOUGHT OFF THE ATTACKERS...
THAT'S IT, BOURNE! WE'LL MAKE YOUR MOTHER PROUD OF YOU YET!
BUT AS THE LAST LIVING GERMAN WAS DRIVEN FROM "THE SCRUBS" SECTOR...*
MORE JERRIES POURING DOWN "PARK LANE"!
QUICK! THROW UP A BARRICADE!
* SEE MAP...EDITOR.
SANDBAGS WERE HURRIEDLY THROWN INTO POSITION...WITH THE ATTACKERS DESPERATELY TRYING TO RIP THEM OUT OF THE WAY!
BLOCK "PARK LANE"... OR THEY'LL GET DOWN "MAYFAIR" INTO OUR SECOND LINE!

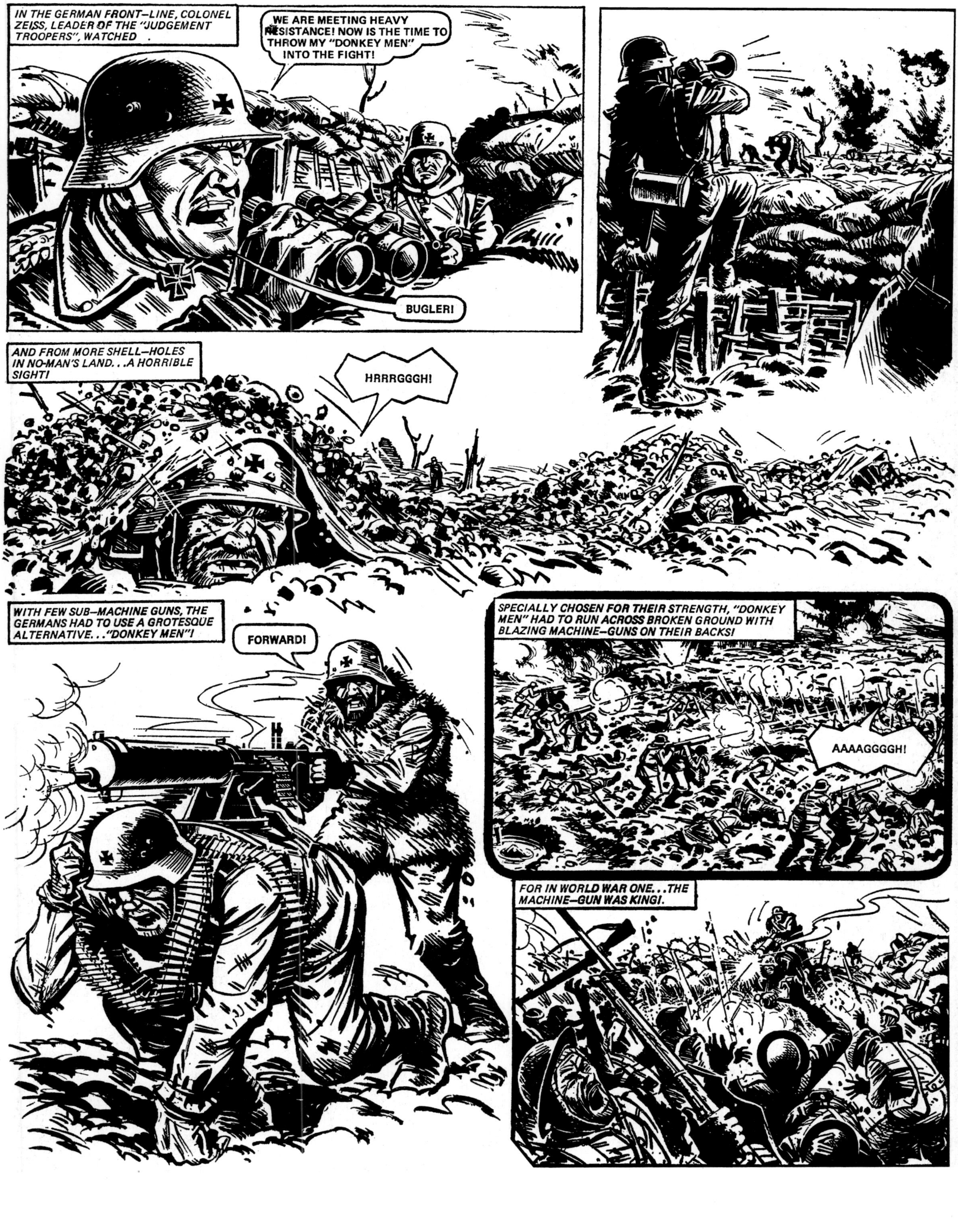
IN THE GERMAN FRONT–LINE, COLONEL ZEISS, LEADER OF THE "JUDGEMENT TROOPERS", WATCHED .
WE ARE MEETING HEAVY RESISTANCE! NOW IS THE TIME TO THROW MY "DONKEY MEN" INTO THE FIGHT!
BUGLER!
AND FROM MORE SHELL–HOLES IN NO-MAN'S LAND. . . A HORRIBLE SIGHT!
HRRRGGGH!
WITH FEW SUB–MACHINE GUNS, THE GERMANS HAD TO USE A GROTESQUE ALTERNATIVE. . . "DONKEY MEN"!
FORWARD!
SPECIALLY CHOSEN FOR THEIR STRENGTH, "DONKEY MEN" HAD TO RUN ACROSS BROKEN GROUND WITH BLAZING MACHINE–GUNS ON THEIR BACKS!
AAAAGGGGH!
FOR IN WORLD WAR ONE. . . THE MACHINE–GUN WAS KING!

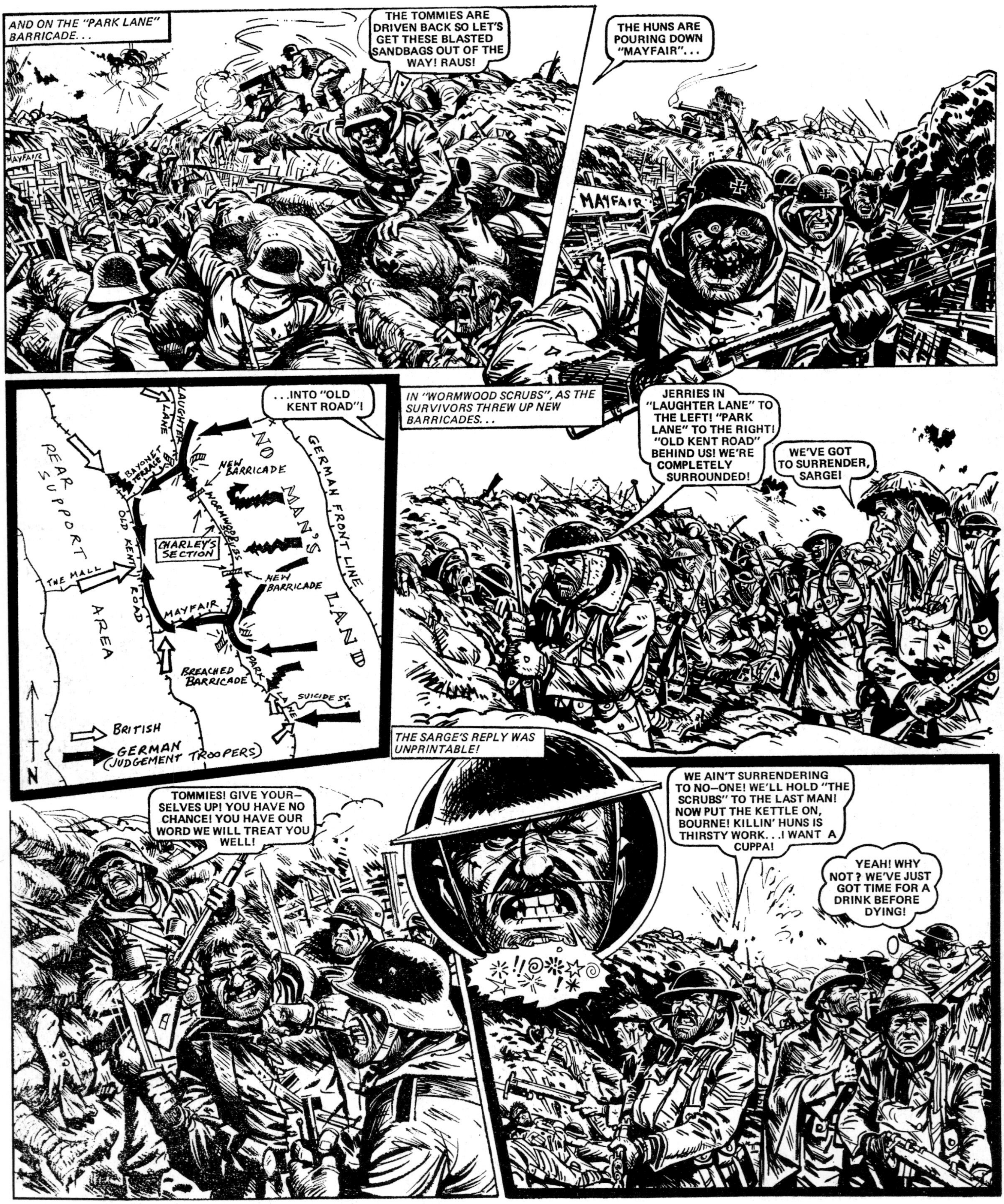

AND ON THE "PARK LANE" BARRICADE...
THE TOMMIES ARE DRIVEN BACK SO LET'S GET THESE BLASTED SANDBAGS OUT OF THE WAY! RAUS!
THE HUNS ARE POURING DOWN "MAYFAIR"...
MAYFAIR
...INTO "OLD KENT ROAD"!
LAUGHTER LANE
NO MAN'S LAND
GERMAN FRONT LINE
REAR SUPPORT AREA
BAYONET TERRACE
NEW BARRICADE
WORMWOOD SCRUBS
OLD KENT ROAD
CHARLEY'S SECTION
THE MALL
NEW BARRICADE
MAYFAIR
BREACHED BARRICADE
PARK LANE
SUICIDE ST.
BRITISH
GERMAN (JUDGEMENT TROOPERS)
N
IN "WORMWOOD SCRUBS", AS THE SURVIVORS THREW UP NEW BARRICADES...
JERRIES IN "LAUGHTER LANE" TO THE LEFT! "PARK LANE" TO THE RIGHT! "OLD KENT ROAD" BEHIND US! WE'RE COMPLETELY SURROUNDED!
WE'VE GOT TO SURRENDER, SARGE!
THE SARGE'S REPLY WAS UNPRINTABLE!
TOMMIES! GIVE YOURSELVES UP! YOU HAVE NO CHANCE! YOU HAVE OUR WORD WE WILL TREAT YOU WELL!
WE AIN'T SURRENDERING TO NO-ONE! WE'LL HOLD "THE SCRUBS" TO THE LAST MAN! NOW PUT THE KETTLE ON, BOURNE! KILLIN' HUNS IS THIRSTY WORK...I WANT A CUPPA!
YEAH! WHY NOT? WE'VE JUST GOT TIME FOR A DRINK BEFORE DYING!

CHARLEY'S WAR

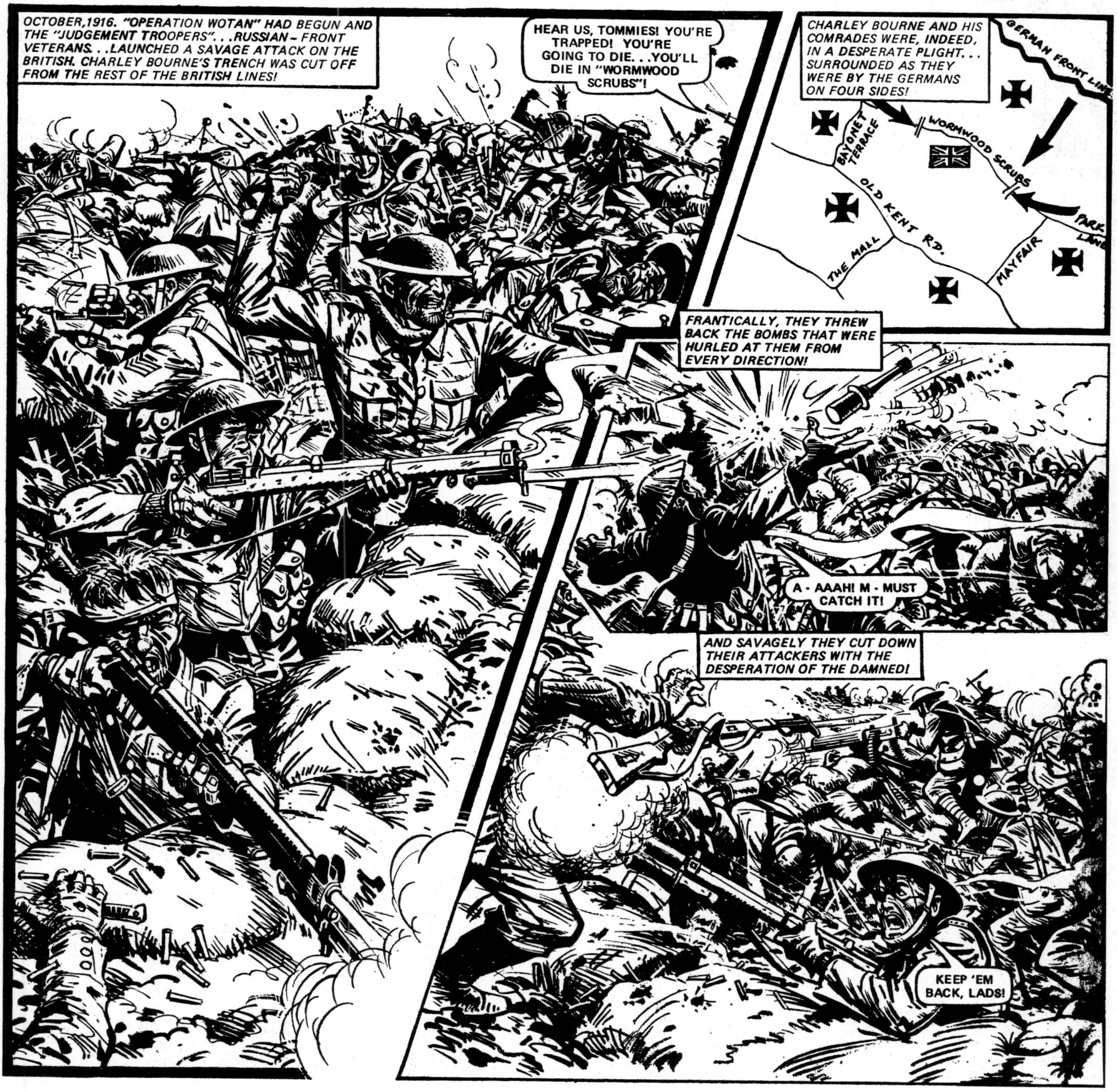

OCTOBER,1916. "OPERATION WOTAN" HAD BEGUN AND THE "JUDGEMENT TROOPERS"...RUSSIAN-FRONT VETERANS...LAUNCHED A SAVAGE ATTACK ON THE BRITISH. CHARLEY BOURNE'S TRENCH WAS CUT OFF FROM THE REST OF THE BRITISH LINES!
HEAR US, TOMMIES! YOU'RE TRAPPED! YOU'RE GOING TO DIE...YOU'LL DIE IN "WORMWOOD SCRUBS"!
CHARLEY BOURNE AND HIS COMRADES WERE, INDEED, IN A DESPERATE PLIGHT... SURROUNDED AS THEY WERE BY THE GERMANS ON FOUR SIDES!
GERMAN FRONT LINE
BAYONET TERRACE
WORMWOOD SCRUBS
OLD KENT RD.
THE MALL
MAYFAIR
PARK LANE
FRANTICALLY, THEY THREW BACK THE BOMBS THAT WERE HURLED AT THEM FROM EVERY DIRECTION!
A-AAAH! M-MUST CATCH IT!
AND SAVAGELY THEY CUT DOWN THEIR ATTACKERS WITH THE DESPERATION OF THE DAMNED!
KEEP 'EM BACK, LADS!

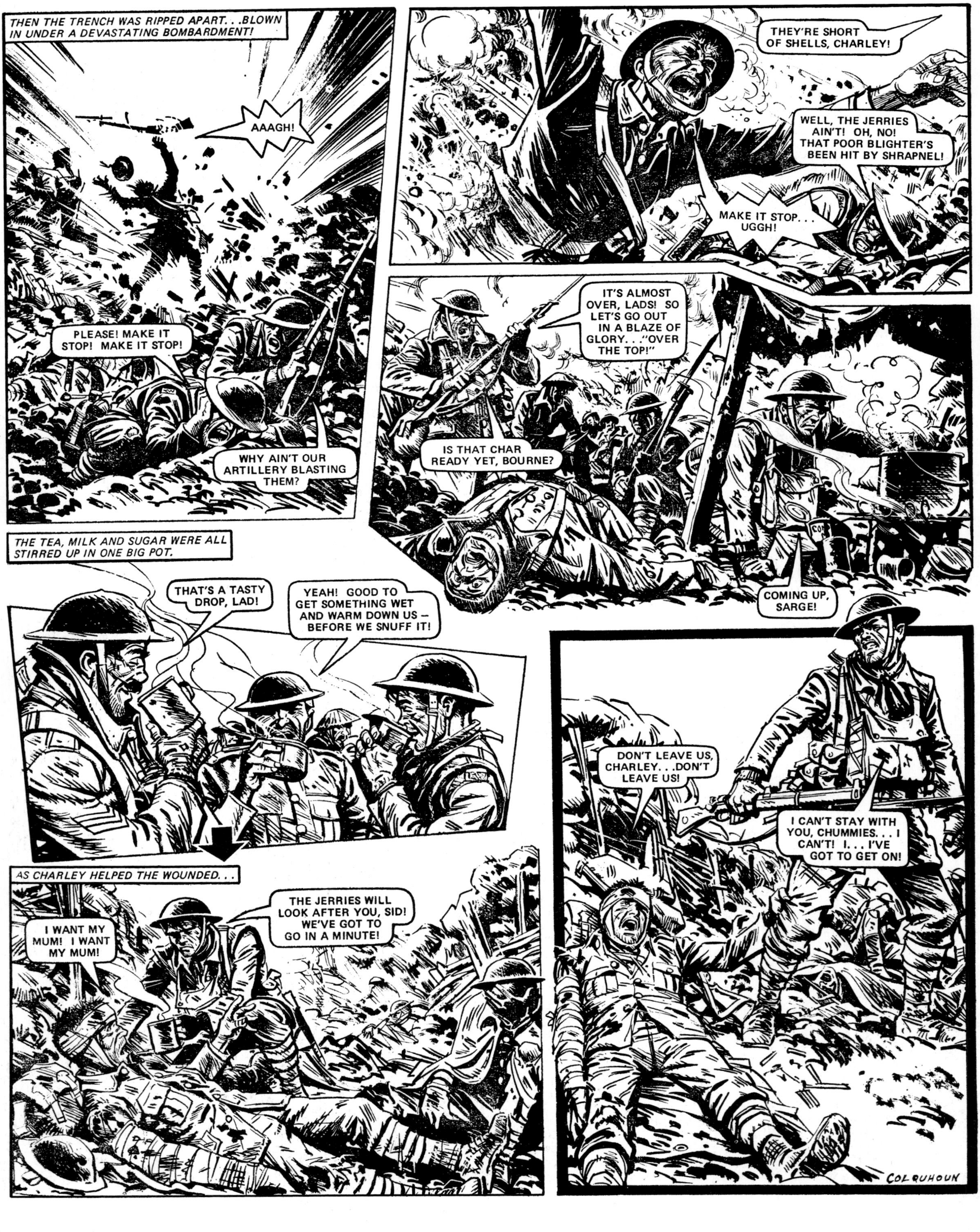
THEN THE TRENCH WAS RIPPED APART. . .BLOWN IN UNDER A DEVASTATING BOMBARDMENT!
AAAGH!
PLEASE! MAKE IT STOP! MAKE IT STOP!
WHY AIN'T OUR ARTILLERY BLASTING THEM?
THEY'RE SHORT OF SHELLS, CHARLEY!
WELL, THE JERRIES AIN'T! OH, NO! THAT POOR BLIGHTER'S BEEN HIT BY SHRAPNEL!
MAKE IT STOP. . . UGGH!
IT'S ALMOST OVER, LADS! SO LET'S GO OUT IN A BLAZE OF GLORY. . ."OVER THE TOP!"
IS THAT CHAR READY YET, BOURNE?
COMING UP, SARGE!
THE TEA, MILK AND SUGAR WERE ALL STIRRED UP IN ONE BIG POT.
THAT'S A TASTY DROP, LAD!
YEAH! GOOD TO GET SOMETHING WET AND WARM DOWN US — BEFORE WE SNUFF IT!
AS CHARLEY HELPED THE WOUNDED. . .
I WANT MY MUM! I WANT MY MUM!
THE JERRIES WILL LOOK AFTER YOU, SID! WE'VE GOT TO GO IN A MINUTE!
DON'T LEAVE US, CHARLEY. . .DON'T LEAVE US!
I CAN'T STAY WITH YOU, CHUMMIES. . . I CAN'T! I. . . I'VE GOT TO GET ON!
COLQUHOUN

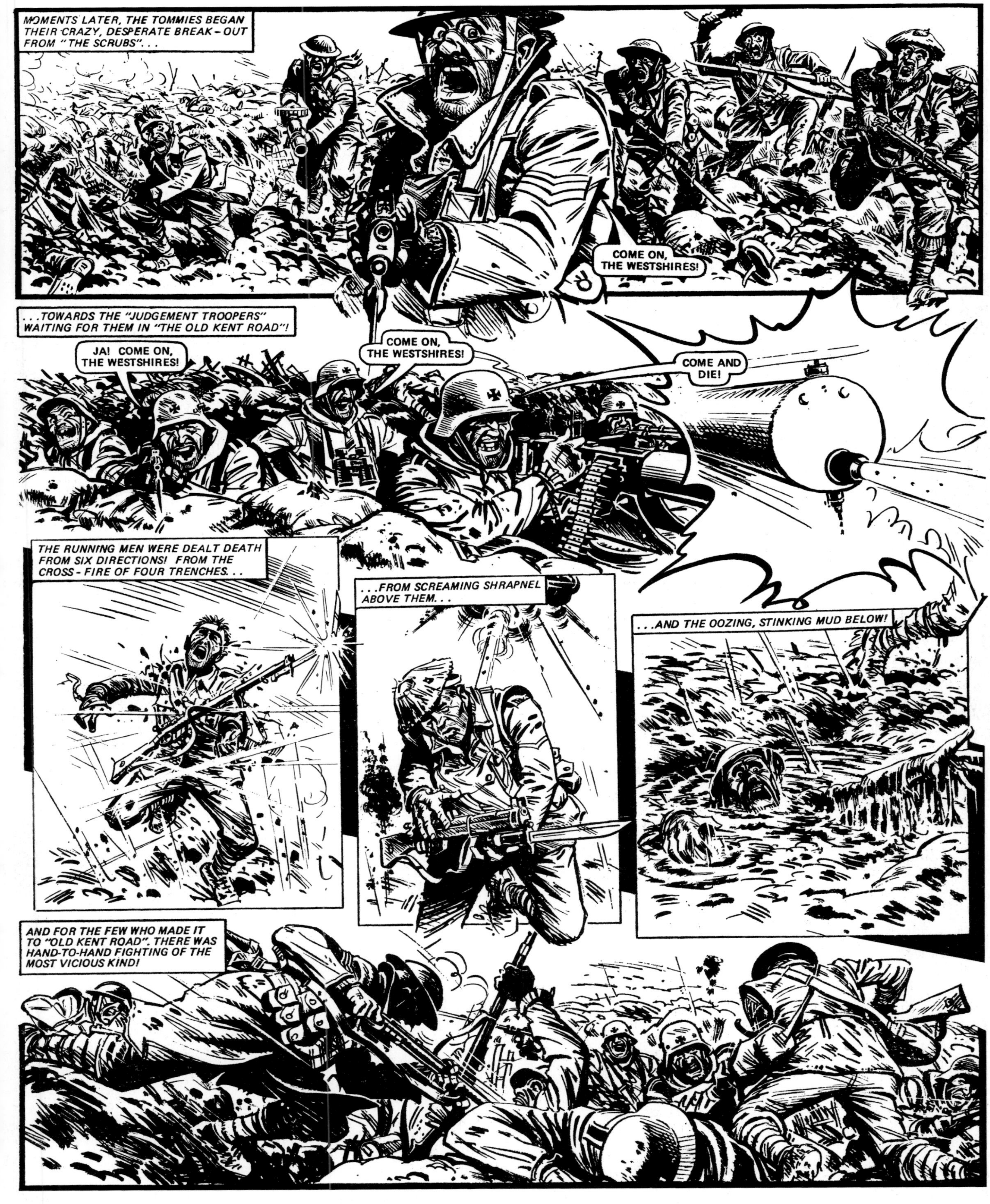
MOMENTS LATER, THE TOMMIES BEGAN THEIR CRAZY, DESPERATE BREAK-OUT FROM "THE SCRUBS"...
COME ON, THE WESTSHIRES!
...TOWARDS THE "JUDGEMENT TROOPERS" WAITING FOR THEM IN "THE OLD KENT ROAD"!
JA! COME ON, THE WESTSHIRES!
COME ON, THE WESTSHIRES!
COME AND DIE!
THE RUNNING MEN WERE DEALT DEATH FROM SIX DIRECTIONS! FROM THE CROSS-FIRE OF FOUR TRENCHES...
...FROM SCREAMING SHRAPNEL ABOVE THEM...
...AND THE OOZING, STINKING MUD BELOW!
AND FOR THE FEW WHO MADE IT TO "OLD KENT ROAD", THERE WAS HAND-TO-HAND FIGHTING OF THE MOST VICIOUS KIND!

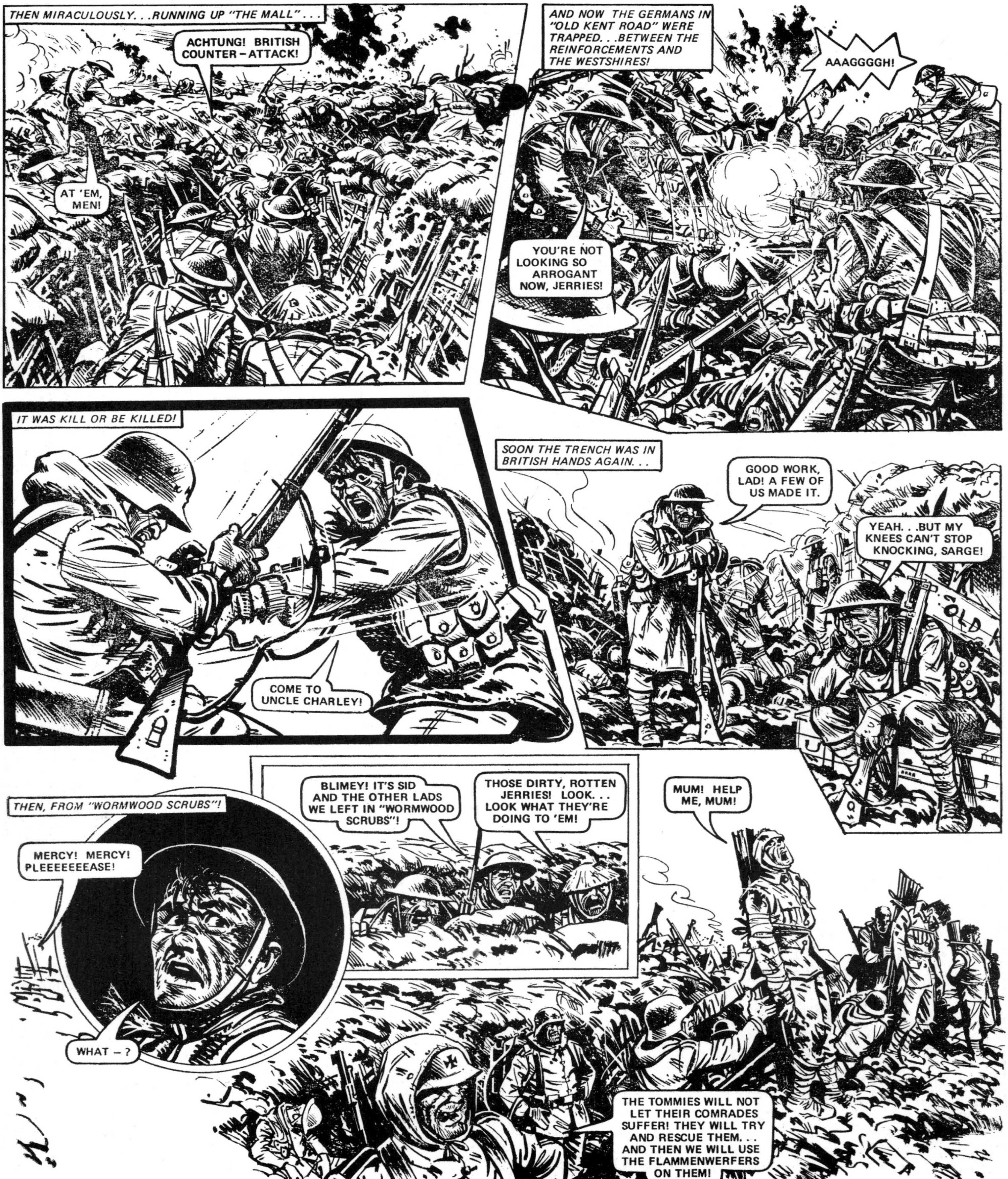
THEN MIRACULOUSLY. . .RUNNING UP "THE MALL" . . .
ACHTUNG! BRITISH COUNTER – ATTACK!
AT 'EM, MEN!
AND NOW THE GERMANS IN "OLD KENT ROAD" WERE TRAPPED. . .BETWEEN THE REINFORCEMENTS AND THE WESTSHIRES!
AAAGGGGH!
YOU'RE NOT LOOKING SO ARROGANT NOW, JERRIES!
IT WAS KILL OR BE KILLED!
COME TO UNCLE CHARLEY!
SOON THE TRENCH WAS IN BRITISH HANDS AGAIN. . .
GOOD WORK, LAD! A FEW OF US MADE IT.
YEAH. . .BUT MY KNEES CAN'T STOP KNOCKING, SARGE!
THEN, FROM "WORMWOOD SCRUBS"!
MERCY! MERCY! PLEEEEEEEASE!
WHAT – ?
BLIMEY! IT'S SID AND THE OTHER LADS WE LEFT IN "WORMWOOD SCRUBS"!
THOSE DIRTY, ROTTEN JERRIES! LOOK. . . LOOK WHAT THEY'RE DOING TO 'EM!
MUM! HELP ME, MUM!
THE TOMMIES WILL NOT LET THEIR COMRADES SUFFER! THEY WILL TRY AND RESCUE THEM. . . AND THEN WE WILL USE THE FLAMMENWERFERS ON THEM!

CHARLEY'S WAR

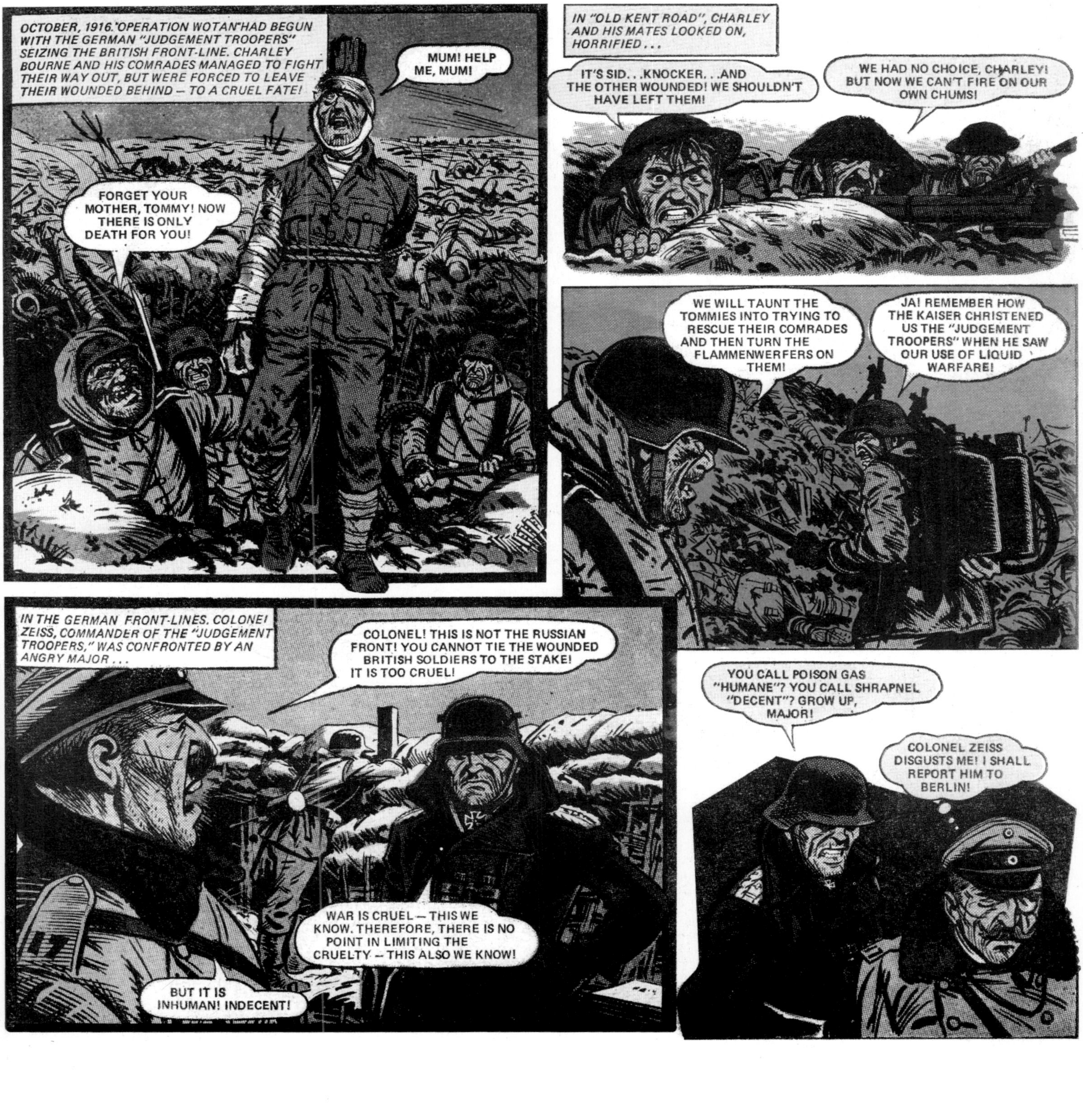

OCTOBER, 1916."OPERATION WOTAN" HAD BEGUN WITH THE GERMAN "JUDGEMENT TROOPERS" SEIZING THE BRITISH FRONT-LINE. CHARLEY BOURNE AND HIS COMRADES MANAGED TO FIGHT THEIR WAY OUT, BUT WERE FORCED TO LEAVE THEIR WOUNDED BEHIND — TO A CRUEL FATE!
MUM! HELP ME, MUM!
FORGET YOUR MOTHER, TOMMY! NOW THERE IS ONLY DEATH FOR YOU!
IN "OLD KENT ROAD", CHARLEY AND HIS MATES LOOKED ON, HORRIFIED . . .
IT'S SID. . .KNOCKER. . .AND THE OTHER WOUNDED! WE SHOULDN'T HAVE LEFT THEM!
WE HAD NO CHOICE, CHARLEY! BUT NOW WE CAN'T FIRE ON OUR OWN CHUMS!
WE WILL TAUNT THE TOMMIES INTO TRYING TO RESCUE THEIR COMRADES AND THEN TURN THE FLAMMENWERFERS ON THEM!
JA! REMEMBER HOW THE KAISER CHRISTENED US THE "JUDGEMENT TROOPERS" WHEN HE SAW OUR USE OF LIQUID WARFARE!
IN THE GERMAN FRONT-LINES. COLONEL ZEISS, COMMANDER OF THE "JUDGEMENT TROOPERS," WAS CONFRONTED BY AN ANGRY MAJOR . . .
COLONEL! THIS IS NOT THE RUSSIAN FRONT! YOU CANNOT TIE THE WOUNDED BRITISH SOLDIERS TO THE STAKE! IT IS TOO CRUEL!
WAR IS CRUEL — THIS WE KNOW. THEREFORE, THERE IS NO POINT IN LIMITING THE CRUELTY — THIS ALSO WE KNOW!
BUT IT IS INHUMAN! INDECENT!
YOU CALL POISON GAS "HUMANE"? YOU CALL SHRAPNEL "DECENT"? GROW UP, MAJOR!
COLONEL ZEISS DISGUSTS ME! I SHALL REPORT HIM TO BERLIN!

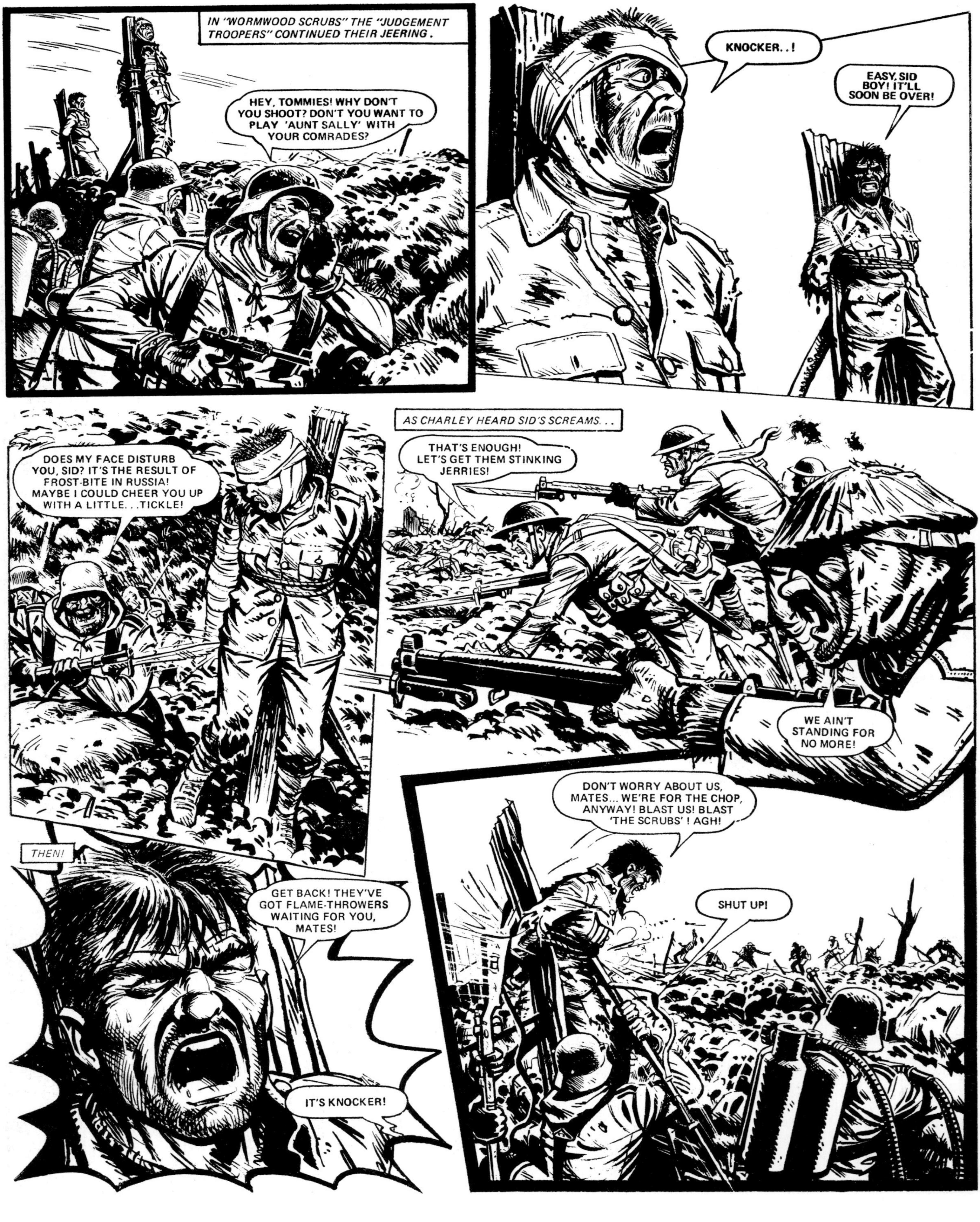
IN "WORMWOOD SCRUBS" THE "JUDGEMENT TROOPERS" CONTINUED THEIR JEERING.
HEY, TOMMIES! WHY DON'T YOU SHOOT? DON'T YOU WANT TO PLAY 'AUNT SALLY' WITH YOUR COMRADES?
KNOCKER..!
EASY, SID BOY! IT'LL SOON BE OVER!
DOES MY FACE DISTURB YOU, SID? IT'S THE RESULT OF FROST-BITE IN RUSSIA! MAYBE I COULD CHEER YOU UP WITH A LITTLE...TICKLE!
AS CHARLEY HEARD SID'S SCREAMS...
THAT'S ENOUGH! LET'S GET THEM STINKING JERRIES!
WE AIN'T STANDING FOR NO MORE!
THEN!
GET BACK! THEY'VE GOT FLAME-THROWERS WAITING FOR YOU, MATES!
IT'S KNOCKER!
DON'T WORRY ABOUT US, MATES... WE'RE FOR THE CHOP, ANYWAY! BLAST US! BLAST 'THE SCRUBS'! AGH!
SHUT UP!

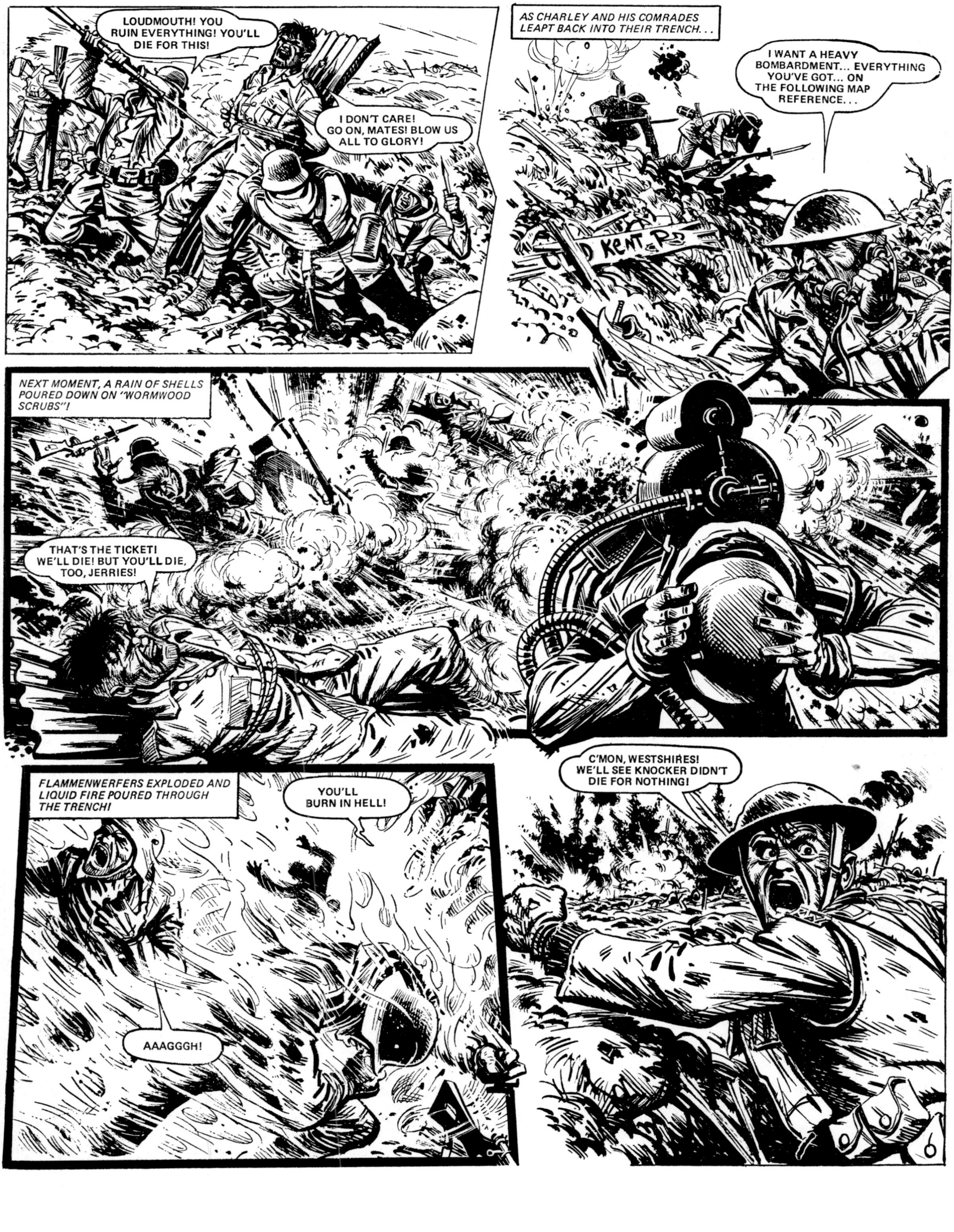
LOUDMOUTH! YOU RUIN EVERYTHING! YOU'LL DIE FOR THIS!
I DON'T CARE! GO ON, MATES! BLOW US ALL TO GLORY!
AS CHARLEY AND HIS COMRADES LEAPT BACK INTO THEIR TRENCH...
I WANT A HEAVY BOMBARDMENT... EVERYTHING YOU'VE GOT... ON THE FOLLOWING MAP REFERENCE...
NEXT MOMENT, A RAIN OF SHELLS POURED DOWN ON "WORMWOOD SCRUBS"!
THAT'S THE TICKET! WE'LL DIE! BUT YOU'LL DIE, TOO, JERRIES!
FLAMMENWERFERS EXPLODED AND LIQUID FIRE POURED THROUGH THE TRENCH!
YOU'LL BURN IN HELL!
AAAGGGH!
C'MON, WESTSHIRES! WE'LL SEE KNOCKER DIDN'T DIE FOR NOTHING!
6

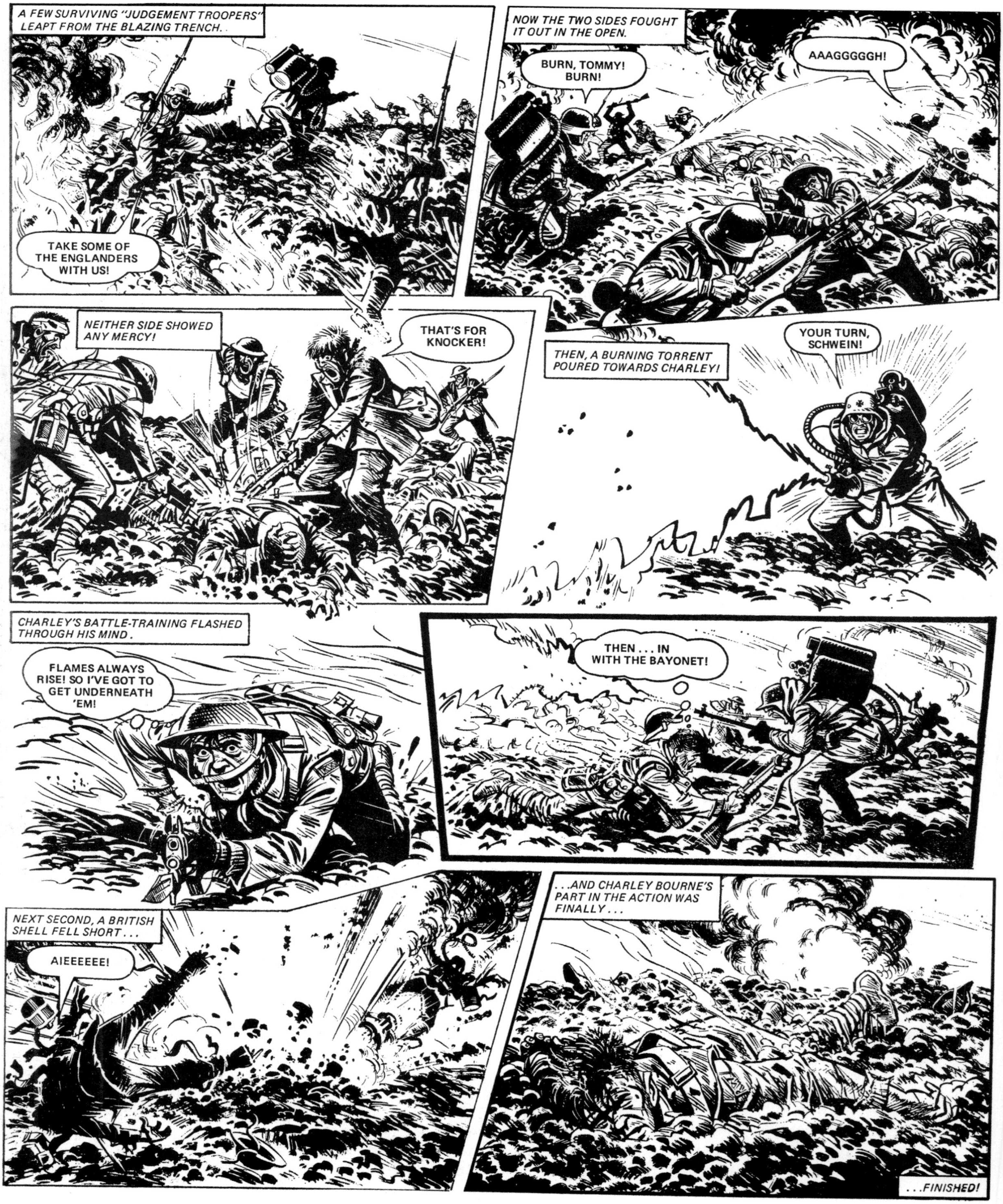
A FEW SURVIVING "JUDGEMENT TROOPERS" LEAPT FROM THE BLAZING TRENCH..
TAKE SOME OF THE ENGLANDERS WITH US!
NOW THE TWO SIDES FOUGHT IT OUT IN THE OPEN.
BURN, TOMMY! BURN!
AAAGGGGGH!
NEITHER SIDE SHOWED ANY MERCY!
THAT'S FOR KNOCKER!
THEN, A BURNING TORRENT POURED TOWARDS CHARLEY!
YOUR TURN, SCHWEIN!
CHARLEY'S BATTLE-TRAINING FLASHED THROUGH HIS MIND.
FLAMES ALWAYS RISE! SO I'VE GOT TO GET UNDERNEATH 'EM!
THEN . . . IN WITH THE BAYONET!
NEXT SECOND, A BRITISH SHELL FELL SHORT . . .
AIEEEEEE!
. . .AND CHARLEY BOURNE'S PART IN THE ACTION WAS FINALLY . . .
. . .FINISHED!

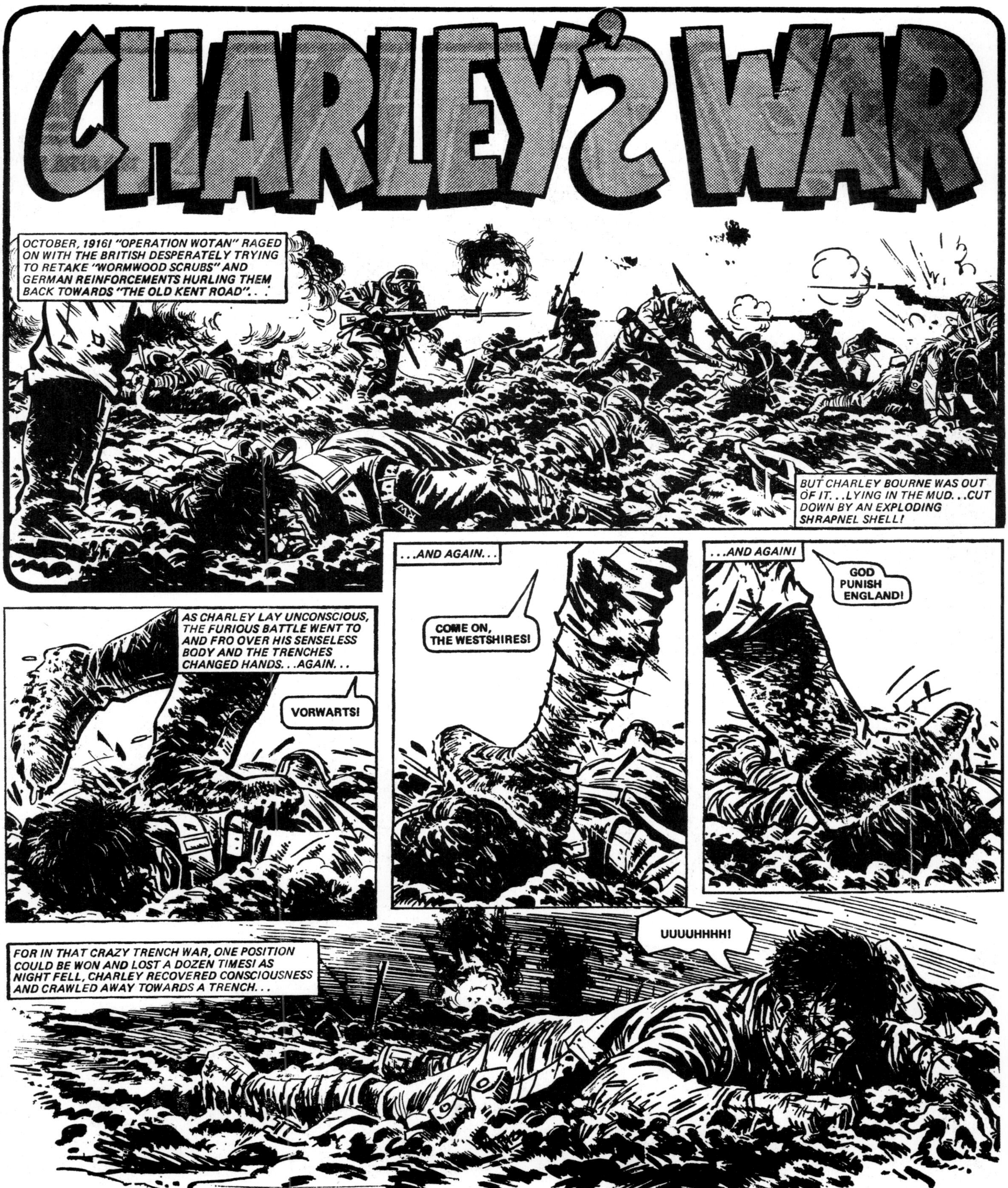
CHARLEY'S WAR
OCTOBER, 1916! "OPERATION WOTAN" RAGED ON WITH THE BRITISH DESPERATELY TRYING TO RETAKE "WORMWOOD SCRUBS" AND GERMAN REINFORCEMENTS HURLING THEM BACK TOWARDS "THE OLD KENT ROAD"...
BUT CHARLEY BOURNE WAS OUT OF IT...LYING IN THE MUD...CUT DOWN BY AN EXPLODING SHRAPNEL SHELL!
AS CHARLEY LAY UNCONSCIOUS, THE FURIOUS BATTLE WENT TO AND FRO OVER HIS SENSELESS BODY AND THE TRENCHES CHANGED HANDS...AGAIN...
VORWARTS!
...AND AGAIN...
COME ON, THE WESTSHIRES!
...AND AGAIN!
GOD PUNISH ENGLAND!
FOR IN THAT CRAZY TRENCH WAR, ONE POSITION COULD BE WON AND LOST A DOZEN TIMES! AS NIGHT FELL, CHARLEY RECOVERED CONSCIOUSNESS AND CRAWLED AWAY TOWARDS A TRENCH...
UUUUHHHH!

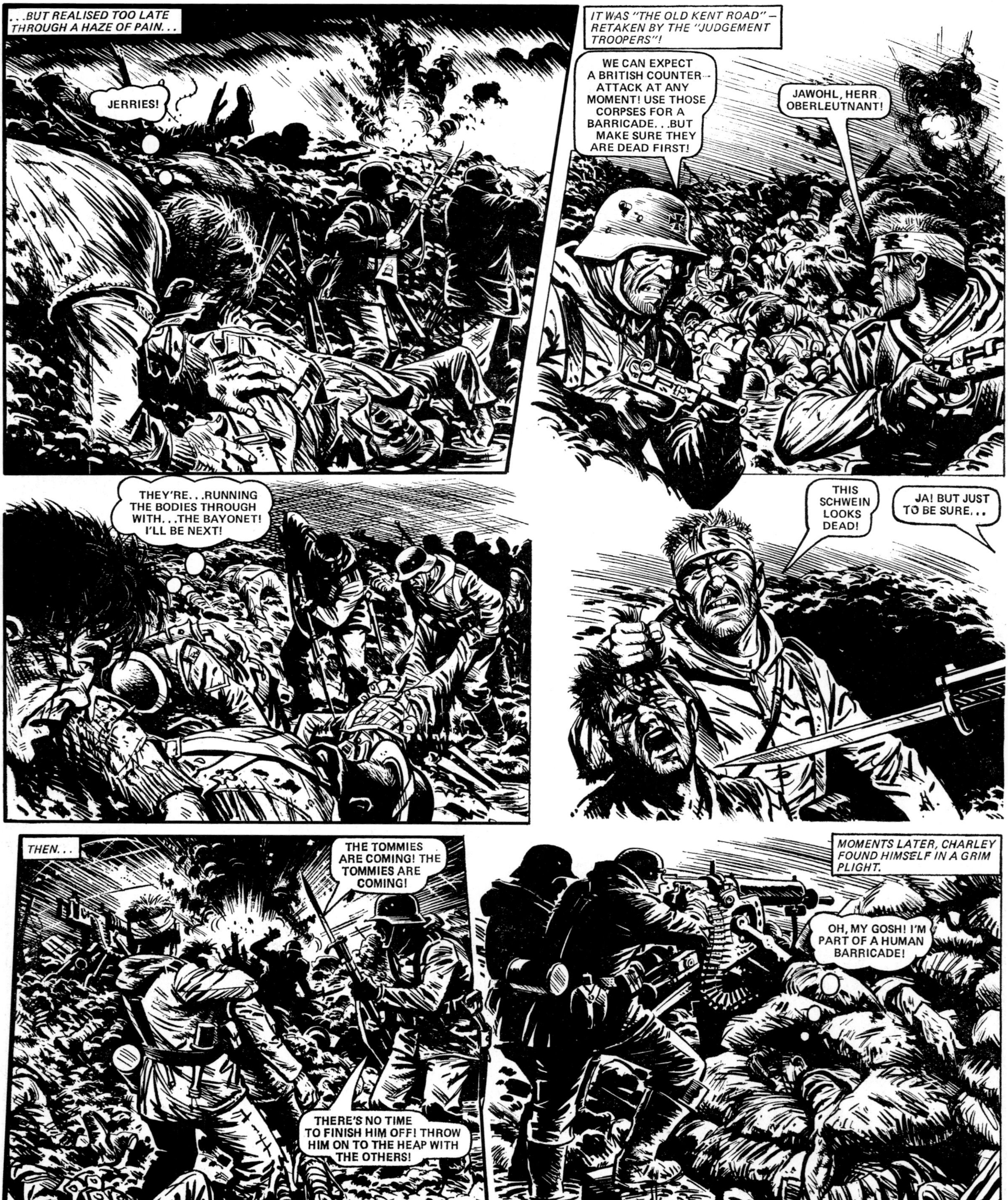
...BUT REALISED TOO LATE THROUGH A HAZE OF PAIN...
JERRIES!
IT WAS "THE OLD KENT ROAD" – RETAKEN BY THE "JUDGEMENT TROOPERS"!
WE CAN EXPECT A BRITISH COUNTER-ATTACK AT ANY MOMENT! USE THOSE CORPSES FOR A BARRICADE...BUT MAKE SURE THEY ARE DEAD FIRST!
JAWOHL, HERR OBERLEUTNANT!
THEY'RE...RUNNING THE BODIES THROUGH WITH...THE BAYONET! I'LL BE NEXT!
THIS SCHWEIN LOOKS DEAD!
JA! BUT JUST TO BE SURE...
THEN...
THE TOMMIES ARE COMING! THE TOMMIES ARE COMING!
THERE'S NO TIME TO FINISH HIM OFF! THROW HIM ON TO THE HEAP WITH THE OTHERS!
MOMENTS LATER, CHARLEY FOUND HIMSELF IN A GRIM PLIGHT.
OH, MY GOSH! I'M PART OF A HUMAN BARRICADE!

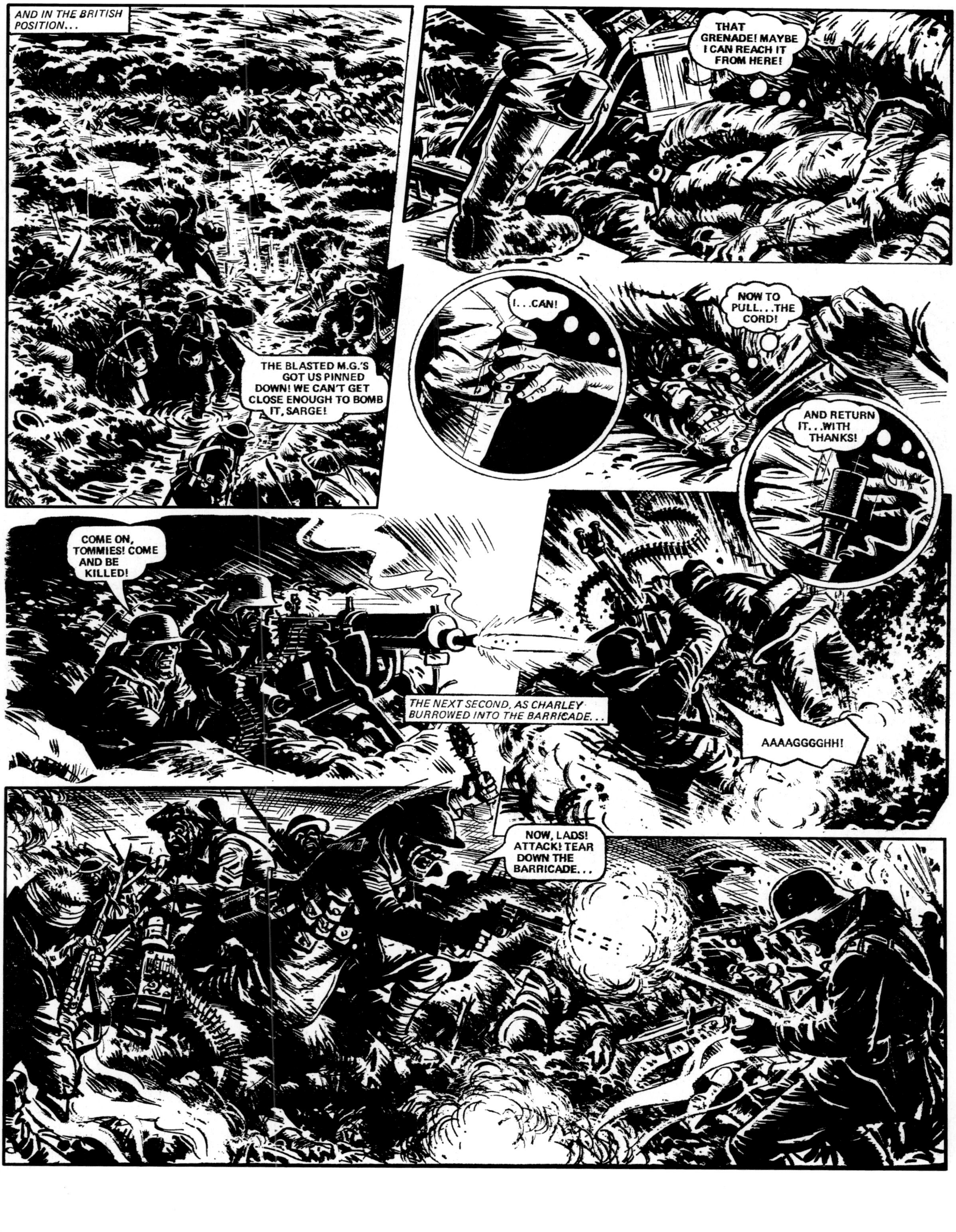
AND IN THE BRITISH POSITION...
THE BLASTED M.G.'S GOT US PINNED DOWN! WE CAN'T GET CLOSE ENOUGH TO BOMB IT, SARGE!
THAT GRENADE! MAYBE I CAN REACH IT FROM HERE!
I...CAN!
NOW TO PULL...THE CORD!
AND RETURN IT...WITH THANKS!
COME ON, TOMMIES! COME AND BE KILLED!
THE NEXT SECOND, AS CHARLEY BURROWED INTO THE BARRICADE...
AAAAGGGGHH!
NOW, LADS! ATTACK! TEAR DOWN THE BARRICADE...

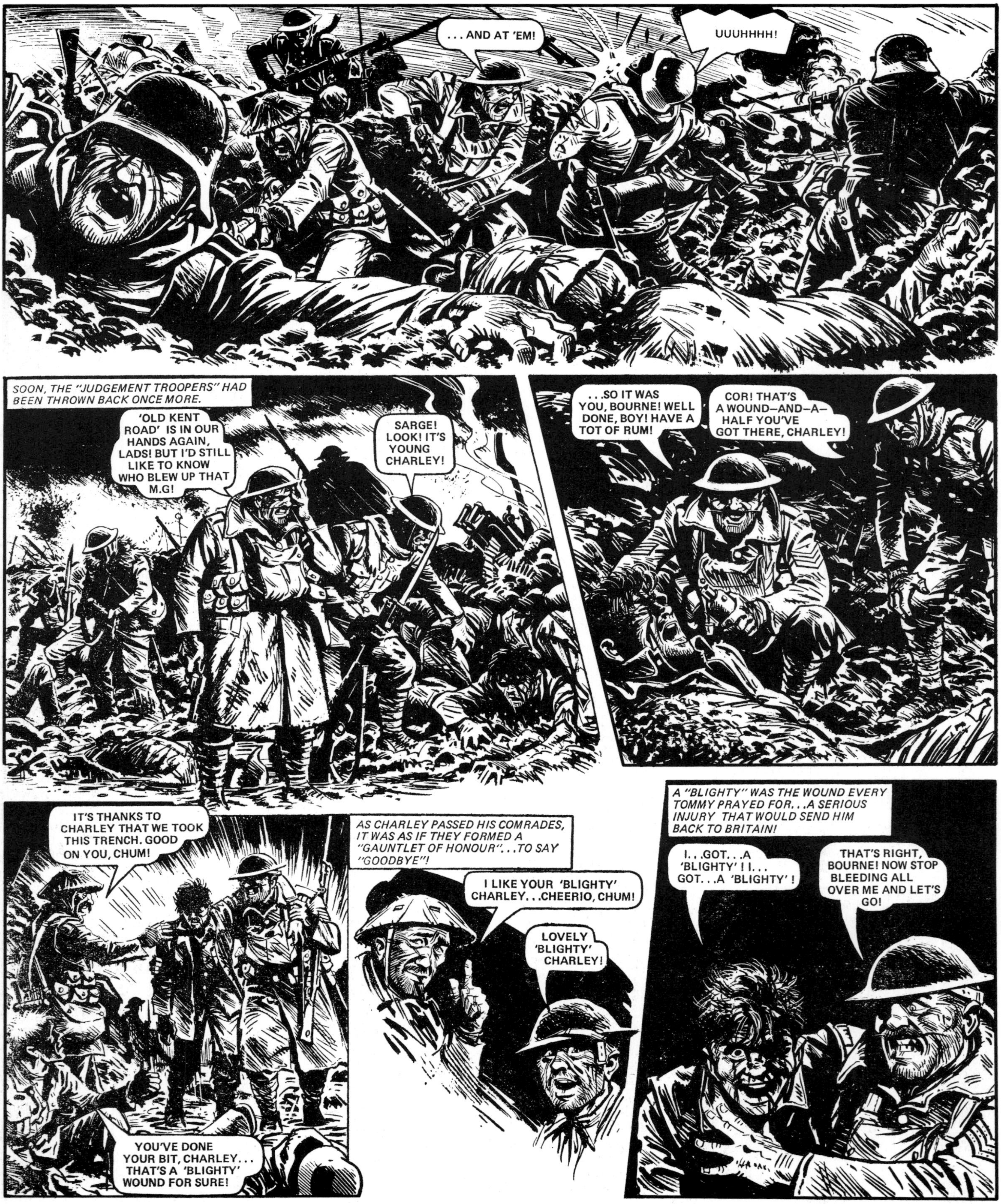

. . . AND AT 'EM!
UUUHHHH!
SOON, THE "JUDGEMENT TROOPERS" HAD BEEN THROWN BACK ONCE MORE.
'OLD KENT ROAD' IS IN OUR HANDS AGAIN, LADS! BUT I'D STILL LIKE TO KNOW WHO BLEW UP THAT M.G!
SARGE! LOOK! IT'S YOUNG CHARLEY!
. . .SO IT WAS YOU, BOURNE! WELL DONE, BOY! HAVE A TOT OF RUM!
COR! THAT'S A WOUND—AND—A—HALF YOU'VE GOT THERE, CHARLEY!
IT'S THANKS TO CHARLEY THAT WE TOOK THIS TRENCH. GOOD ON YOU, CHUM!
YOU'VE DONE YOUR BIT, CHARLEY. . . THAT'S A 'BLIGHTY' WOUND FOR SURE!
AS CHARLEY PASSED HIS COMRADES, IT WAS AS IF THEY FORMED A "GAUNTLET OF HONOUR". . .TO SAY "GOODBYE"!
I LIKE YOUR 'BLIGHTY' CHARLEY. . .CHEERIO, CHUM!
LOVELY 'BLIGHTY' CHARLEY!
A "BLIGHTY" WAS THE WOUND EVERY TOMMY PRAYED FOR. . .A SERIOUS INJURY THAT WOULD SEND HIM BACK TO BRITAIN!
I. . GOT. . .A 'BLIGHTY'! I. . . GOT. . .A 'BLIGHTY'!
THAT'S RIGHT, BOURNE! NOW STOP BLEEDING ALL OVER ME AND LET'S GO!

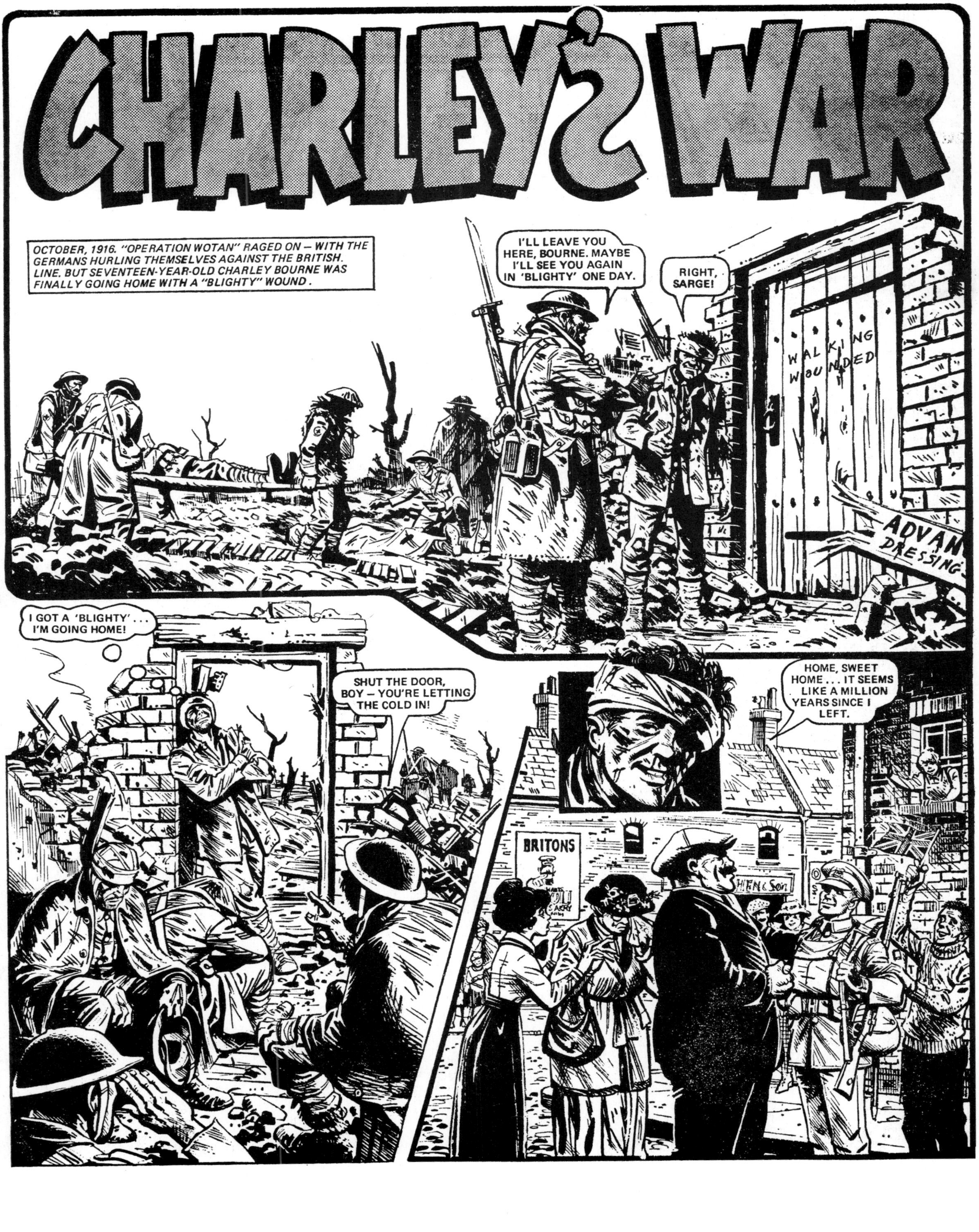
CHARLEY'S WAR
OCTOBER, 1916. "OPERATION WOTAN" RAGED ON — WITH THE GERMANS HURLING THEMSELVES AGAINST THE BRITISH LINE. BUT SEVENTEEN-YEAR-OLD CHARLEY BOURNE WAS FINALLY GOING HOME WITH A "BLIGHTY" WOUND.
I'LL LEAVE YOU HERE, BOURNE. MAYBE I'LL SEE YOU AGAIN IN 'BLIGHTY' ONE DAY.
RIGHT, SARGE!
WALKING WOUNDED
ADVAN DRESSING
I GOT A 'BLIGHTY'... I'M GOING HOME!
SHUT THE DOOR, BOY — YOU'RE LETTING THE COLD IN!
HOME, SWEET HOME... IT SEEMS LIKE A MILLION YEARS SINCE I LEFT.
BRITONS

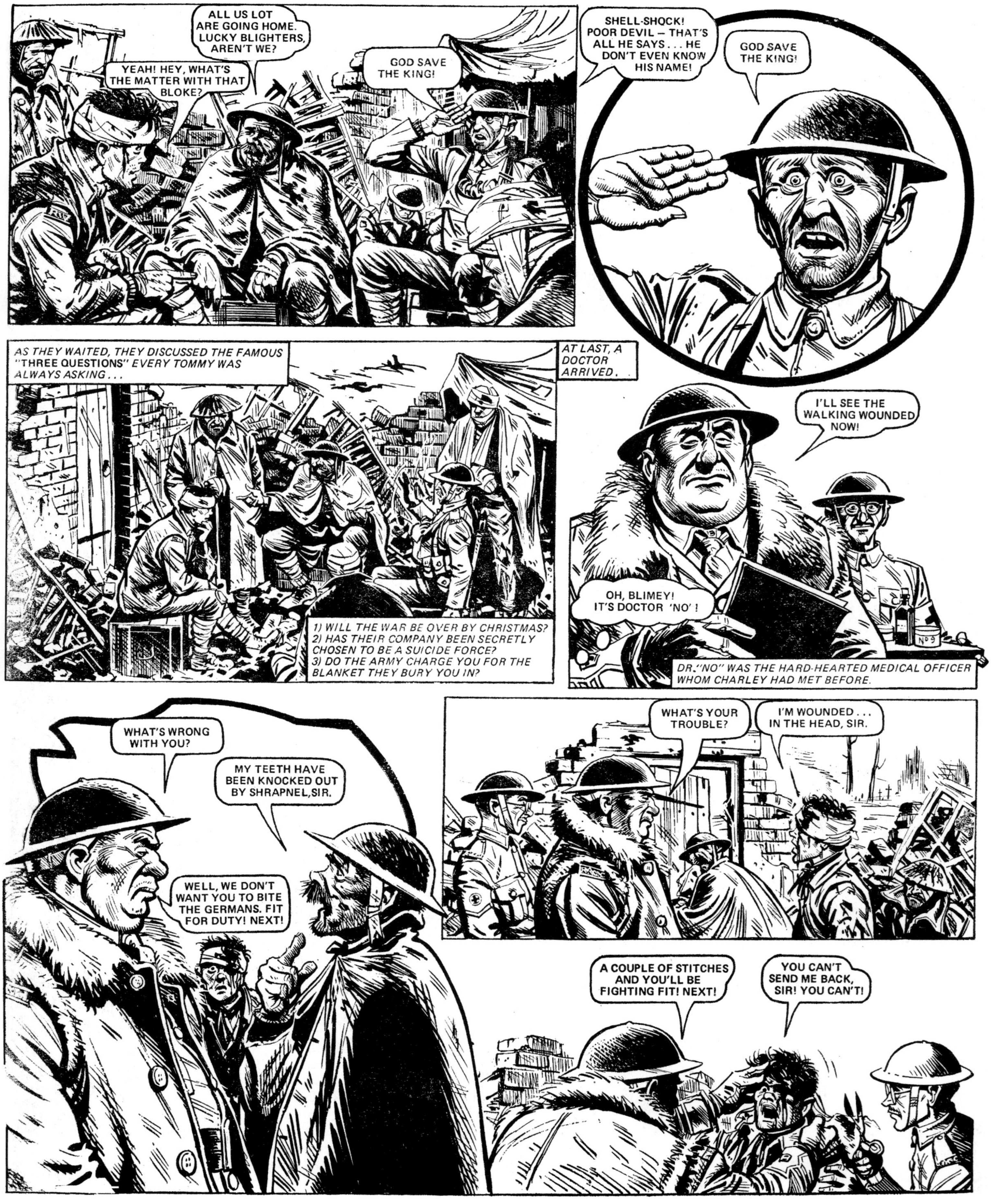
ALL US LOT ARE GOING HOME. LUCKY BLIGHTERS, AREN'T WE?
YEAH! HEY, WHAT'S THE MATTER WITH THAT BLOKE?
GOD SAVE THE KING!
SHELL-SHOCK! POOR DEVIL — THAT'S ALL HE SAYS . . . HE DON'T EVEN KNOW HIS NAME!
GOD SAVE THE KING!
AS THEY WAITED, THEY DISCUSSED THE FAMOUS "THREE QUESTIONS" EVERY TOMMY WAS ALWAYS ASKING . . .
1) WILL THE WAR BE OVER BY CHRISTMAS? 2) HAS THEIR COMPANY BEEN SECRETLY CHOSEN TO BE A SUICIDE FORCE? 3) DO THE ARMY CHARGE YOU FOR THE BLANKET THEY BURY YOU IN?
AT LAST, A DOCTOR ARRIVED.
I'LL SEE THE WALKING WOUNDED NOW!
OH, BLIMEY! IT'S DOCTOR 'NO'!
DR."NO" WAS THE HARD-HEARTED MEDICAL OFFICER WHOM CHARLEY HAD MET BEFORE.
WHAT'S WRONG WITH YOU?
MY TEETH HAVE BEEN KNOCKED OUT BY SHRAPNEL, SIR.
WELL, WE DON'T WANT YOU TO BITE THE GERMANS. FIT FOR DUTY! NEXT!
WHAT'S YOUR TROUBLE?
I'M WOUNDED . . . IN THE HEAD, SIR.
A COUPLE OF STITCHES AND YOU'LL BE FIGHTING FIT! NEXT!
YOU CAN'T SEND ME BACK, SIR! YOU CAN'T!

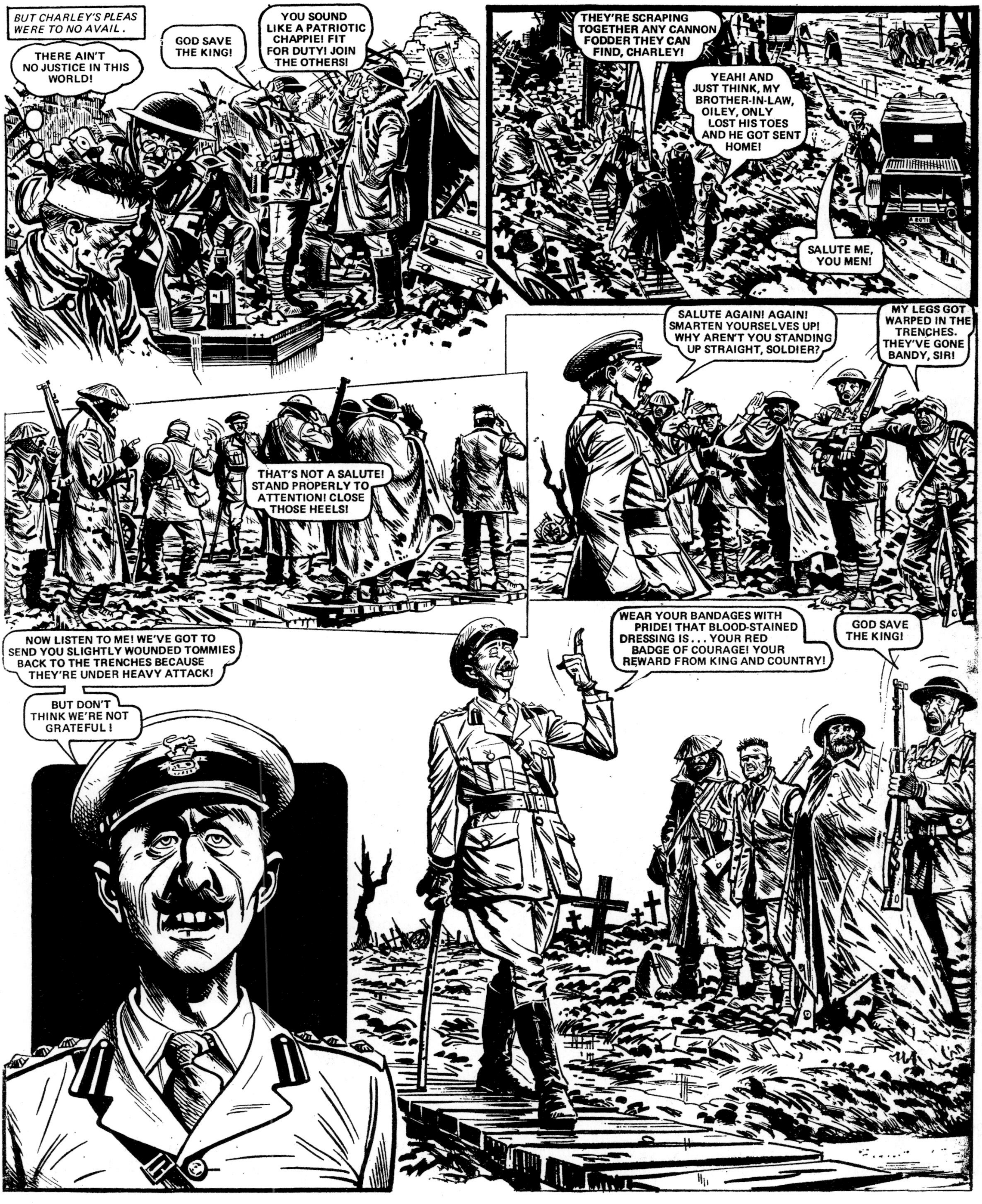

BUT CHARLEY'S PLEAS WERE TO NO AVAIL.
THERE AIN'T NO JUSTICE IN THIS WORLD!
GOD SAVE THE KING!
YOU SOUND LIKE A PATRIOTIC CHAPPIE! FIT FOR DUTY! JOIN THE OTHERS!
THEY'RE SCRAPING TOGETHER ANY CANNON FODDER THEY CAN FIND, CHARLEY!
YEAH! AND JUST THINK, MY BROTHER-IN-LAW, OILEY, ONLY LOST HIS TOES AND HE GOT SENT HOME!
SALUTE ME, YOU MEN!
THAT'S NOT A SALUTE! STAND PROPERLY TO ATTENTION! CLOSE THOSE HEELS!
SALUTE AGAIN! AGAIN! SMARTEN YOURSELVES UP! WHY AREN'T YOU STANDING UP STRAIGHT, SOLDIER?
MY LEGS GOT WARPED IN THE TRENCHES. THEY'VE GONE BANDY, SIR!
NOW LISTEN TO ME! WE'VE GOT TO SEND YOU SLIGHTLY WOUNDED TOMMIES BACK TO THE TRENCHES BECAUSE THEY'RE UNDER HEAVY ATTACK!
BUT DON'T THINK WE'RE NOT GRATEFUL!
WEAR YOUR BANDAGES WITH PRIDE! THAT BLOOD-STAINED DRESSING IS . . . YOUR RED BADGE OF COURAGE! YOUR REWARD FROM KING AND COUNTRY!
GOD SAVE THE KING!

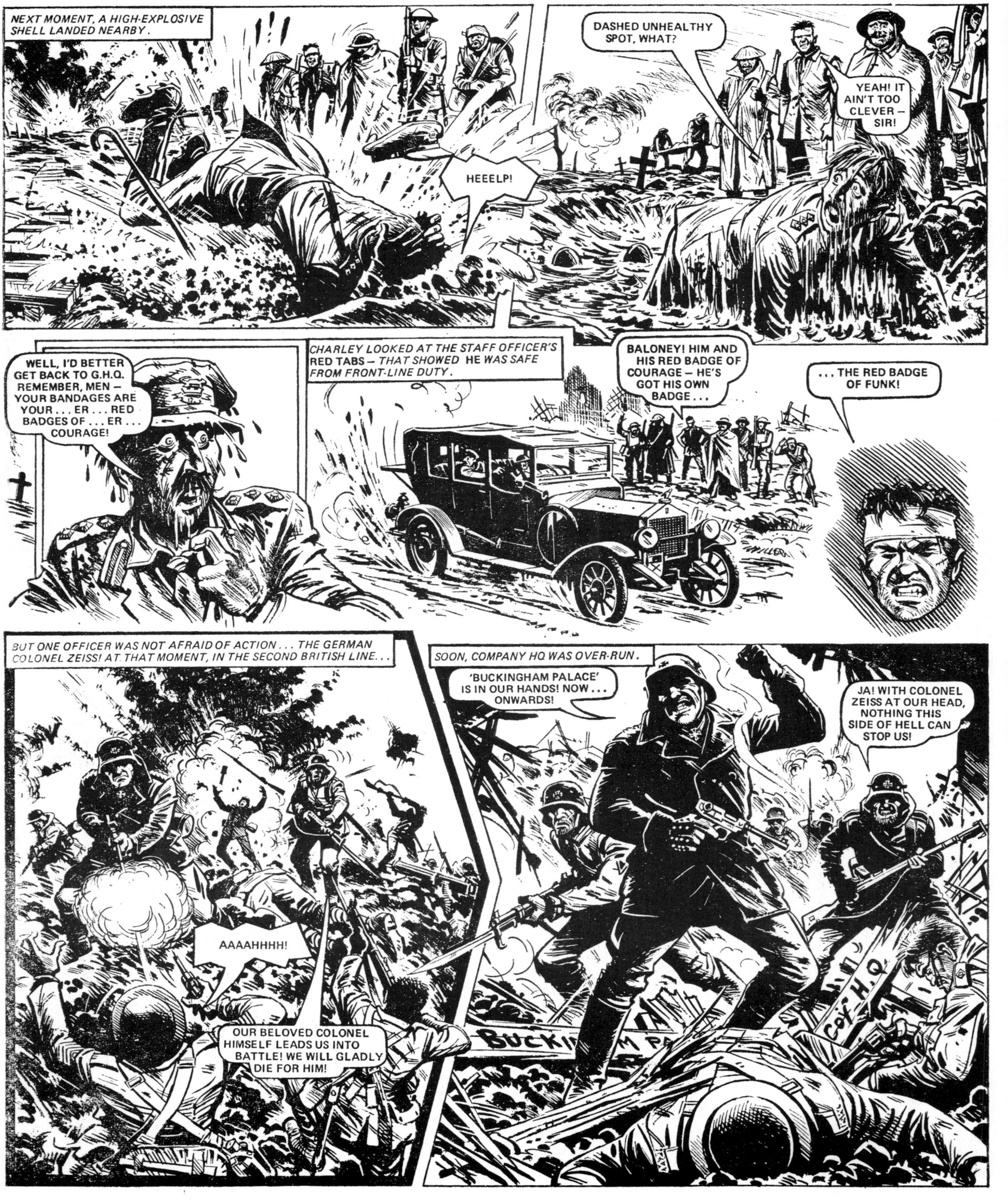
NEXT MOMENT, A HIGH-EXPLOSIVE SHELL LANDED NEARBY.
HEEELP!
DASHED UNHEALTHY SPOT, WHAT?
YEAH! IT AIN'T TOO CLEVER — SIR!
WELL, I'D BETTER GET BACK TO G.H.Q. REMEMBER, MEN — YOUR BANDAGES ARE YOUR . . . ER . . . RED BADGES OF . . . ER . . . COURAGE!
CHARLEY LOOKED AT THE STAFF OFFICER'S RED TABS — THAT SHOWED HE WAS SAFE FROM FRONT-LINE DUTY.
BALONEY! HIM AND HIS RED BADGE OF COURAGE — HE'S GOT HIS OWN BADGE . . .
. . . THE RED BADGE OF FUNK!
BUT ONE OFFICER WAS NOT AFRAID OF ACTION . . . THE GERMAN COLONEL ZEISS! AT THAT MOMENT, IN THE SECOND BRITISH LINE . . .
AAAAHHHH!
OUR BELOVED COLONEL HIMSELF LEADS US INTO BATTLE! WE WILL GLADLY DIE FOR HIM!
SOON, COMPANY HQ WAS OVER-RUN.
'BUCKINGHAM PALACE' IS IN OUR HANDS! NOW . . . ONWARDS!
JA! WITH COLONEL ZEISS AT OUR HEAD, NOTHING THIS SIDE OF HELL CAN STOP US!
COY H.Q.

CHARLEY'S WAR

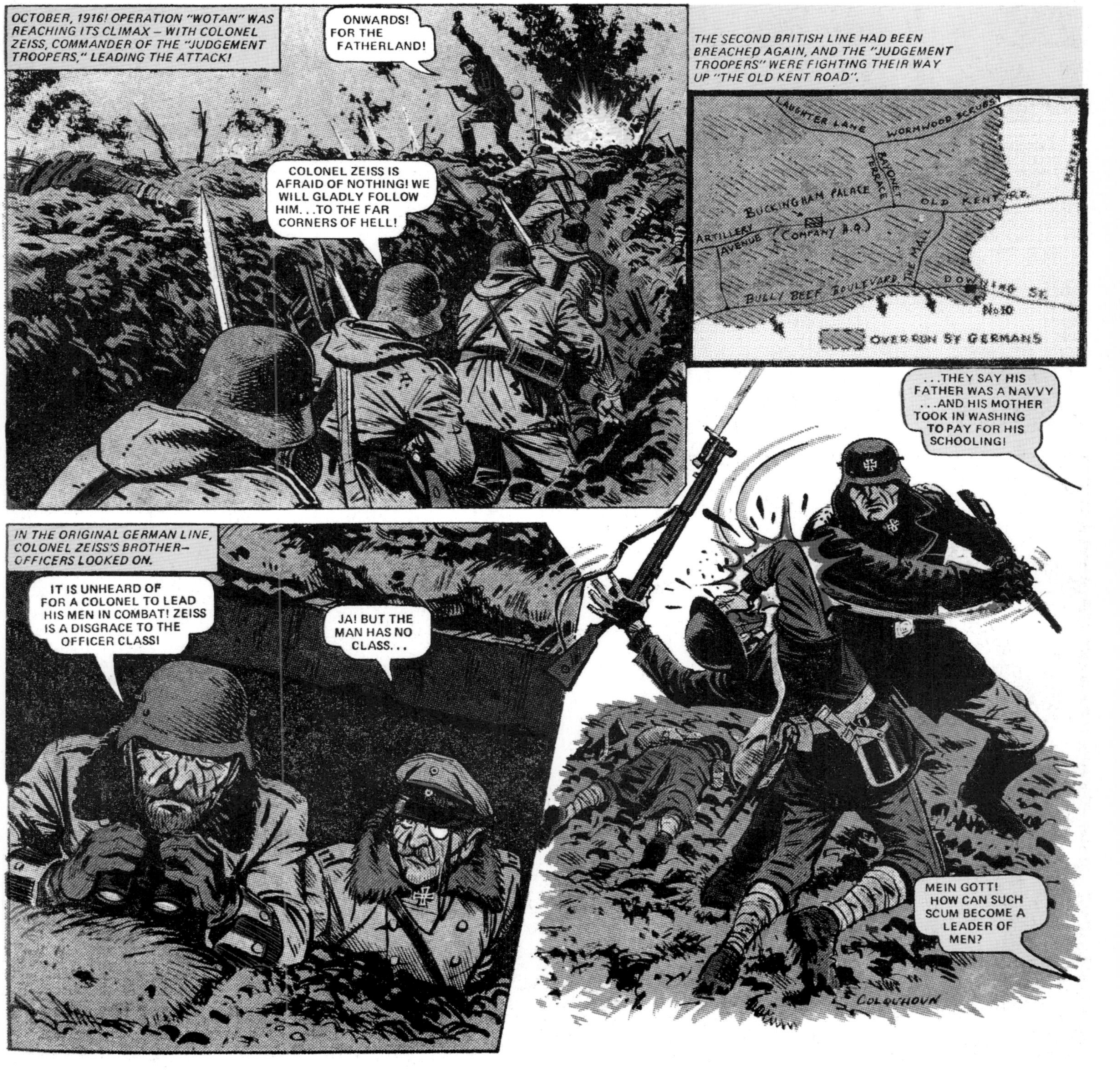
OCTOBER, 1916! OPERATION "WOTAN" WAS REACHING ITS CLIMAX – WITH COLONEL ZEISS, COMMANDER OF THE "JUDGEMENT TROOPERS," LEADING THE ATTACK!
ONWARDS! FOR THE FATHERLAND!
COLONEL ZEISS IS AFRAID OF NOTHING! WE WILL GLADLY FOLLOW HIM. . .TO THE FAR CORNERS OF HELL!
THE SECOND BRITISH LINE HAD BEEN BREACHED AGAIN, AND THE "JUDGEMENT TROOPERS" WERE FIGHTING THEIR WAY UP "THE OLD KENT ROAD".
WORMWOOD SCRUBS
BAYONET TERRACE
BUCKINGHAM PALACE
OLD KENT RD.
ARTILLERY AVENUE
(COMPANY H.Q.)
THE MALL
BULLY BEEF BOULEVARD
DOWNING ST.
No10
OVER RUN BY GERMANS
IN THE ORIGINAL GERMAN LINE, COLONEL ZEISS'S BROTHER-OFFICERS LOOKED ON.
IT IS UNHEARD OF FOR A COLONEL TO LEAD HIS MEN IN COMBAT! ZEISS IS A DISGRACE TO THE OFFICER CLASS!
JA! BUT THE MAN HAS NO CLASS. . .
. . .THEY SAY HIS FATHER WAS A NAVVY . . .AND HIS MOTHER TOOK IN WASHING TO PAY FOR HIS SCHOOLING!
MEIN GOTT! HOW CAN SUCH SCUM BECOME A LEADER OF MEN?
COLQUHOUN

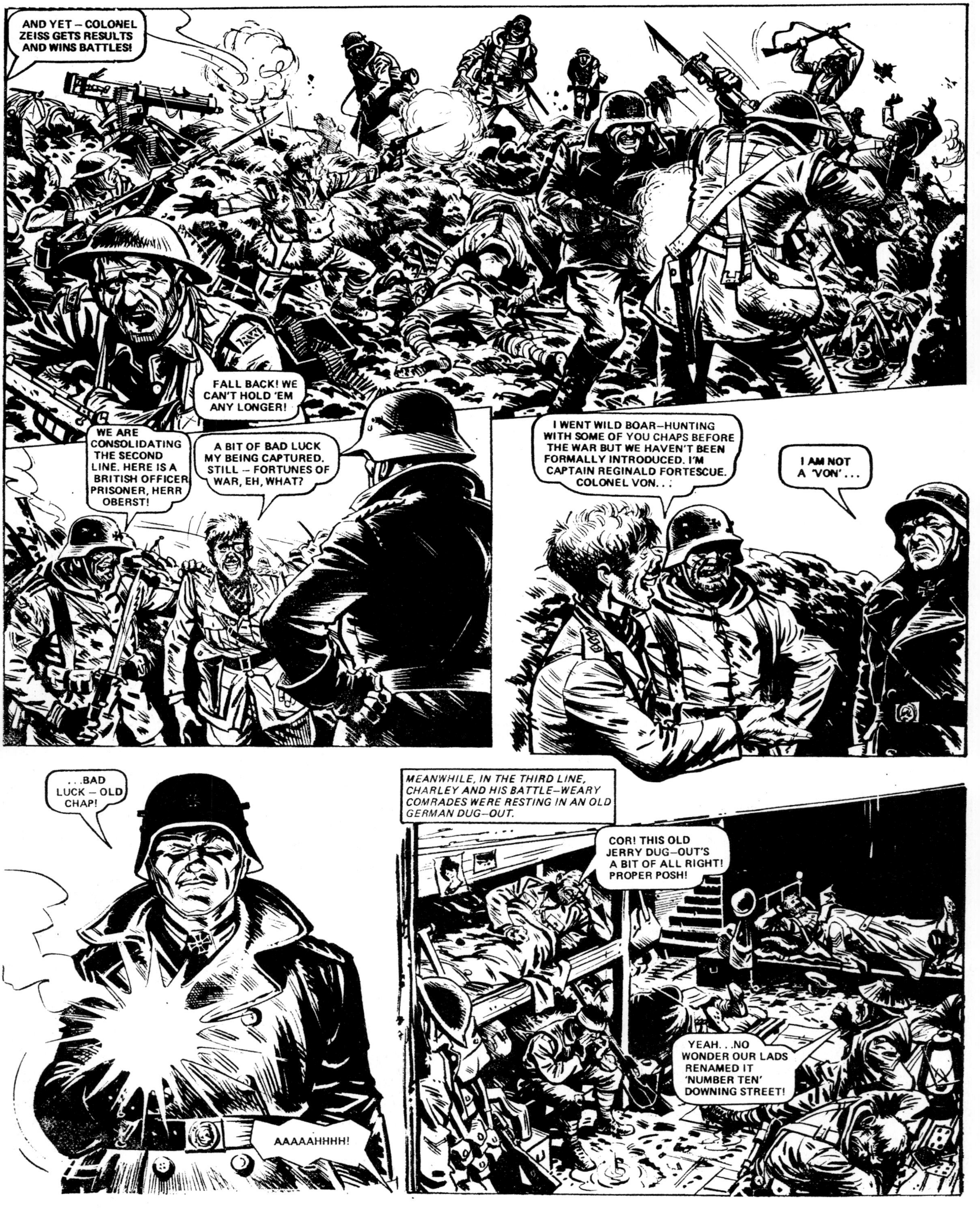

AND YET – COLONEL ZEISS GETS RESULTS AND WINS BATTLES!
FALL BACK! WE CAN'T HOLD 'EM ANY LONGER!
WE ARE CONSOLIDATING THE SECOND LINE. HERE IS A BRITISH OFFICER PRISONER, HERR OBERST!
A BIT OF BAD LUCK MY BEING CAPTURED. STILL – FORTUNES OF WAR, EH, WHAT?
I WENT WILD BOAR-HUNTING WITH SOME OF YOU CHAPS BEFORE THE WAR BUT WE HAVEN'T BEEN FORMALLY INTRODUCED. I'M CAPTAIN REGINALD FORTESCUE. COLONEL VON. . .
I AM NOT A 'VON'. . .
. . .BAD LUCK – OLD CHAP!
AAAAAHHHH!
MEANWHILE, IN THE THIRD LINE, CHARLEY AND HIS BATTLE-WEARY COMRADES WERE RESTING IN AN OLD GERMAN DUG-OUT.
COR! THIS OLD JERRY DUG-OUT'S A BIT OF ALL RIGHT! PROPER POSH!
YEAH. . .NO WONDER OUR LADS RENAMED IT 'NUMBER TEN' DOWNING STREET!

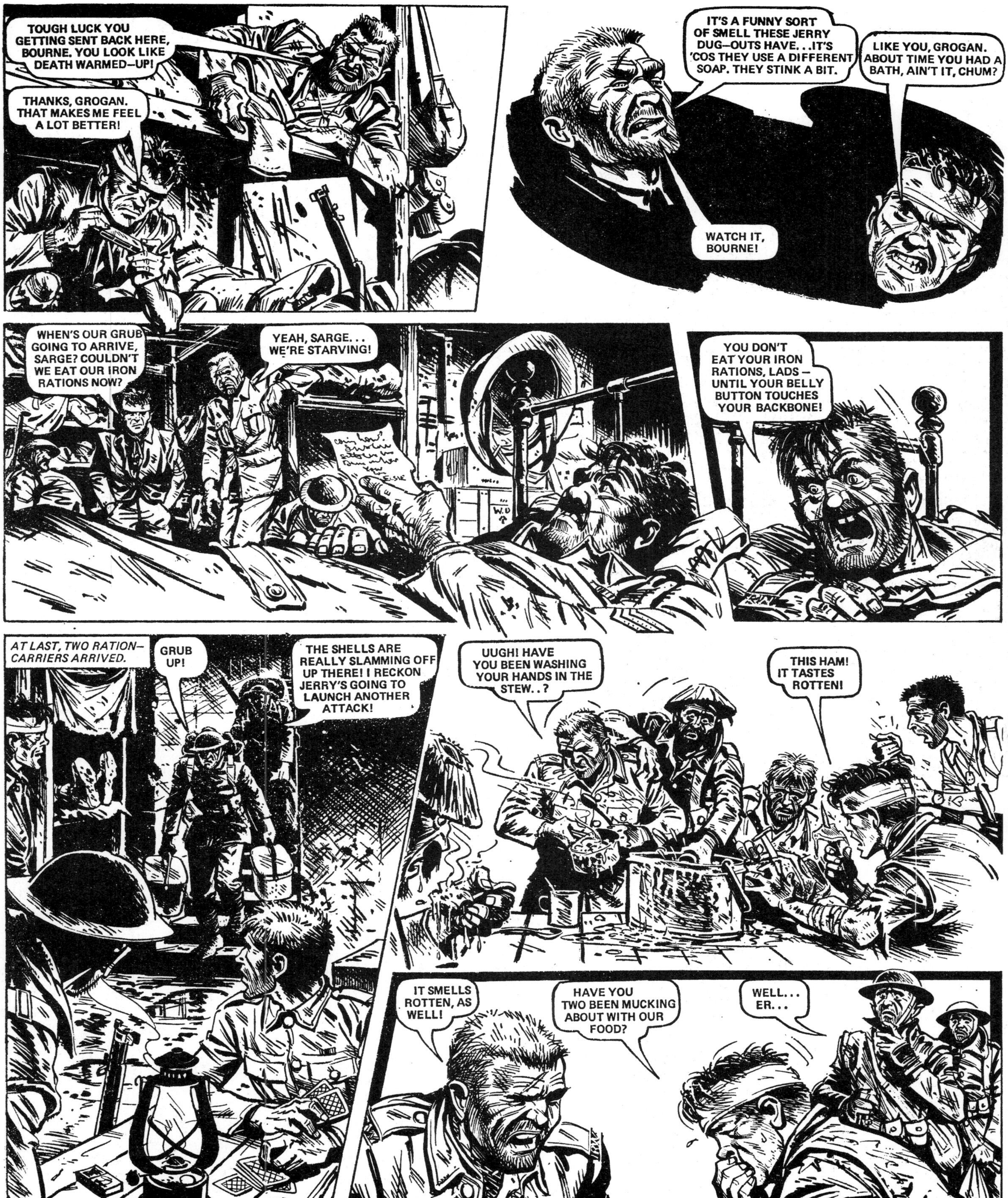
TOUGH LUCK YOU GETTING SENT BACK HERE, BOURNE. YOU LOOK LIKE DEATH WARMED—UP!
THANKS, GROGAN. THAT MAKES ME FEEL A LOT BETTER!
IT'S A FUNNY SORT OF SMELL THESE JERRY DUG—OUTS HAVE. . .IT'S 'COS THEY USE A DIFFERENT SOAP. THEY STINK A BIT.
LIKE YOU, GROGAN. ABOUT TIME YOU HAD A BATH, AIN'T IT, CHUM?
WATCH IT, BOURNE!
WHEN'S OUR GRUB GOING TO ARRIVE, SARGE? COULDN'T WE EAT OUR IRON RATIONS NOW?
YEAH, SARGE. . . WE'RE STARVING!
YOU DON'T EAT YOUR IRON RATIONS, LADS — UNTIL YOUR BELLY BUTTON TOUCHES YOUR BACKBONE!
AT LAST, TWO RATION—CARRIERS ARRIVED.
GRUB UP!
THE SHELLS ARE REALLY SLAMMING OFF UP THERE! I RECKON JERRY'S GOING TO LAUNCH ANOTHER ATTACK!
UUGH! HAVE YOU BEEN WASHING YOUR HANDS IN THE STEW. . ?
THIS HAM! IT TASTES ROTTEN!
IT SMELLS ROTTEN, AS WELL!
HAVE YOU TWO BEEN MUCKING ABOUT WITH OUR FOOD?
WELL. . . ER. . .

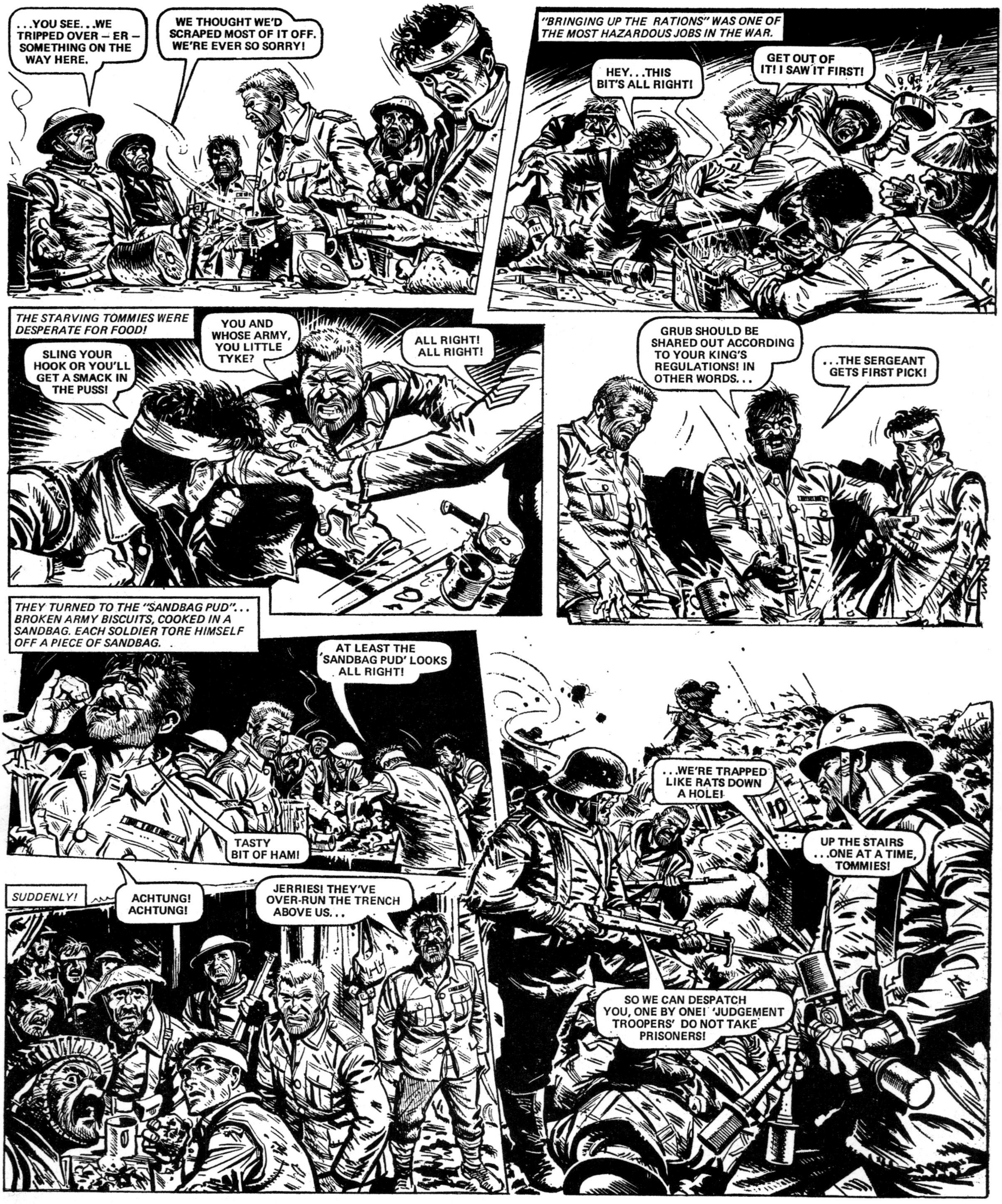
...YOU SEE...WE TRIPPED OVER — ER — SOMETHING ON THE WAY HERE.
WE THOUGHT WE'D SCRAPED MOST OF IT OFF. WE'RE EVER SO SORRY!
"BRINGING UP THE RATIONS" WAS ONE OF THE MOST HAZARDOUS JOBS IN THE WAR.
HEY...THIS BIT'S ALL RIGHT!
GET OUT OF IT! I SAW IT FIRST!
THE STARVING TOMMIES WERE DESPERATE FOR FOOD!
SLING YOUR HOOK OR YOU'LL GET A SMACK IN THE PUSS!
YOU AND WHOSE ARMY, YOU LITTLE TYKE?
ALL RIGHT! ALL RIGHT!
GRUB SHOULD BE SHARED OUT ACCORDING TO YOUR KING'S REGULATIONS! IN OTHER WORDS...
...THE SERGEANT GETS FIRST PICK!
THEY TURNED TO THE "SANDBAG PUD"... BROKEN ARMY BISCUITS, COOKED IN A SANDBAG. EACH SOLDIER TORE HIMSELF OFF A PIECE OF SANDBAG.
AT LEAST THE 'SANDBAG PUD' LOOKS ALL RIGHT!
TASTY BIT OF HAM!
SUDDENLY!
ACHTUNG! ACHTUNG!
JERRIES! THEY'VE OVER-RUN THE TRENCH ABOVE US...
...WE'RE TRAPPED LIKE RATS DOWN A HOLE!
UP THE STAIRS ...ONE AT A TIME, TOMMIES!
SO WE CAN DESPATCH YOU, ONE BY ONE! 'JUDGEMENT TROOPERS' DO NOT TAKE PRISONERS!

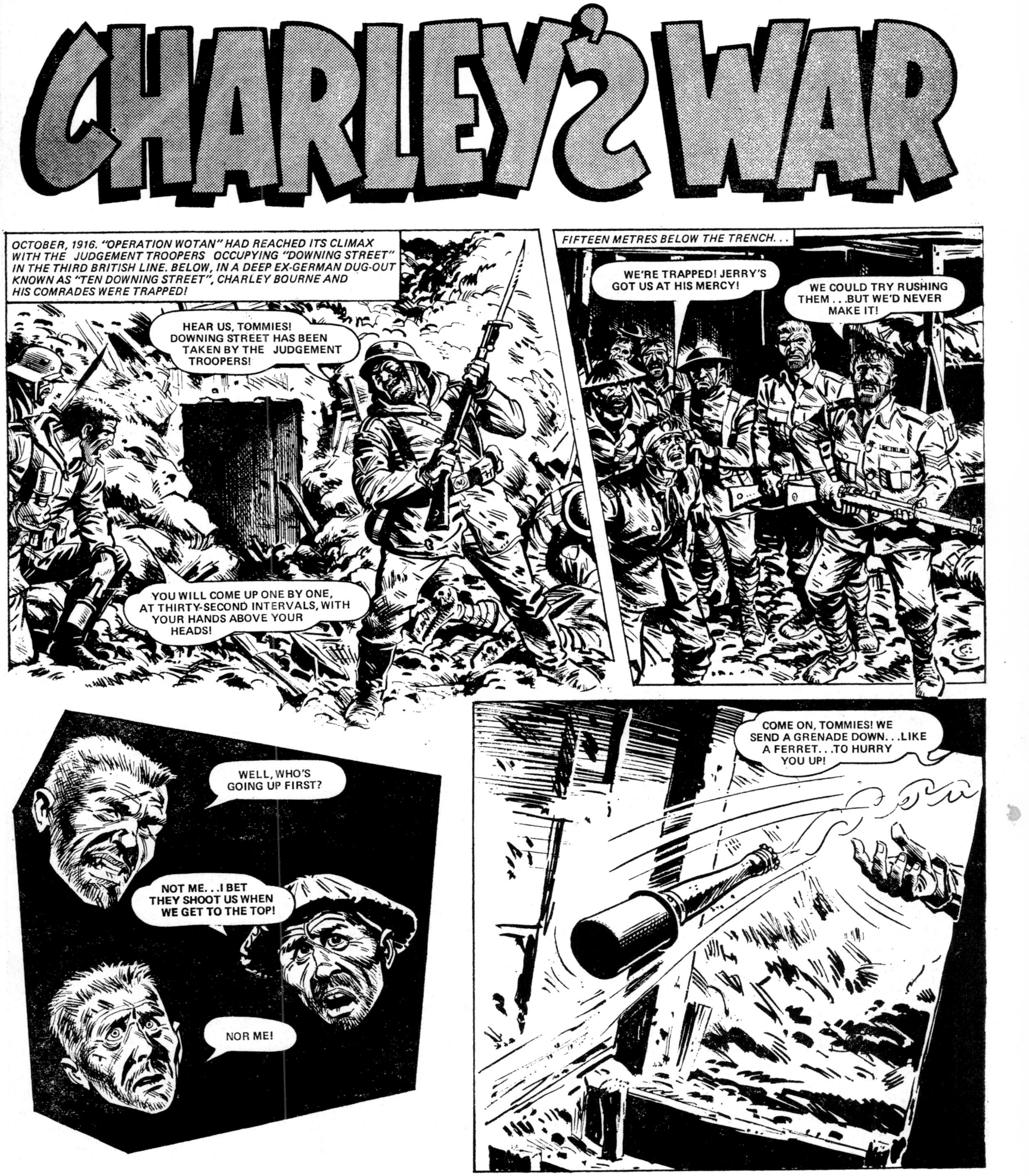
CHARLEY'S WAR
OCTOBER, 1916. "OPERATION WOTAN" HAD REACHED ITS CLIMAX WITH THE JUDGEMENT TROOPERS OCCUPYING "DOWNING STREET" IN THE THIRD BRITISH LINE. BELOW, IN A DEEP EX-GERMAN DUG-OUT KNOWN AS "TEN DOWNING STREET", CHARLEY BOURNE AND HIS COMRADES WERE TRAPPED!
HEAR US, TOMMIES! DOWNING STREET HAS BEEN TAKEN BY THE JUDGEMENT TROOPERS!
YOU WILL COME UP ONE BY ONE, AT THIRTY-SECOND INTERVALS, WITH YOUR HANDS ABOVE YOUR HEADS!
FIFTEEN METRES BELOW THE TRENCH. . .
WE'RE TRAPPED! JERRY'S GOT US AT HIS MERCY!
WE COULD TRY RUSHING THEM . . .BUT WE'D NEVER MAKE IT!
WELL, WHO'S GOING UP FIRST?
NOT ME. . .I BET THEY SHOOT US WHEN WE GET TO THE TOP!
NOR ME!
COME ON, TOMMIES! WE SEND A GRENADE DOWN. . .LIKE A FERRET. . .TO HURRY YOU UP!

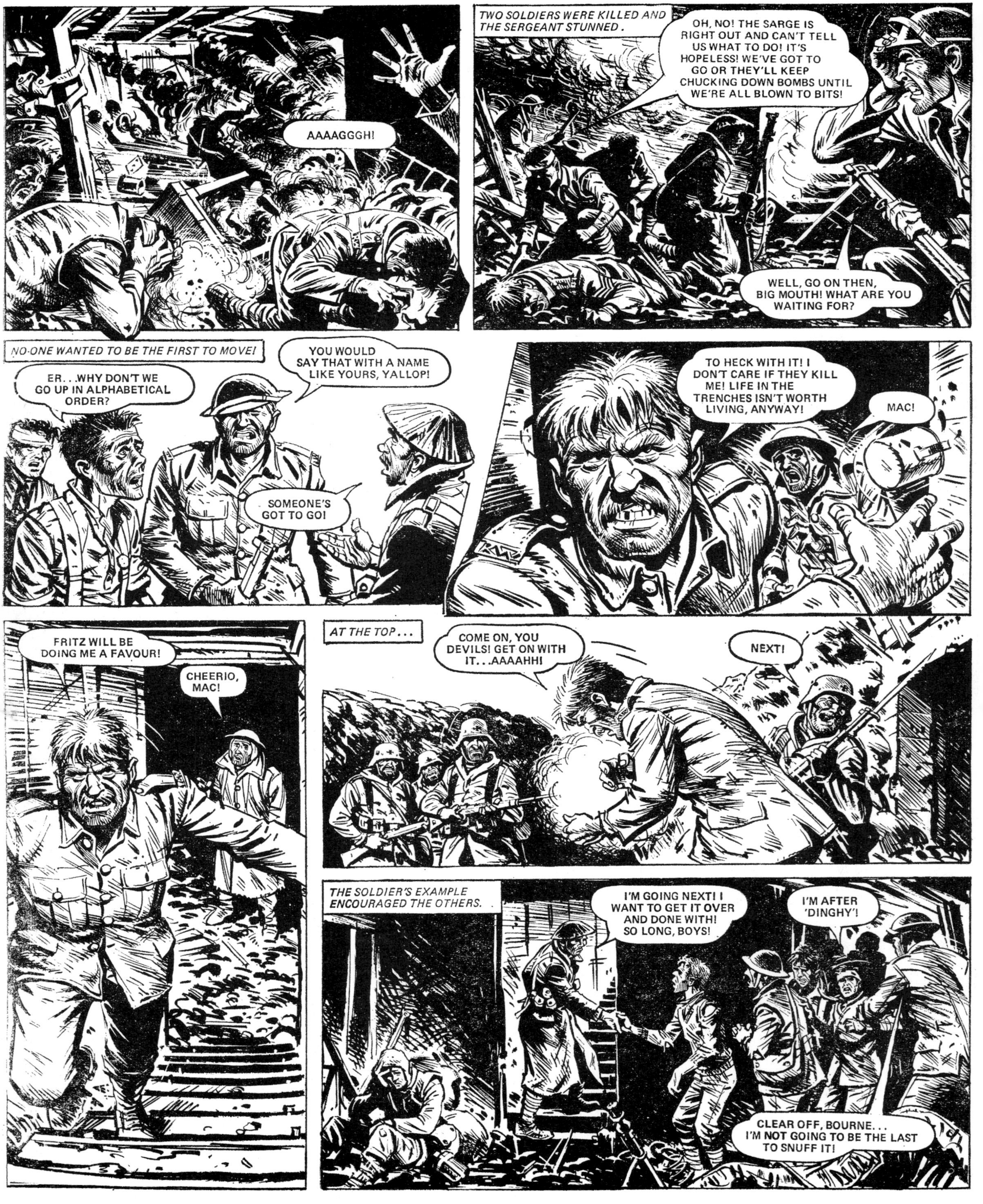
AAAAGGGH!
TWO SOLDIERS WERE KILLED AND THE SERGEANT STUNNED.
OH, NO! THE SARGE IS RIGHT OUT AND CAN'T TELL US WHAT TO DO! IT'S HOPELESS! WE'VE GOT TO GO OR THEY'LL KEEP CHUCKING DOWN BOMBS UNTIL WE'RE ALL BLOWN TO BITS!
WELL, GO ON THEN, BIG MOUTH! WHAT ARE YOU WAITING FOR?
NO-ONE WANTED TO BE THE FIRST TO MOVE!
ER. . .WHY DON'T WE GO UP IN ALPHABETICAL ORDER?
YOU WOULD SAY THAT WITH A NAME LIKE YOURS, YALLOP!
SOMEONE'S GOT TO GO!
TO HECK WITH IT! I DON'T CARE IF THEY KILL ME! LIFE IN THE TRENCHES ISN'T WORTH LIVING, ANYWAY!
MAC!
FRITZ WILL BE DOING ME A FAVOUR!
CHEERIO, MAC!
AT THE TOP...
COME ON, YOU DEVILS! GET ON WITH IT. . .AAAAHH!
NEXT!
THE SOLDIER'S EXAMPLE ENCOURAGED THE OTHERS.
I'M GOING NEXT! I WANT TO GET IT OVER AND DONE WITH! SO LONG, BOYS!
I'M AFTER 'DINGHY'!
CLEAR OFF, BOURNE... I'M NOT GOING TO BE THE LAST TO SNUFF IT!

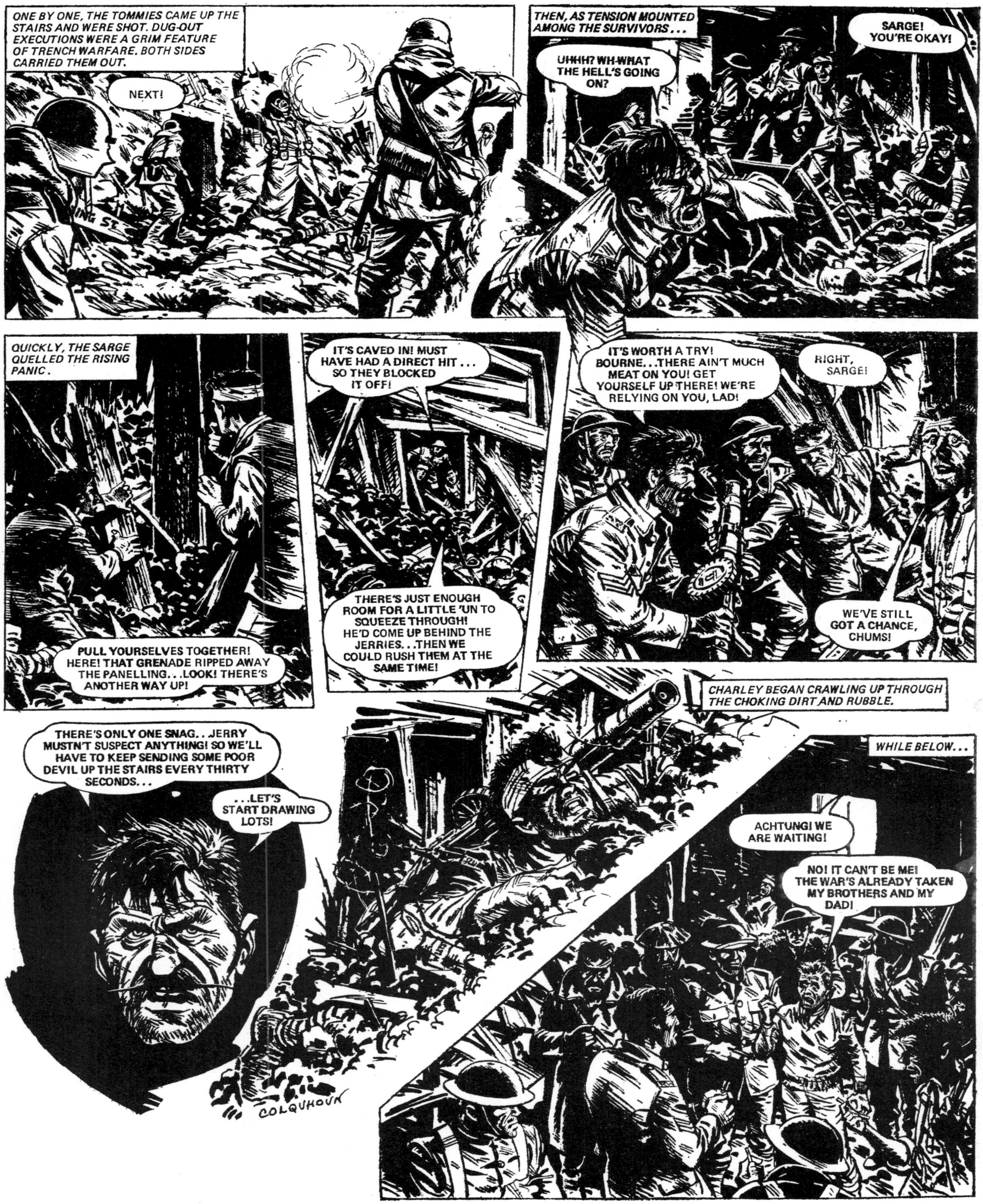
ONE BY ONE, THE TOMMIES CAME UP THE STAIRS AND WERE SHOT. DUG-OUT EXECUTIONS WERE A GRIM FEATURE OF TRENCH WARFARE. BOTH SIDES CARRIED THEM OUT.
NEXT!
THEN, AS TENSION MOUNTED AMONG THE SURVIVORS . . .
UHHH? WH-WHAT THE HELL'S GOING ON?
SARGE! YOU'RE OKAY!
QUICKLY, THE SARGE QUELLED THE RISING PANIC.
PULL YOURSELVES TOGETHER! HERE! THAT GRENADE RIPPED AWAY THE PANELLING. . .LOOK! THERE'S ANOTHER WAY UP!
IT'S CAVED IN! MUST HAVE HAD A DIRECT HIT . . . SO THEY BLOCKED IT OFF!
THERE'S JUST ENOUGH ROOM FOR A LITTLE 'UN TO SQUEEZE THROUGH! HE'D COME UP BEHIND THE JERRIES. . .THEN WE COULD RUSH THEM AT THE SAME TIME!
IT'S WORTH A TRY! BOURNE. . .THERE AIN'T MUCH MEAT ON YOU! GET YOURSELF UP THERE! WE'RE RELYING ON YOU, LAD!
RIGHT, SARGE!
WE'VE STILL GOT A CHANCE, CHUMS!
THERE'S ONLY ONE SNAG. . JERRY MUSTN'T SUSPECT ANYTHING! SO WE'LL HAVE TO KEEP SENDING SOME POOR DEVIL UP THE STAIRS EVERY THIRTY SECONDS. . .
. . .LET'S START DRAWING LOTS!
CHARLEY BEGAN CRAWLING UP THROUGH THE CHOKING DIRT AND RUBBLE.
COLQUHOUN
WHILE BELOW. . .
ACHTUNG! WE ARE WAITING!
NO! IT CAN'T BE ME! THE WAR'S ALREADY TAKEN MY BROTHERS AND MY DAD!

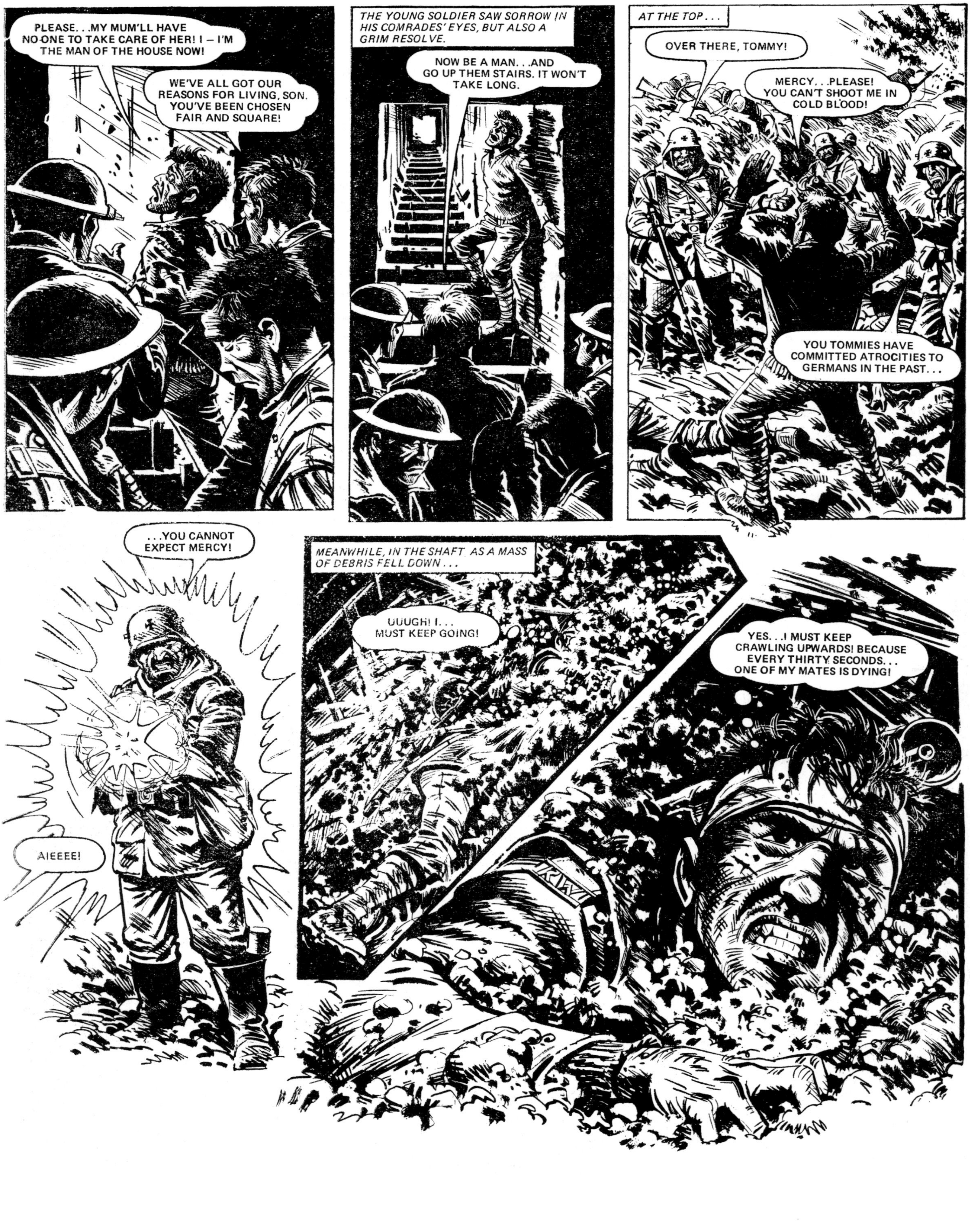
PLEASE. . .MY MUM'LL HAVE NO-ONE TO TAKE CARE OF HER! I — I'M THE MAN OF THE HOUSE NOW!
WE'VE ALL GOT OUR REASONS FOR LIVING, SON. YOU'VE BEEN CHOSEN FAIR AND SQUARE!
THE YOUNG SOLDIER SAW SORROW IN HIS COMRADES' EYES, BUT ALSO A GRIM RESOLVE.
NOW BE A MAN. . .AND GO UP THEM STAIRS. IT WON'T TAKE LONG.
AT THE TOP . . .
OVER THERE, TOMMY!
MERCY. . .PLEASE! YOU CAN'T SHOOT ME IN COLD BLOOD!
YOU TOMMIES HAVE COMMITTED ATROCITIES TO GERMANS IN THE PAST. . .
. . .YOU CANNOT EXPECT MERCY!
AIEEEE!
MEANWHILE, IN THE SHAFT AS A MASS OF DEBRIS FELL DOWN . . .
UUUGH! I . . . MUST KEEP GOING!
YES. . .I MUST KEEP CRAWLING UPWARDS! BECAUSE EVERY THIRTY SECONDS. . . ONE OF MY MATES IS DYING!

CHARLEY'S WAR

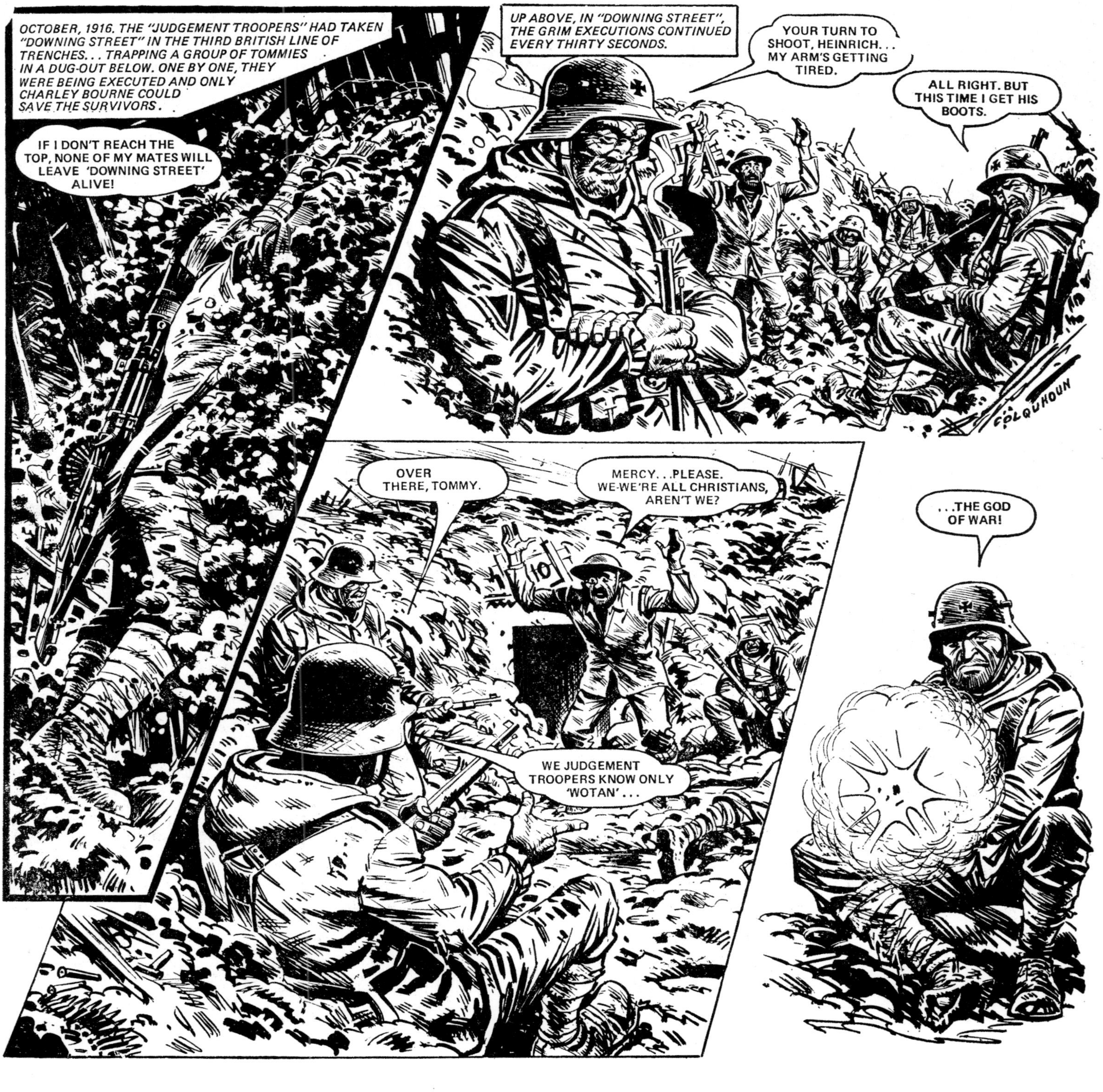

OCTOBER, 1916. THE "JUDGEMENT TROOPERS" HAD TAKEN "DOWNING STREET" IN THE THIRD BRITISH LINE OF TRENCHES... TRAPPING A GROUP OF TOMMIES IN A DUG-OUT BELOW. ONE BY ONE, THEY WERE BEING EXECUTED AND ONLY CHARLEY BOURNE COULD SAVE THE SURVIVORS.
IF I DON'T REACH THE TOP, NONE OF MY MATES WILL LEAVE 'DOWNING STREET' ALIVE!
UP ABOVE, IN "DOWNING STREET", THE GRIM EXECUTIONS CONTINUED EVERY THIRTY SECONDS.
YOUR TURN TO SHOOT, HEINRICH... MY ARM'S GETTING TIRED.
ALL RIGHT. BUT THIS TIME I GET HIS BOOTS.
COLQUHOUN
OVER THERE, TOMMY.
MERCY...PLEASE. WE-WE'RE ALL CHRISTIANS, AREN'T WE?
10
WE JUDGEMENT TROOPERS KNOW ONLY 'WOTAN'...
...THE GOD OF WAR!

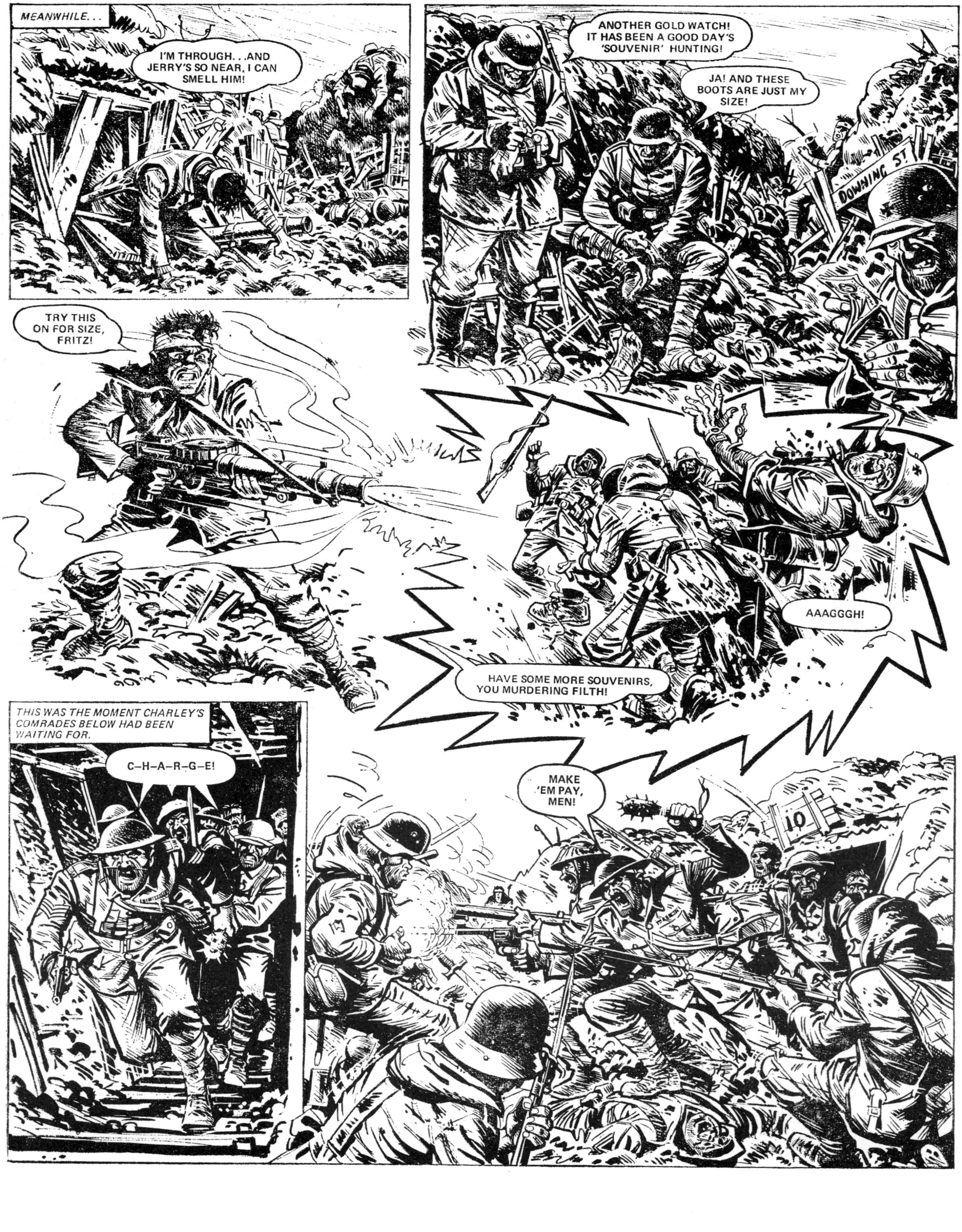
MEANWHILE...
I'M THROUGH...AND JERRY'S SO NEAR, I CAN SMELL HIM!
ANOTHER GOLD WATCH! IT HAS BEEN A GOOD DAY'S 'SOUVENIR' HUNTING!
JA! AND THESE BOOTS ARE JUST MY SIZE!
DOWNING ST.
TRY THIS ON FOR SIZE, FRITZ!
AAAGGGH!
HAVE SOME MORE SOUVENIRS, YOU MURDERING FILTH!
THIS WAS THE MOMENT CHARLEY'S COMRADES BELOW HAD BEEN WAITING FOR.
C-H-A-R-G-E!
MAKE 'EM PAY, MEN!
10

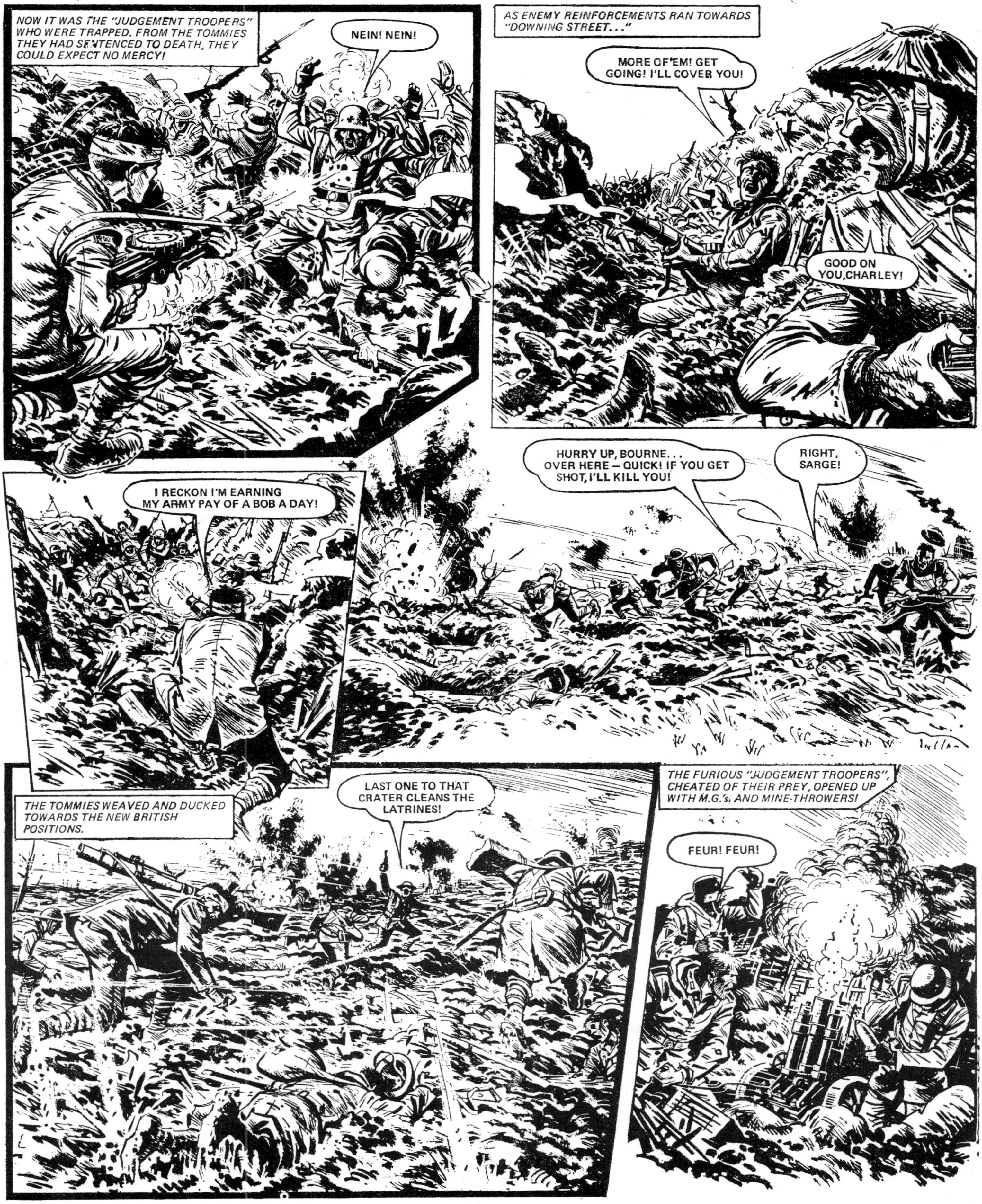
NOW IT WAS THE "JUDGEMENT TROOPERS" WHO WERE TRAPPED. FROM THE TOMMIES THEY HAD SENTENCED TO DEATH, THEY COULD EXPECT NO MERCY!
NEIN! NEIN!
AS ENEMY REINFORCEMENTS RAN TOWARDS "DOWNING STREET..."
MORE OF 'EM! GET GOING! I'LL COVER YOU!
GOOD ON YOU,CHARLEY!
I RECKON I'M EARNING MY ARMY PAY OF A BOB A DAY!
HURRY UP, BOURNE... OVER HERE — QUICK! IF YOU GET SHOT, I'LL KILL YOU!
RIGHT, SARGE!
THE TOMMIES WEAVED AND DUCKED TOWARDS THE NEW BRITISH POSITIONS.
LAST ONE TO THAT CRATER CLEANS THE LATRINES!
THE FURIOUS "JUDGEMENT TROOPERS", CHEATED OF THEIR PREY, OPENED UP WITH M.G.'s. AND MINE-THROWERS!
FEUR! FEUR!

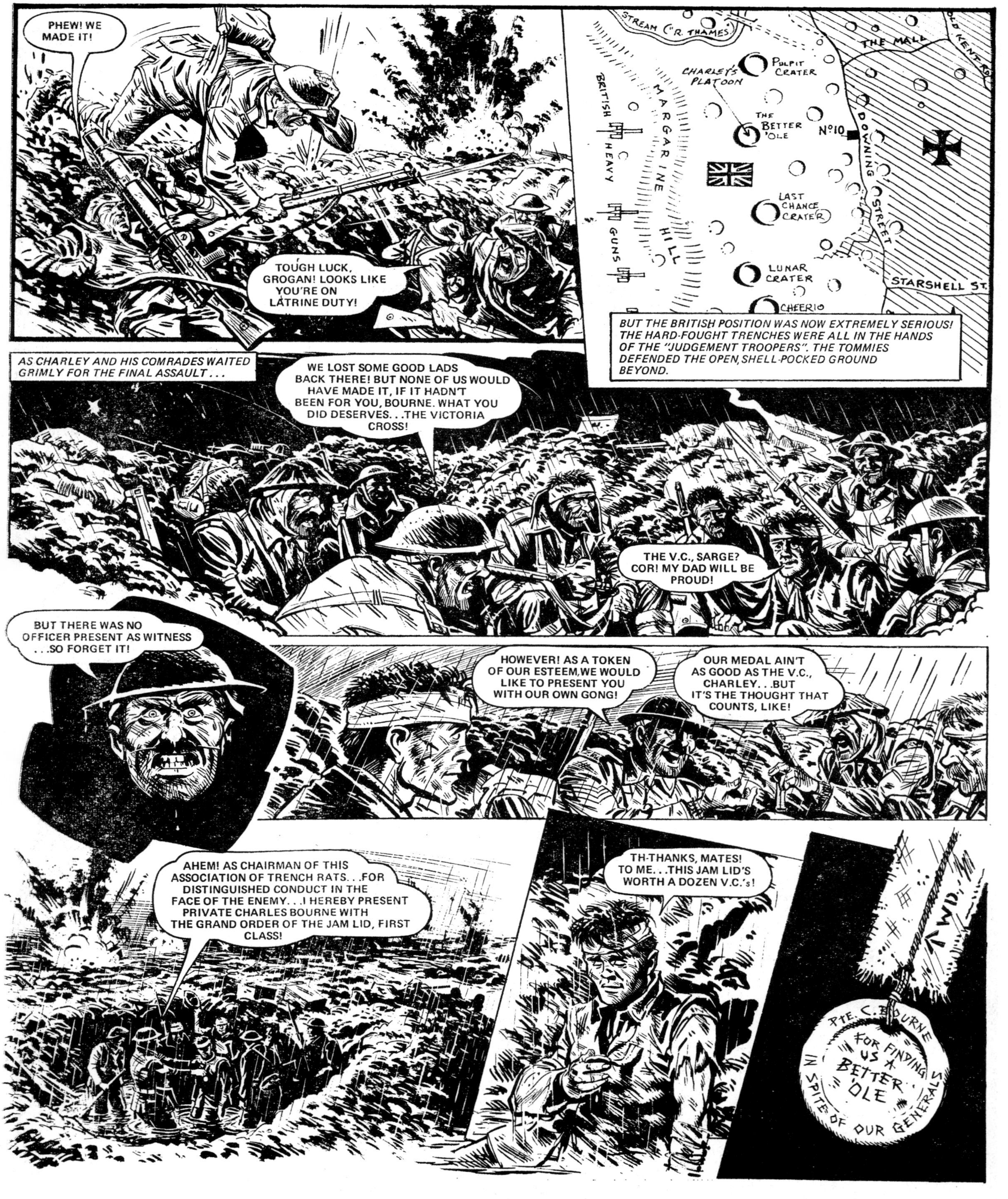
PHEW! WE MADE IT!
TOUGH LUCK, GROGAN! LOOKS LIKE YOU'RE ON LATRINE DUTY!
STREAM ("R. THAMES)
THE MALL
PULPIT CRATER
CHARLEY'S PLATOON
BRITISH HEAVY GUNS
MARGARINE HILL
THE BETTER 'OLE
Nº10
DOWNING STREET
LAST CHANCE CRATER
LUNAR CRATER
STARSHELL ST.
CHEERIO
BUT THE BRITISH POSITION WAS NOW EXTREMELY SERIOUS! THE HARD-FOUGHT TRENCHES WERE ALL IN THE HANDS OF THE "JUDGEMENT TROOPERS". THE TOMMIES DEFENDED THE OPEN, SHELL-POCKED GROUND BEYOND.
AS CHARLEY AND HIS COMRADES WAITED GRIMLY FOR THE FINAL ASSAULT . . .
WE LOST SOME GOOD LADS BACK THERE! BUT NONE OF US WOULD HAVE MADE IT, IF IT HADN'T BEEN FOR YOU, BOURNE. WHAT YOU DID DESERVES. . .THE VICTORIA CROSS!
THE V.C., SARGE? COR! MY DAD WILL BE PROUD!
BUT THERE WAS NO OFFICER PRESENT AS WITNESS . . .SO FORGET IT!
HOWEVER! AS A TOKEN OF OUR ESTEEM, WE WOULD LIKE TO PRESENT YOU WITH OUR OWN GONG!
OUR MEDAL AIN'T AS GOOD AS THE V.C., CHARLEY. . .BUT IT'S THE THOUGHT THAT COUNTS, LIKE!
AHEM! AS CHAIRMAN OF THIS ASSOCIATION OF TRENCH RATS. . .FOR DISTINGUISHED CONDUCT IN THE FACE OF THE ENEMY. . .I HEREBY PRESENT PRIVATE CHARLES BOURNE WITH THE GRAND ORDER OF THE JAM LID, FIRST CLASS!
TH-THANKS, MATES! TO ME. . .THIS JAM LID'S WORTH A DOZEN V.C.'s!
PTE. C. BOURNE
FOR FINDING US A BETTER 'OLE
IN SPITE OF OUR GENERALS

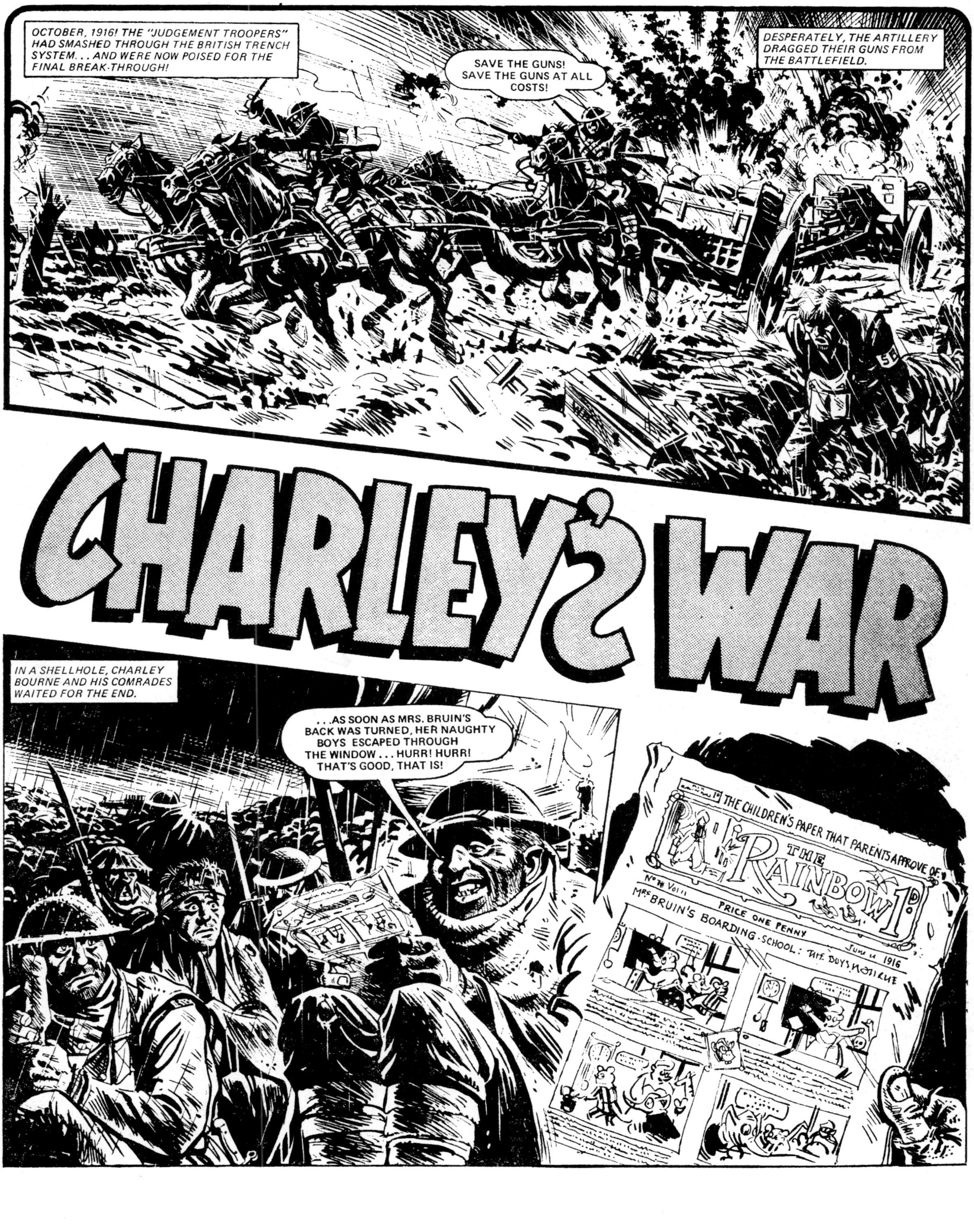
OCTOBER, 1916! THE "JUDGEMENT TROOPERS" HAD SMASHED THROUGH THE BRITISH TRENCH SYSTEM... AND WERE NOW POISED FOR THE FINAL BREAK-THROUGH!
SAVE THE GUNS! SAVE THE GUNS AT ALL COSTS!
DESPERATELY, THE ARTILLERY DRAGGED THEIR GUNS FROM THE BATTLEFIELD.
CHARLEY'S WAR
IN A SHELLHOLE, CHARLEY BOURNE AND HIS COMRADES WAITED FOR THE END.
...AS SOON AS MRS. BRUIN'S BACK WAS TURNED, HER NAUGHTY BOYS ESCAPED THROUGH THE WINDOW... HURR! HURR! THAT'S GOOD, THAT IS!
THE CHILDREN'S PAPER THAT PARENTS APPROVE OF
THE RAINBOW 1d.
PRICE ONE PENNY
MRS BRUIN'S BOARDING-SCHOOL:
1916

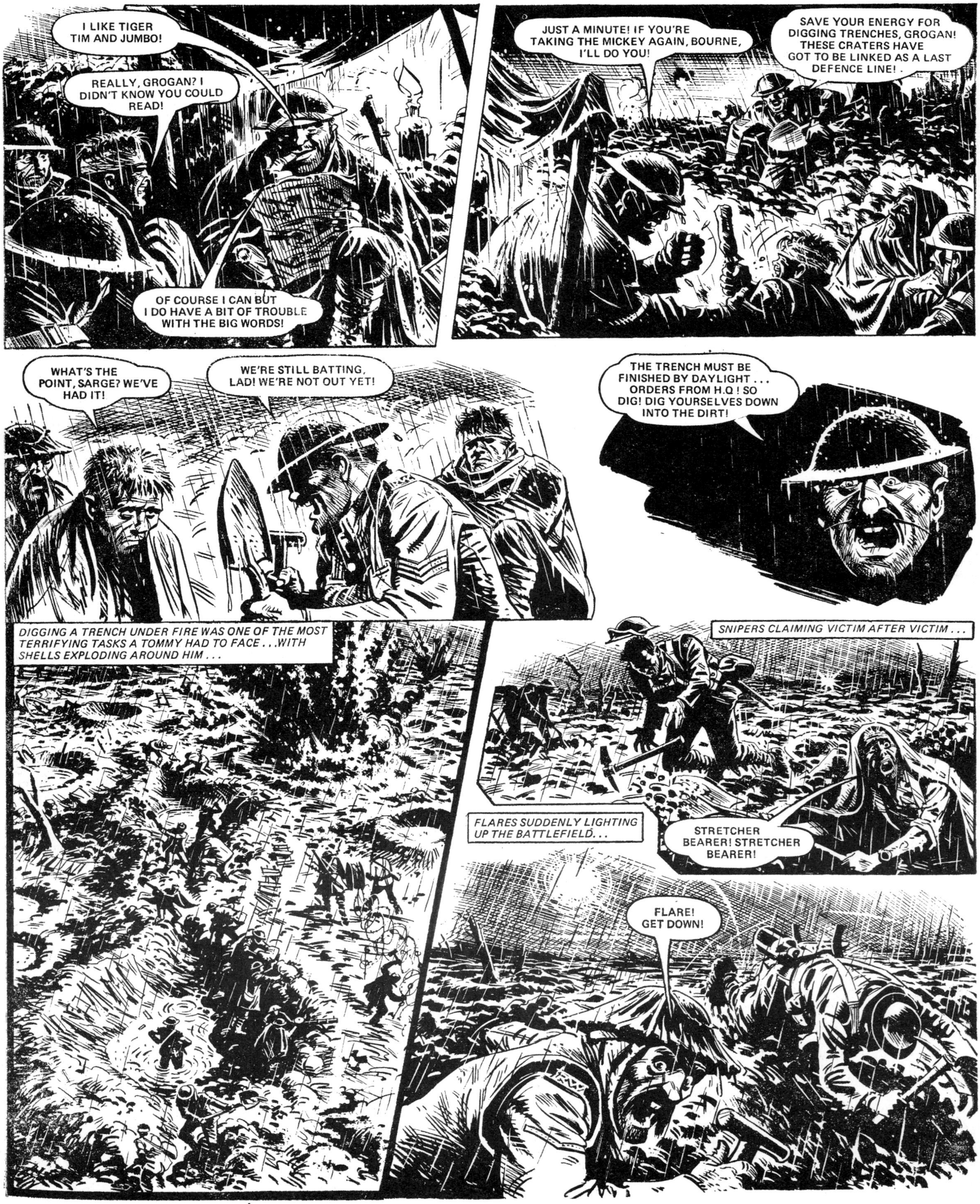
I LIKE TIGER TIM AND JUMBO!
REALLY, GROGAN? I DIDN'T KNOW YOU COULD READ!
OF COURSE I CAN BUT I DO HAVE A BIT OF TROUBLE WITH THE BIG WORDS!
JUST A MINUTE! IF YOU'RE TAKING THE MICKEY AGAIN, BOURNE, I'LL DO YOU!
SAVE YOUR ENERGY FOR DIGGING TRENCHES, GROGAN! THESE CRATERS HAVE GOT TO BE LINKED AS A LAST DEFENCE LINE!
WHAT'S THE POINT, SARGE? WE'VE HAD IT!
WE'RE STILL BATTING, LAD! WE'RE NOT OUT YET!
THE TRENCH MUST BE FINISHED BY DAYLIGHT . . . ORDERS FROM H.Q ! SO DIG! DIG YOURSELVES DOWN INTO THE DIRT!
DIGGING A TRENCH UNDER FIRE WAS ONE OF THE MOST TERRIFYING TASKS A TOMMY HAD TO FACE . . .WITH SHELLS EXPLODING AROUND HIM . . .
SNIPERS CLAIMING VICTIM AFTER VICTIM . . .
STRETCHER BEARER! STRETCHER BEARER!
FLARES SUDDENLY LIGHTING UP THE BATTLEFIELD. . .
FLARE! GET DOWN!

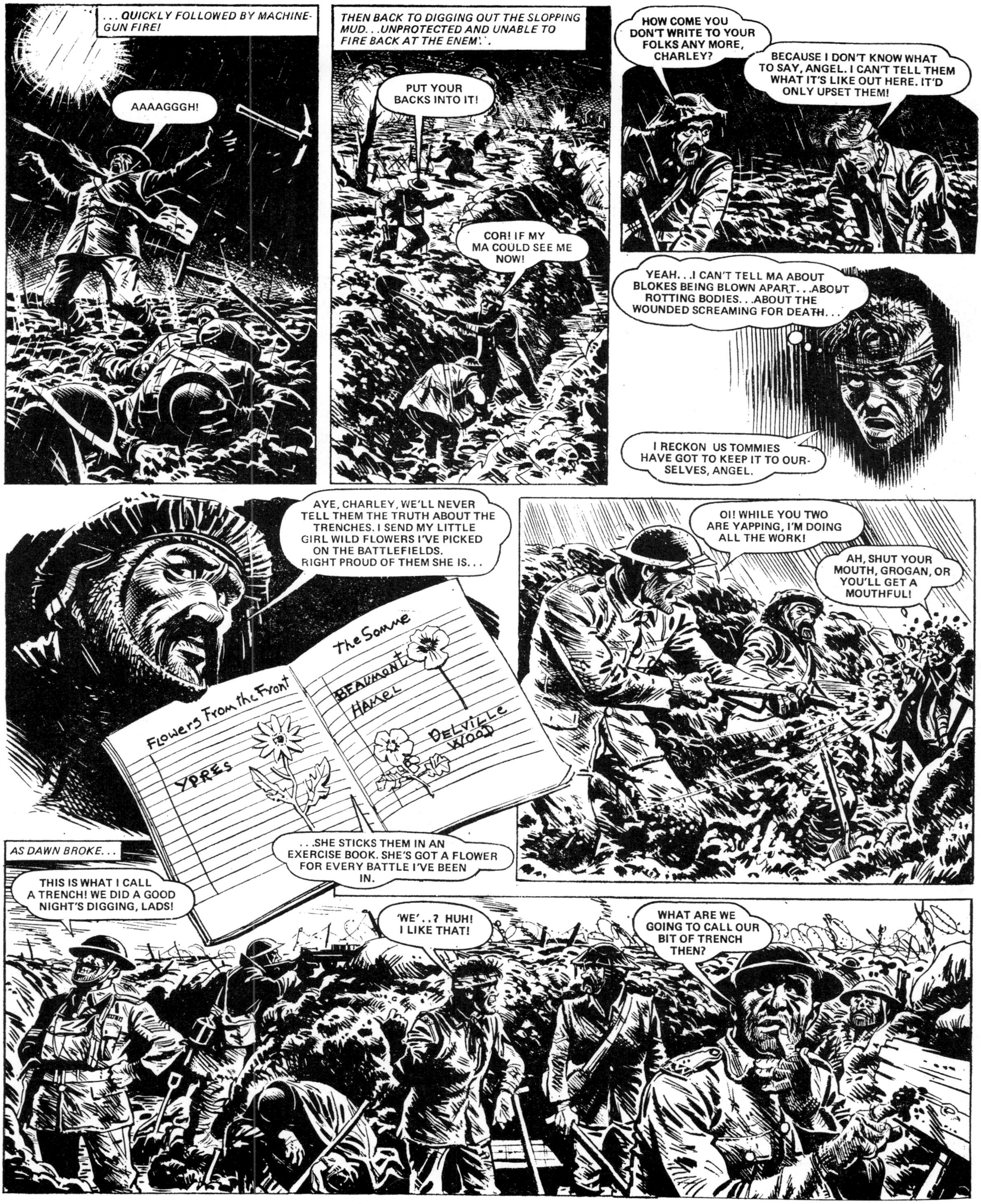

...QUICKLY FOLLOWED BY MACHINE-GUN FIRE!
AAAAGGGH!
THEN BACK TO DIGGING OUT THE SLOPPING MUD...UNPROTECTED AND UNABLE TO FIRE BACK AT THE ENEMY...
PUT YOUR BACKS INTO IT!
COR! IF MY MA COULD SEE ME NOW!
HOW COME YOU DON'T WRITE TO YOUR FOLKS ANY MORE, CHARLEY?
BECAUSE I DON'T KNOW WHAT TO SAY, ANGEL. I CAN'T TELL THEM WHAT IT'S LIKE OUT HERE. IT'D ONLY UPSET THEM!
YEAH...I CAN'T TELL MA ABOUT BLOKES BEING BLOWN APART...ABOUT ROTTING BODIES...ABOUT THE WOUNDED SCREAMING FOR DEATH...
I RECKON US TOMMIES HAVE GOT TO KEEP IT TO OURSELVES, ANGEL.
AYE, CHARLEY, WE'LL NEVER TELL THEM THE TRUTH ABOUT THE TRENCHES. I SEND MY LITTLE GIRL WILD FLOWERS I'VE PICKED ON THE BATTLEFIELDS. RIGHT PROUD OF THEM SHE IS...
Flowers From the Front
YPRES
The Somme
BEAUMONT HAMEL
DELVILLE WOOD
...SHE STICKS THEM IN AN EXERCISE BOOK. SHE'S GOT A FLOWER FOR EVERY BATTLE I'VE BEEN IN.
OI! WHILE YOU TWO ARE YAPPING, I'M DOING ALL THE WORK!
AH, SHUT YOUR MOUTH, GROGAN, OR YOU'LL GET A MOUTHFUL!
AS DAWN BROKE...
THIS IS WHAT I CALL A TRENCH! WE DID A GOOD NIGHT'S DIGGING, LADS!
'WE'..? HUH! I LIKE THAT!
WHAT ARE WE GOING TO CALL OUR BIT OF TRENCH THEN?

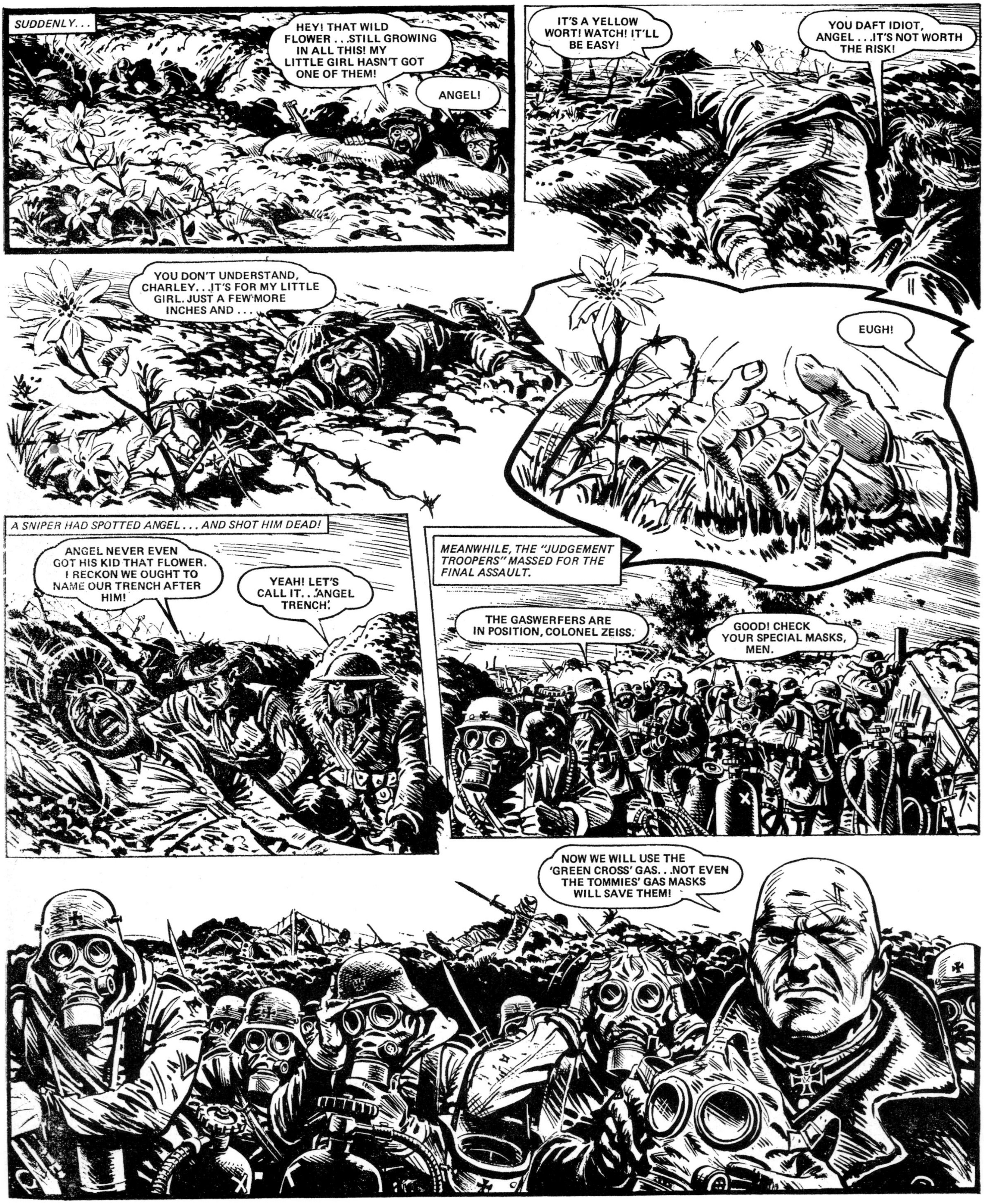

SUDDENLY . . .
HEY! THAT WILD FLOWER . . .STILL GROWING IN ALL THIS! MY LITTLE GIRL HASN'T GOT ONE OF THEM!
ANGEL!
IT'S A YELLOW WORT! WATCH! IT'LL BE EASY!
YOU DAFT IDIOT, ANGEL . . .IT'S NOT WORTH THE RISK!
YOU DON'T UNDERSTAND, CHARLEY. . .IT'S FOR MY LITTLE GIRL. JUST A FEW MORE INCHES AND . . .
EUGH!
A SNIPER HAD SPOTTED ANGEL . . . AND SHOT HIM DEAD!
ANGEL NEVER EVEN GOT HIS KID THAT FLOWER. I RECKON WE OUGHT TO NAME OUR TRENCH AFTER HIM!
YEAH! LET'S CALL IT. . .'ANGEL TRENCH'.
MEANWHILE, THE "JUDGEMENT TROOPERS" MASSED FOR THE FINAL ASSAULT.
THE GASWERFERS ARE IN POSITION, COLONEL ZEISS.
GOOD! CHECK YOUR SPECIAL MASKS, MEN.
NOW WE WILL USE THE 'GREEN CROSS' GAS. . .NOT EVEN THE TOMMIES' GAS MASKS WILL SAVE THEM!

CHARLEY'S WAR

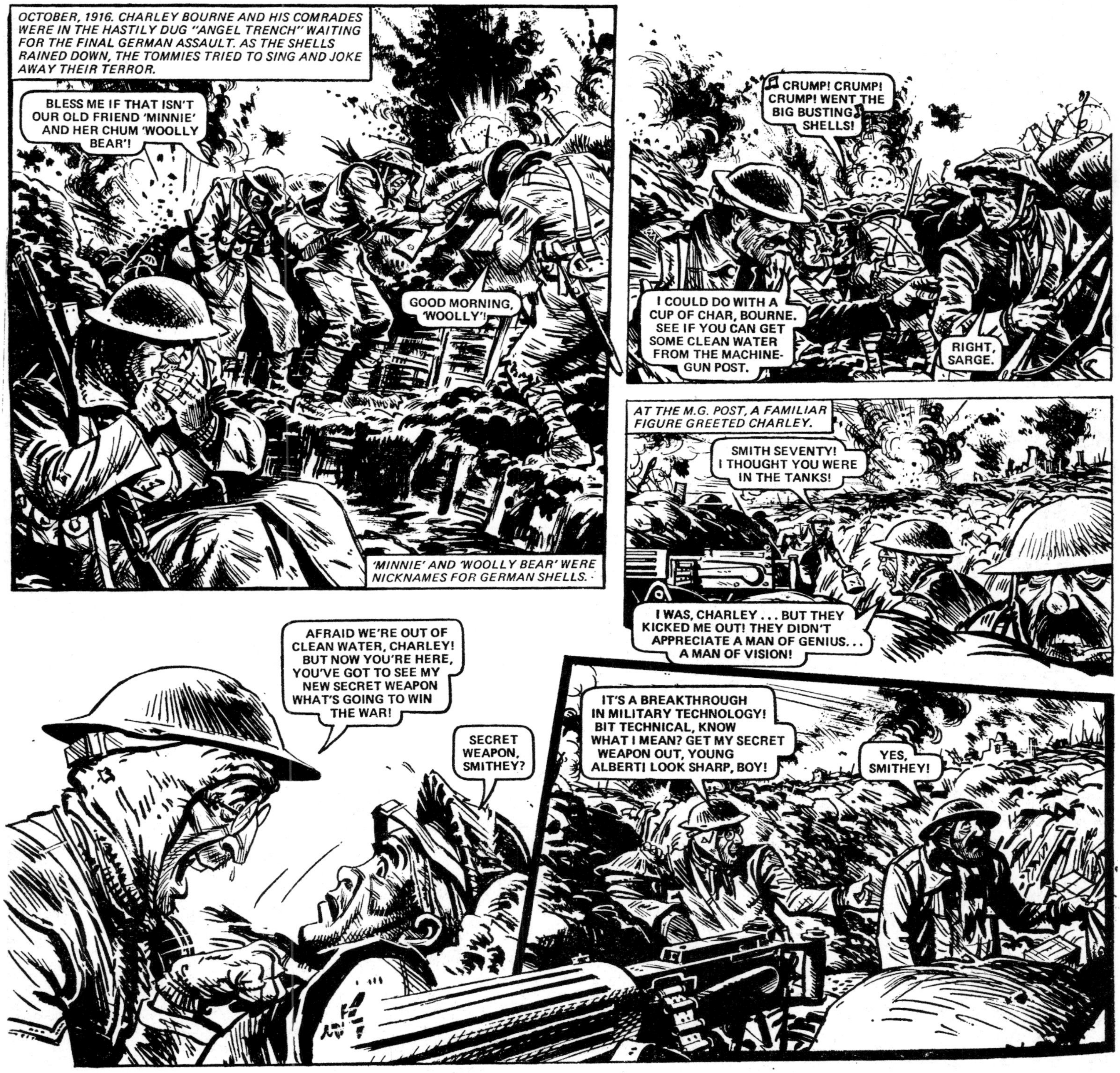

OCTOBER, 1916. CHARLEY BOURNE AND HIS COMRADES WERE IN THE HASTILY DUG "ANGEL TRENCH" WAITING FOR THE FINAL GERMAN ASSAULT. AS THE SHELLS RAINED DOWN, THE TOMMIES TRIED TO SING AND JOKE AWAY THEIR TERROR.
BLESS ME IF THAT ISN'T OUR OLD FRIEND 'MINNIE' AND HER CHUM 'WOOLLY BEAR'!
GOOD MORNING, 'WOOLLY'!
'MINNIE' AND 'WOOLLY BEAR' WERE NICKNAMES FOR GERMAN SHELLS.
♪ CRUMP! CRUMP! CRUMP! WENT THE BIG BUSTING SHELLS! ♪
I COULD DO WITH A CUP OF CHAR, BOURNE. SEE IF YOU CAN GET SOME CLEAN WATER FROM THE MACHINE-GUN POST.
RIGHT, SARGE.
AT THE M.G. POST, A FAMILIAR FIGURE GREETED CHARLEY.
SMITH SEVENTY! I THOUGHT YOU WERE IN THE TANKS!
I WAS, CHARLEY . . . BUT THEY KICKED ME OUT! THEY DIDN'T APPRECIATE A MAN OF GENIUS. . . A MAN OF VISION!
AFRAID WE'RE OUT OF CLEAN WATER, CHARLEY! BUT NOW YOU'RE HERE, YOU'VE GOT TO SEE MY NEW SECRET WEAPON WHAT'S GOING TO WIN THE WAR!
SECRET WEAPON, SMITHEY?
IT'S A BREAKTHROUGH IN MILITARY TECHNOLOGY! BIT TECHNICAL, KNOW WHAT I MEAN? GET MY SECRET WEAPON OUT, YOUNG ALBERT! LOOK SHARP, BOY!
YES, SMITHEY!

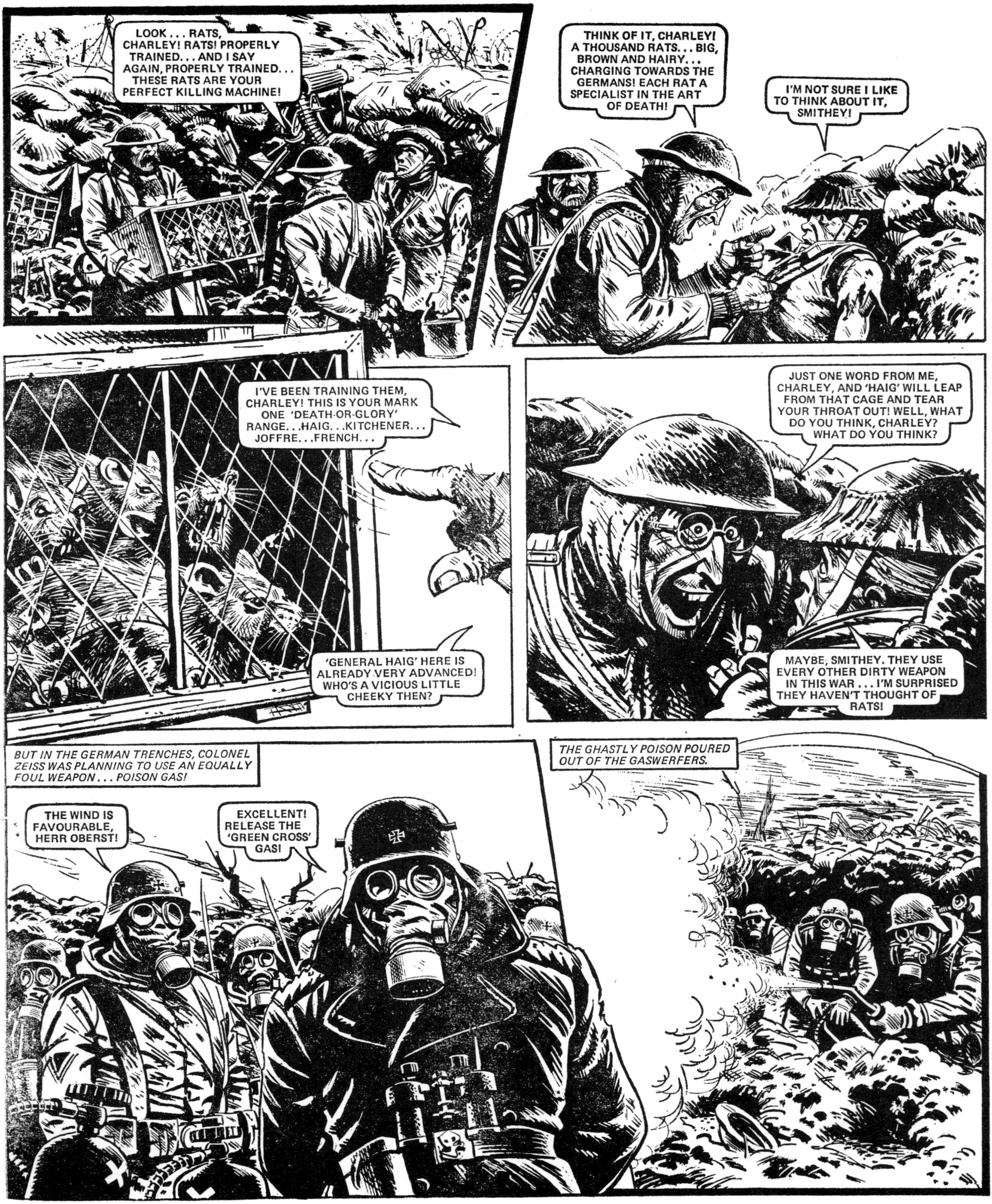
LOOK... RATS, CHARLEY! RATS! PROPERLY TRAINED... AND I SAY AGAIN, PROPERLY TRAINED... THESE RATS ARE YOUR PERFECT KILLING MACHINE!
THINK OF IT, CHARLEY! A THOUSAND RATS... BIG, BROWN AND HAIRY... CHARGING TOWARDS THE GERMANS! EACH RAT A SPECIALIST IN THE ART OF DEATH!
I'M NOT SURE I LIKE TO THINK ABOUT IT, SMITHEY!
I'VE BEEN TRAINING THEM, CHARLEY! THIS IS YOUR MARK ONE 'DEATH-OR-GLORY' RANGE...HAIG...KITCHENER... JOFFRE...FRENCH...
'GENERAL HAIG' HERE IS ALREADY VERY ADVANCED! WHO'S A VICIOUS LITTLE CHEEKY THEN?
JUST ONE WORD FROM ME, CHARLEY, AND 'HAIG' WILL LEAP FROM THAT CAGE AND TEAR YOUR THROAT OUT! WELL, WHAT DO YOU THINK, CHARLEY? WHAT DO YOU THINK?
MAYBE, SMITHEY. THEY USE EVERY OTHER DIRTY WEAPON IN THIS WAR... I'M SURPRISED THEY HAVEN'T THOUGHT OF RATS!
BUT IN THE GERMAN TRENCHES, COLONEL ZEISS WAS PLANNING TO USE AN EQUALLY FOUL WEAPON... POISON GAS!
THE WIND IS FAVOURABLE, HERR OBERST!
EXCELLENT! RELEASE THE 'GREEN CROSS' GAS!
THE GHASTLY POISON POURED OUT OF THE GASWERFERS.

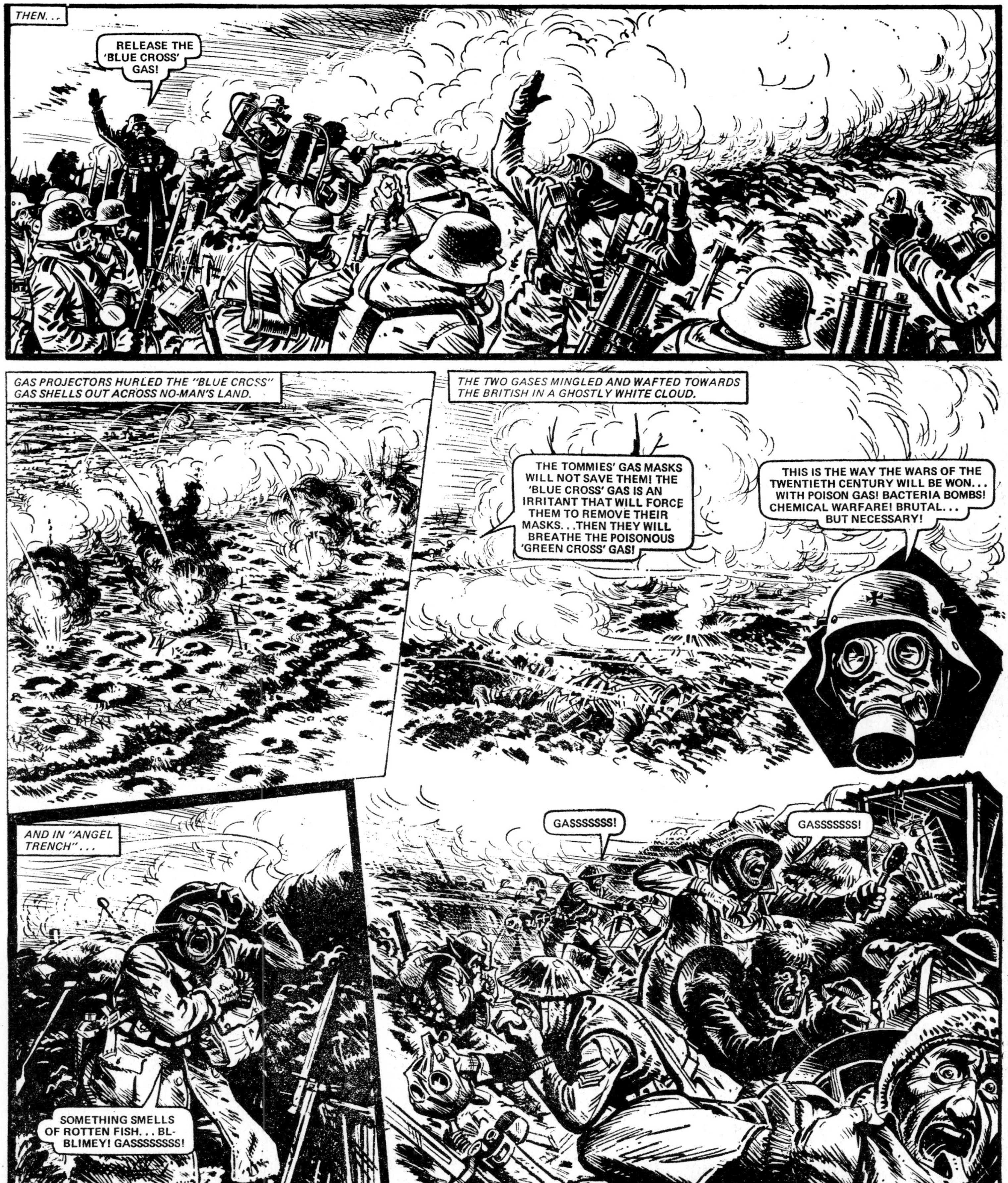
THEN...
RELEASE THE 'BLUE CROSS' GAS!
GAS PROJECTORS HURLED THE "BLUE CROSS" GAS SHELLS OUT ACROSS NO-MAN'S LAND.
THE TWO GASES MINGLED AND WAFTED TOWARDS THE BRITISH IN A GHOSTLY WHITE CLOUD.
THE TOMMIES' GAS MASKS WILL NOT SAVE THEM! THE 'BLUE CROSS' GAS IS AN IRRITANT THAT WILL FORCE THEM TO REMOVE THEIR MASKS...THEN THEY WILL BREATHE THE POISONOUS 'GREEN CROSS' GAS!
THIS IS THE WAY THE WARS OF THE TWENTIETH CENTURY WILL BE WON... WITH POISON GAS! BACTERIA BOMBS! CHEMICAL WARFARE! BRUTAL... BUT NECESSARY!
AND IN "ANGEL TRENCH"...
SOMETHING SMELLS OF ROTTEN FISH... BL-BLIMEY! GASSSSSSSS!
GASSSSSSS!
GASSSSSSS!

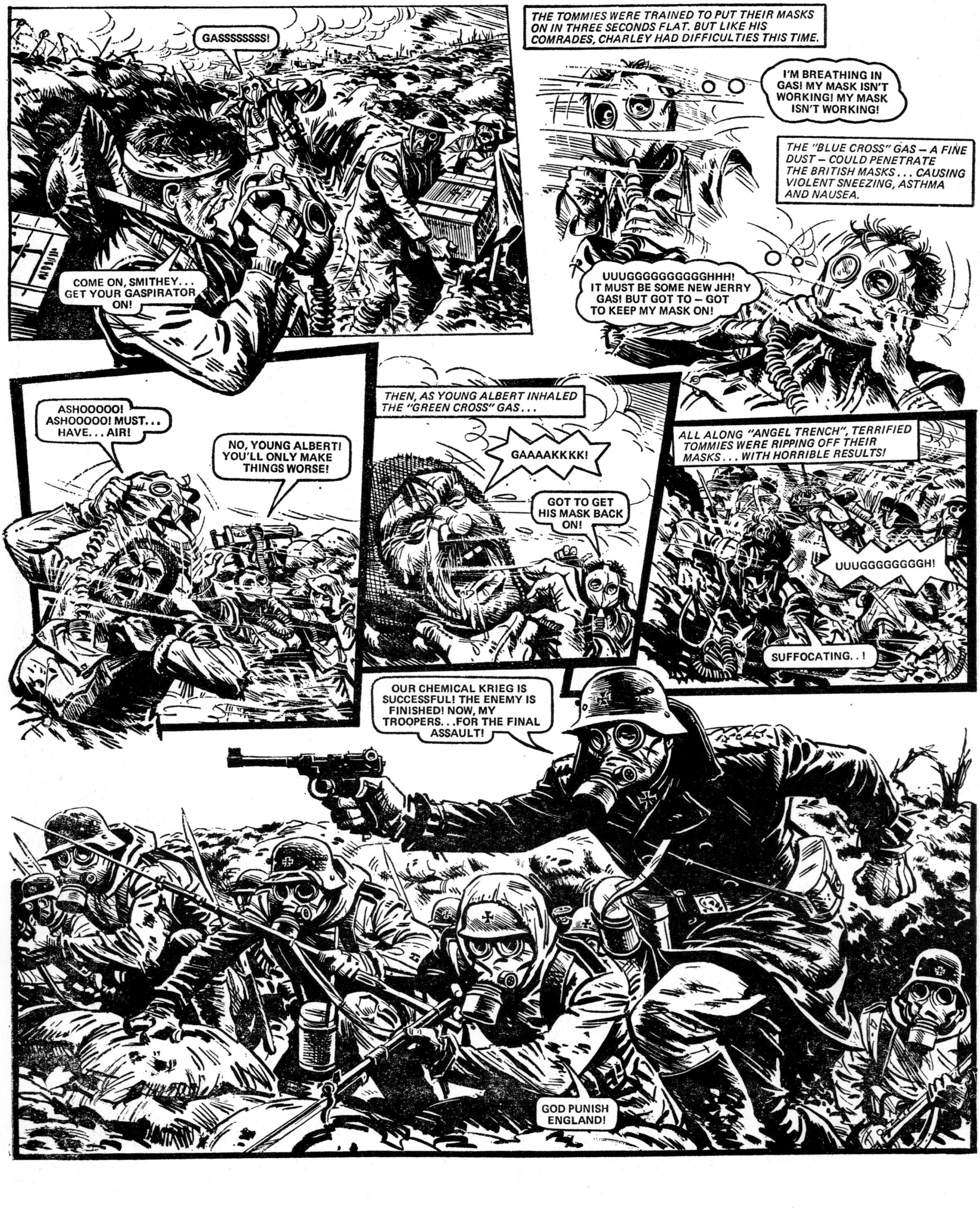
GASSSSSSSS!
COME ON, SMITHEY... GET YOUR GASPIRATOR ON!
THE TOMMIES WERE TRAINED TO PUT THEIR MASKS ON IN THREE SECONDS FLAT. BUT LIKE HIS COMRADES, CHARLEY HAD DIFFICULTIES THIS TIME.
I'M BREATHING IN GAS! MY MASK ISN'T WORKING! MY MASK ISN'T WORKING!
THE "BLUE CROSS" GAS – A FINE DUST – COULD PENETRATE THE BRITISH MASKS... CAUSING VIOLENT SNEEZING, ASTHMA AND NAUSEA.
UUUGGGGGGGGGGHHH! IT MUST BE SOME NEW JERRY GAS! BUT GOT TO – GOT TO KEEP MY MASK ON!
ASHOOOOO! ASHOOOOO! MUST... HAVE... AIR!
NO, YOUNG ALBERT! YOU'LL ONLY MAKE THINGS WORSE!
THEN, AS YOUNG ALBERT INHALED THE "GREEN CROSS" GAS...
GAAAAKKKK!
GOT TO GET HIS MASK BACK ON!
ALL ALONG "ANGEL TRENCH", TERRIFIED TOMMIES WERE RIPPING OFF THEIR MASKS... WITH HORRIBLE RESULTS!
UUUGGGGGGGGH!
SUFFOCATING..!
OUR CHEMICAL KRIEG IS SUCCESSFUL! THE ENEMY IS FINISHED! NOW, MY TROOPERS...FOR THE FINAL ASSAULT!
GOD PUNISH ENGLAND!

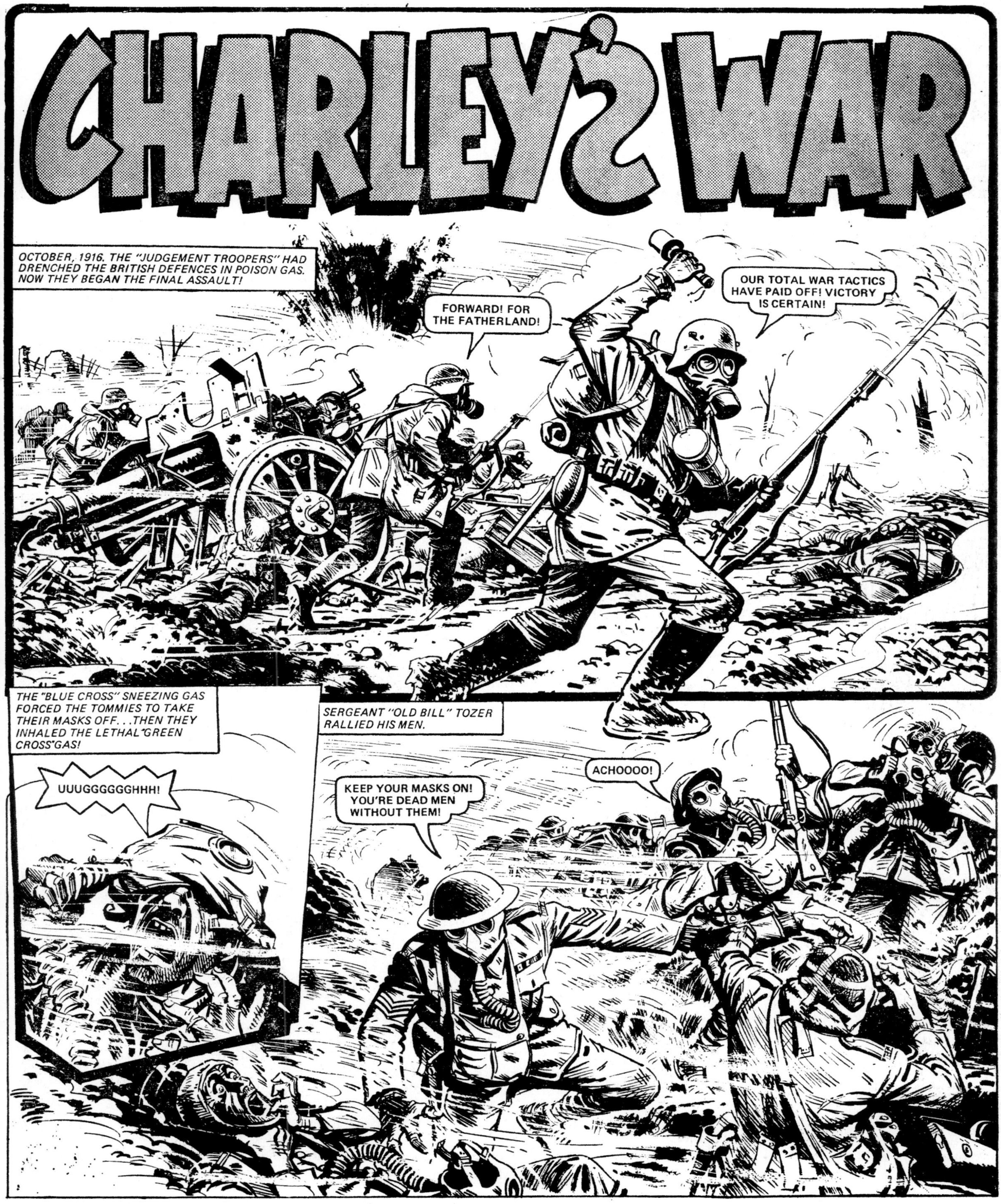

CHARLEY'S WAR
OCTOBER, 1916. THE "JUDGEMENT TROOPERS" HAD DRENCHED THE BRITISH DEFENCES IN POISON GAS. NOW THEY BEGAN THE FINAL ASSAULT!
FORWARD! FOR THE FATHERLAND!
OUR TOTAL WAR TACTICS HAVE PAID OFF! VICTORY IS CERTAIN!
THE "BLUE CROSS" SNEEZING GAS FORCED THE TOMMIES TO TAKE THEIR MASKS OFF. . .THEN THEY INHALED THE LETHAL "GREEN CROSS" GAS!
UUUGGGGGGHHH!
SERGEANT "OLD BILL" TOZER RALLIED HIS MEN.
KEEP YOUR MASKS ON! YOU'RE DEAD MEN WITHOUT THEM!
ACHOOOO!

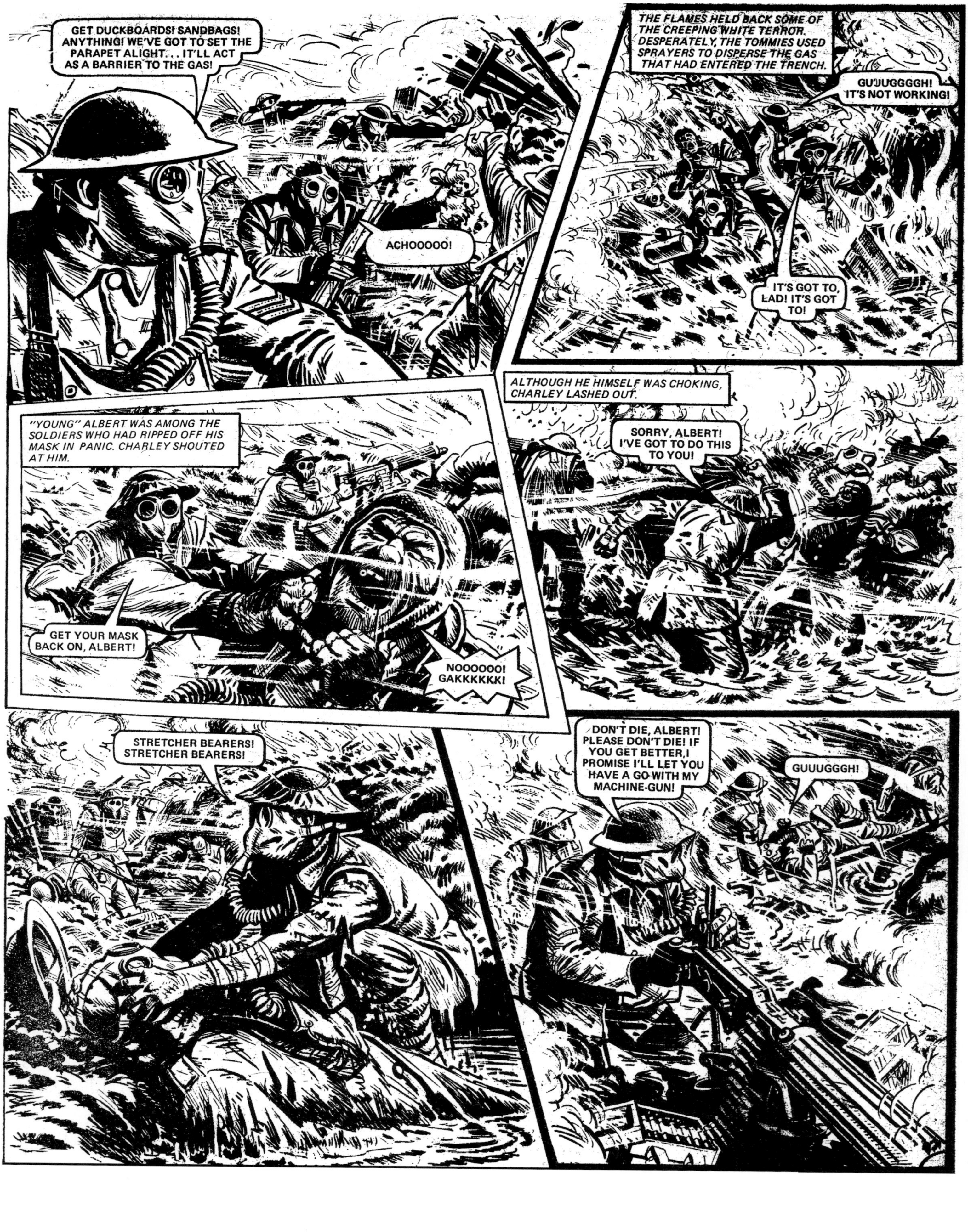
GET DUCKBOARDS! SANDBAGS! ANYTHING! WE'VE GOT TO SET THE PARAPET ALIGHT. . . IT'LL ACT AS A BARRIER TO THE GAS!
ACHOOOOO!
THE FLAMES HELD BACK SOME OF THE CREEPING WHITE TERROR. DESPERATELY, THE TOMMIES USED SPRAYERS TO DISPERSE THE GAS THAT HAD ENTERED THE TRENCH.
GUJUUGGGGH! IT'S NOT WORKING!
IT'S GOT TO, LAD! IT'S GOT TO!
"YOUNG" ALBERT WAS AMONG THE SOLDIERS WHO HAD RIPPED OFF HIS MASK IN PANIC. CHARLEY SHOUTED AT HIM.
GET YOUR MASK BACK ON, ALBERT!
NOOOOOO! GAKKKKKK!
ALTHOUGH HE HIMSELF WAS CHOKING, CHARLEY LASHED OUT.
SORRY, ALBERT! I'VE GOT TO DO THIS TO YOU!
STRETCHER BEARERS! STRETCHER BEARERS!
DON'T DIE, ALBERT! PLEASE DON'T DIE! IF YOU GET BETTER, I PROMISE I'LL LET YOU HAVE A GO WITH MY MACHINE-GUN!
GUUUGGGH!

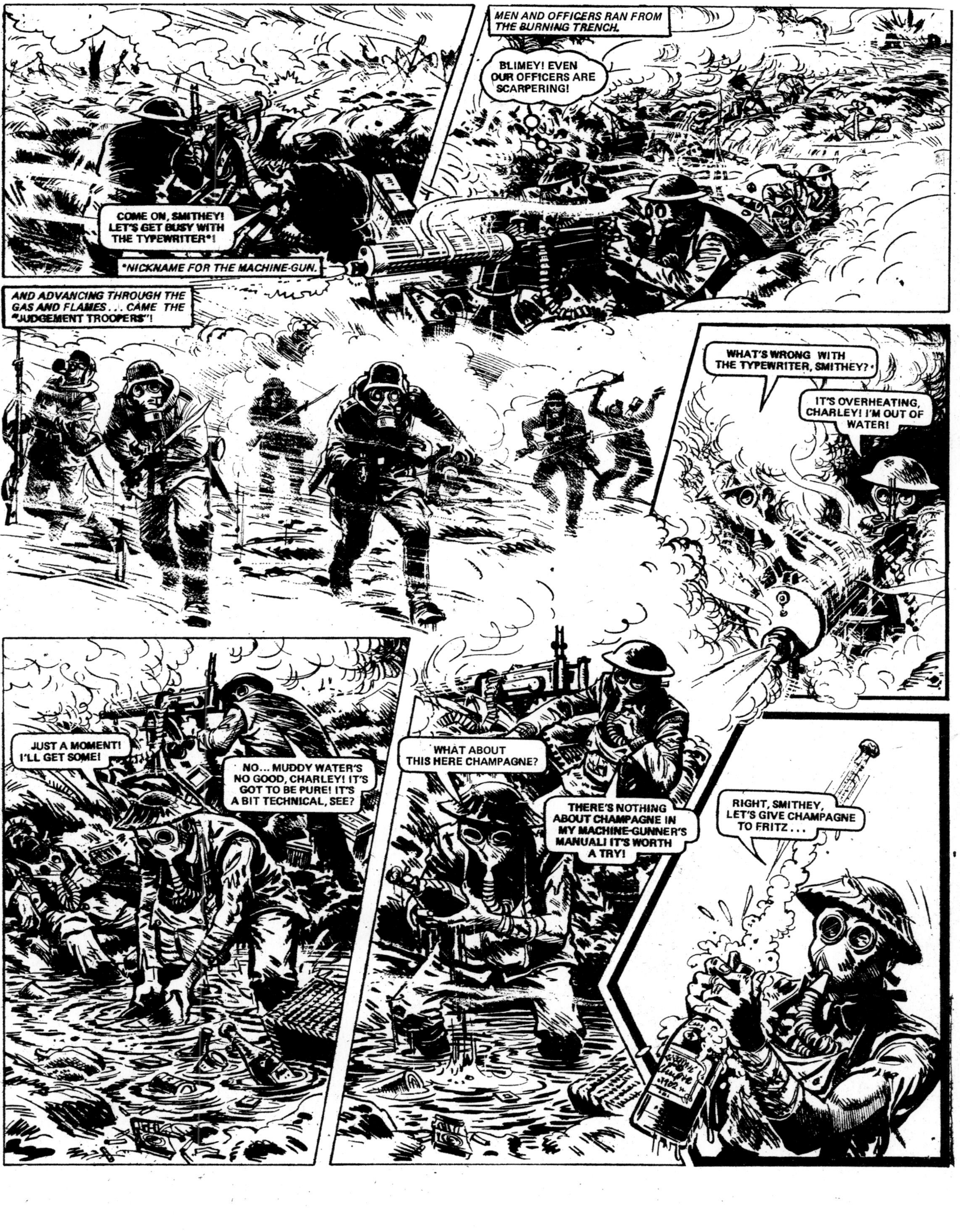
COME ON, SMITHEY! LET'S GET BUSY WITH THE TYPEWRITER*!
*NICKNAME FOR THE MACHINE-GUN.
MEN AND OFFICERS RAN FROM THE BURNING TRENCH.
BLIMEY! EVEN OUR OFFICERS ARE SCARPERING!
AND ADVANCING THROUGH THE GAS AND FLAMES . . . CAME THE "JUDGEMENT TROOPERS"!
WHAT'S WRONG WITH THE TYPEWRITER, SMITHEY?
IT'S OVERHEATING, CHARLEY! I'M OUT OF WATER!
JUST A MOMENT! I'LL GET SOME!
NO... MUDDY WATER'S NO GOOD, CHARLEY! IT'S GOT TO BE PURE! IT'S A BIT TECHNICAL, SEE?
WHAT ABOUT THIS HERE CHAMPAGNE?
THERE'S NOTHING ABOUT CHAMPAGNE IN MY MACHINE-GUNNER'S MANUAL! IT'S WORTH A TRY!
RIGHT, SMITHEY, LET'S GIVE CHAMPAGNE TO FRITZ . . .

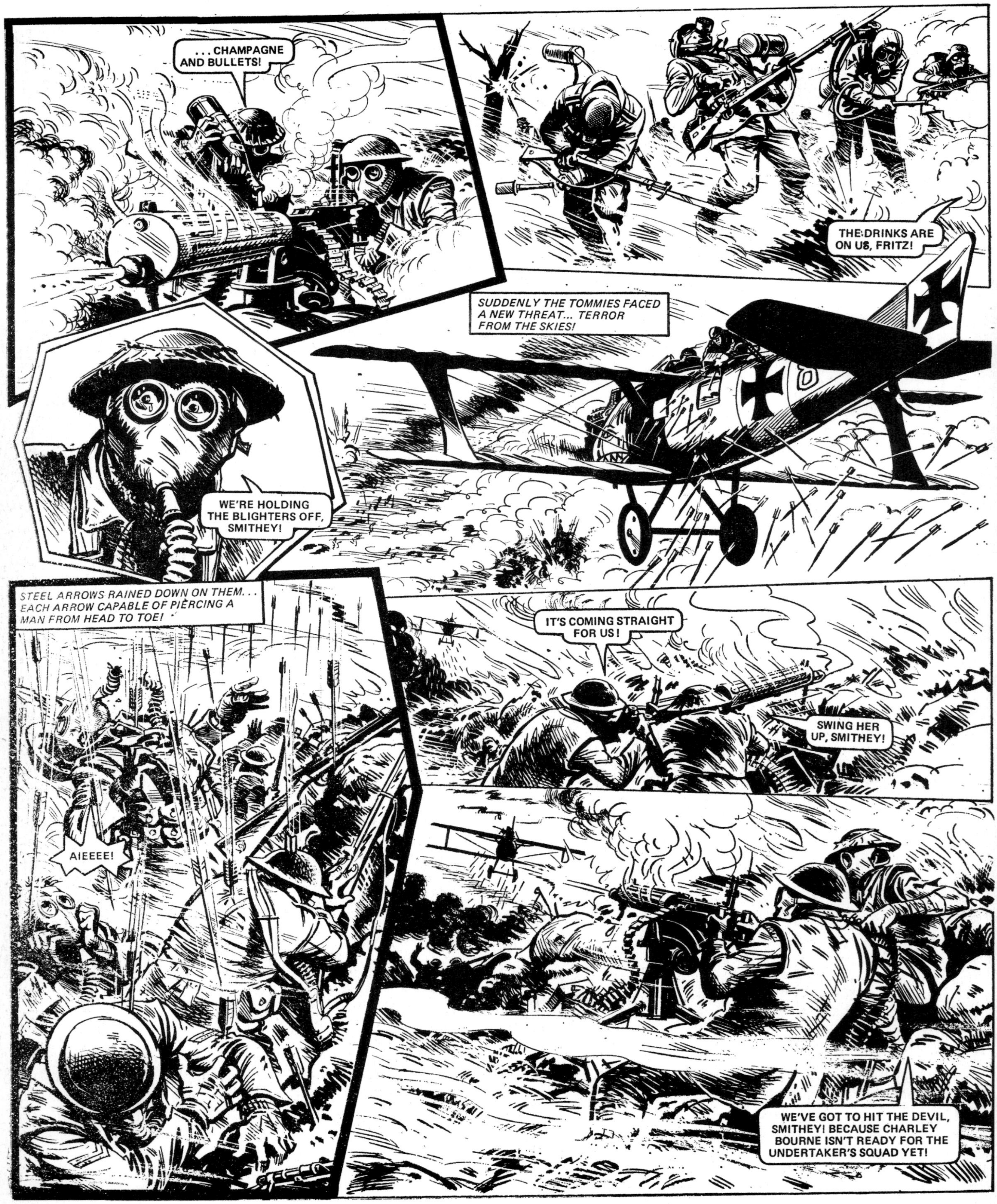

. . . CHAMPAGNE AND BULLETS!
THE DRINKS ARE ON US, FRITZ!
SUDDENLY THE TOMMIES FACED A NEW THREAT... TERROR FROM THE SKIES!
WE'RE HOLDING THE BLIGHTERS OFF, SMITHEY!
STEEL ARROWS RAINED DOWN ON THEM. . . EACH ARROW CAPABLE OF PIERCING A MAN FROM HEAD TO TOE!
AIEEEE!
IT'S COMING STRAIGHT FOR US!
SWING HER UP, SMITHEY!
WE'VE GOT TO HIT THE DEVIL, SMITHEY! BECAUSE CHARLEY BOURNE ISN'T READY FOR THE UNDERTAKER'S SQUAD YET!

CHARLEY'S WAR

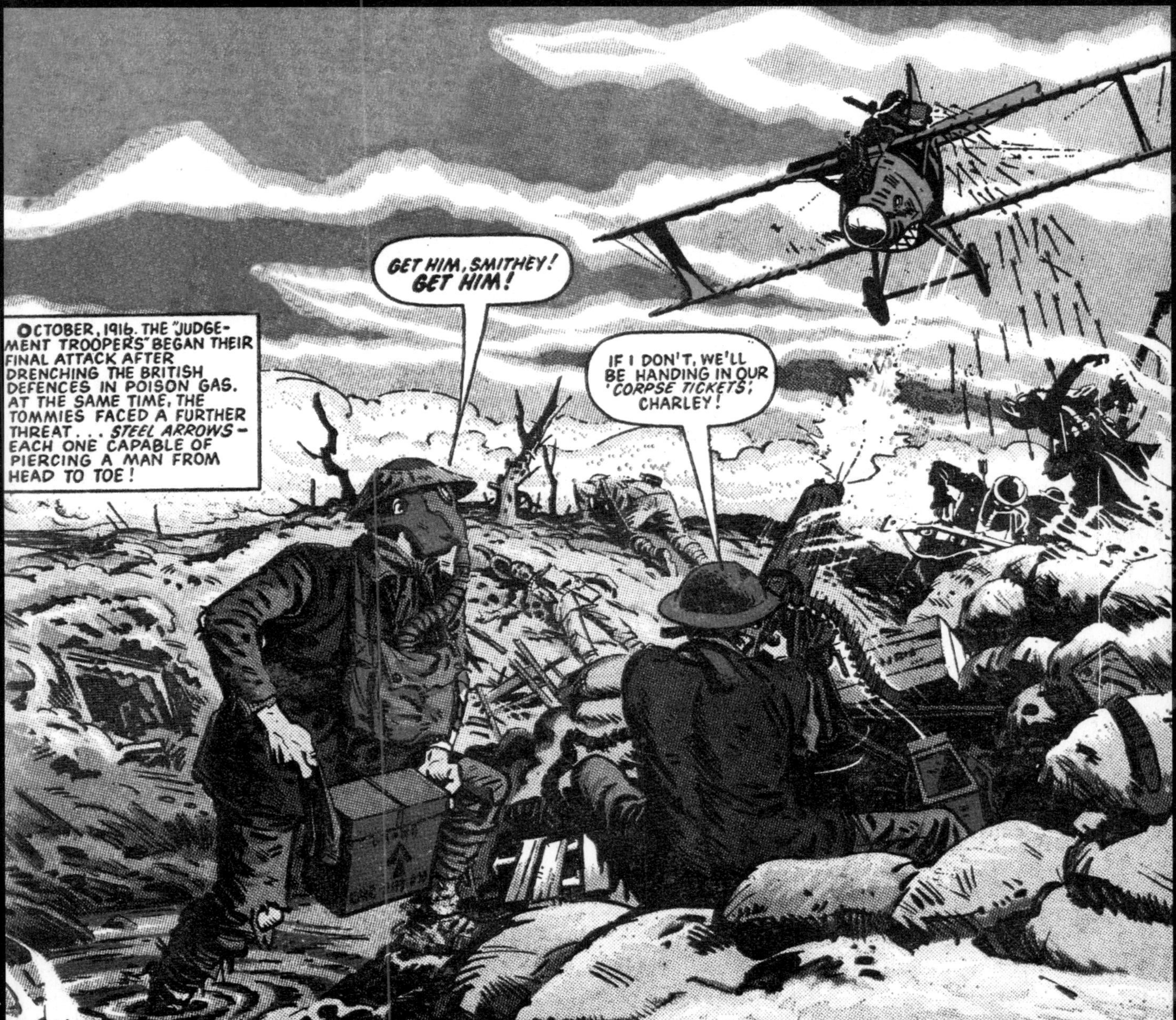

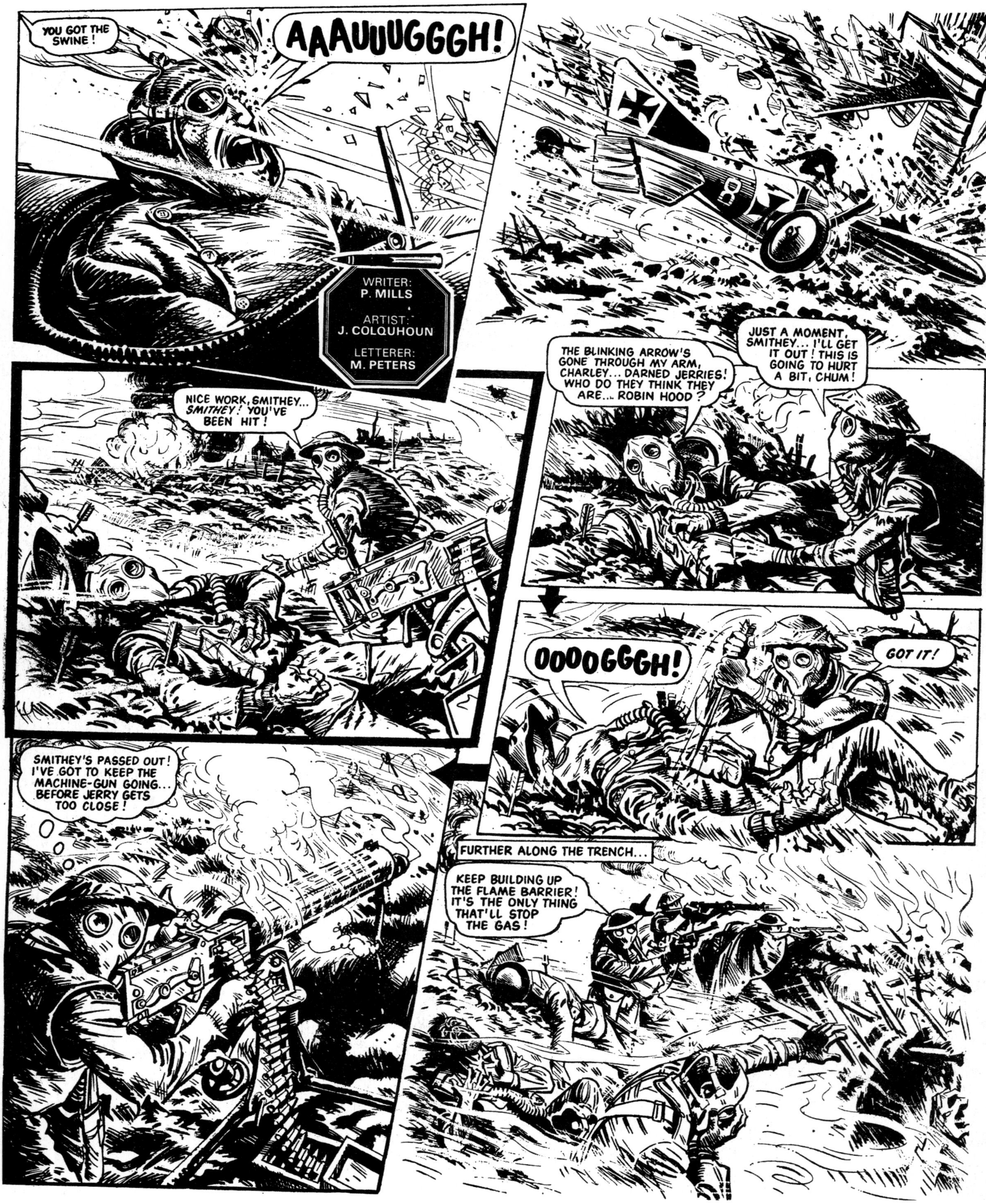
YOU GOT THE SWINE!
AAAUUUGGGH!
WRITER: P. MILLS
ARTIST: J. COLQUHOUN
LETTERER: M. PETERS
NICE WORK, SMITHEY... SMITHEY! YOU'VE BEEN HIT!
THE BLINKING ARROW'S GONE THROUGH MY ARM, CHARLEY... DARNED JERRIES! WHO DO THEY THINK THEY ARE... ROBIN HOOD?
JUST A MOMENT, SMITHEY... I'LL GET IT OUT! THIS IS GOING TO HURT A BIT, CHUM!
OOOOGGGH!
GOT IT!
SMITHEY'S PASSED OUT! I'VE GOT TO KEEP THE MACHINE-GUN GOING... BEFORE JERRY GETS TOO CLOSE!
FURTHER ALONG THE TRENCH...
KEEP BUILDING UP THE FLAME BARRIER! IT'S THE ONLY THING THAT'LL STOP THE GAS!

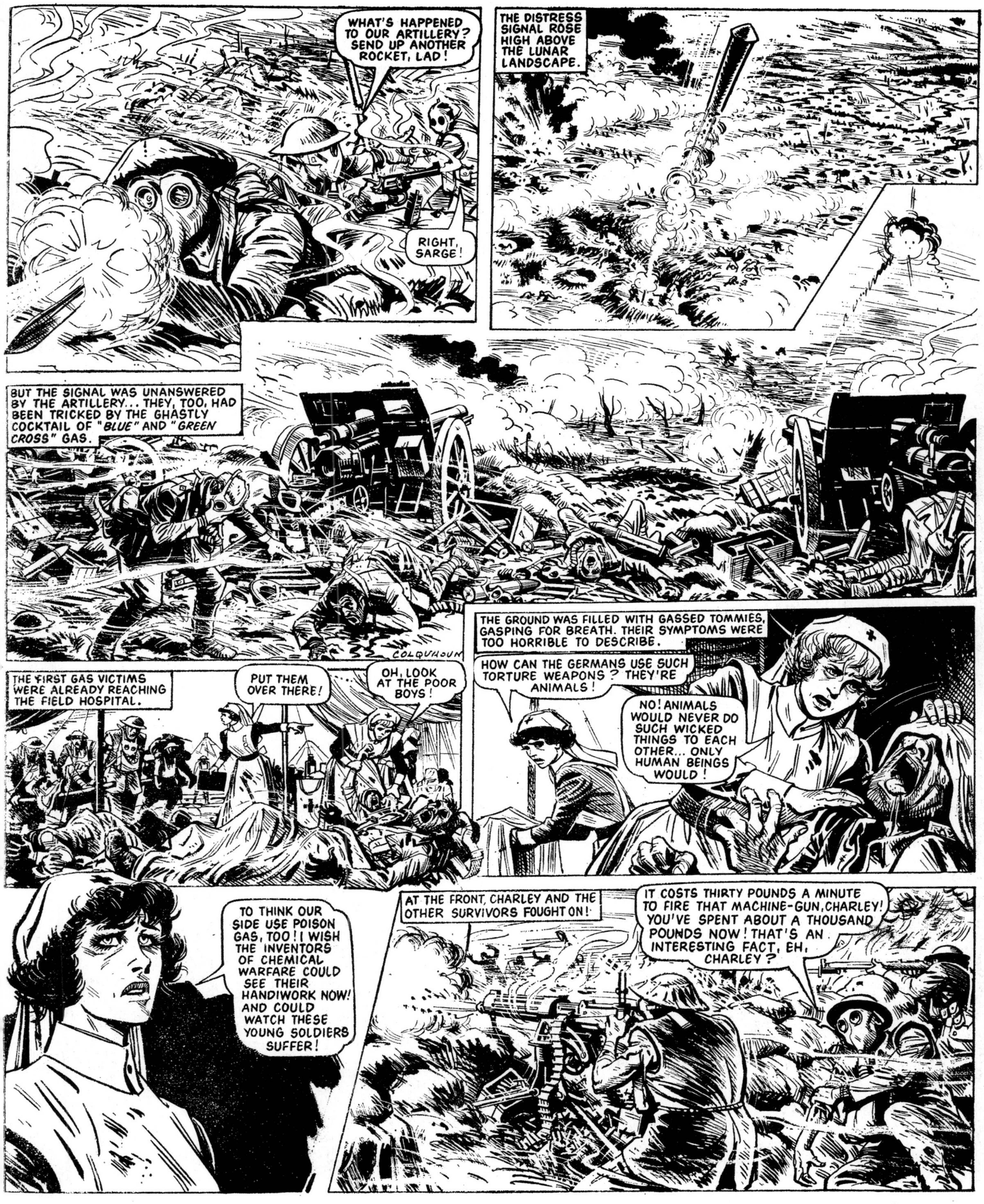
WHAT'S HAPPENED TO OUR ARTILLERY? SEND UP ANOTHER ROCKET, LAD!
RIGHT, SARGE!
THE DISTRESS SIGNAL ROSE HIGH ABOVE THE LUNAR LANDSCAPE.
BUT THE SIGNAL WAS UNANSWERED BY THE ARTILLERY... THEY, TOO, HAD BEEN TRICKED BY THE GHASTLY COCKTAIL OF "BLUE" AND "GREEN CROSS" GAS.
COLQUHOUN
THE FIRST GAS VICTIMS WERE ALREADY REACHING THE FIELD HOSPITAL.
PUT THEM OVER THERE!
OH, LOOK AT THE POOR BOYS!
THE GROUND WAS FILLED WITH GASSED TOMMIES, GASPING FOR BREATH. THEIR SYMPTOMS WERE TOO HORRIBLE TO DESCRIBE.
HOW CAN THE GERMANS USE SUCH TORTURE WEAPONS? THEY'RE ANIMALS!
NO! ANIMALS WOULD NEVER DO SUCH WICKED THINGS TO EACH OTHER... ONLY HUMAN BEINGS WOULD!
TO THINK OUR SIDE USE POISON GAS, TOO! I WISH THE INVENTORS OF CHEMICAL WARFARE COULD SEE THEIR HANDIWORK NOW! AND COULD WATCH THESE YOUNG SOLDIERS SUFFER!
AT THE FRONT, CHARLEY AND THE OTHER SURVIVORS FOUGHT ON!
IT COSTS THIRTY POUNDS A MINUTE TO FIRE THAT MACHINE-GUN, CHARLEY! YOU'VE SPENT ABOUT A THOUSAND POUNDS NOW! THAT'S AN INTERESTING FACT, EH, CHARLEY?

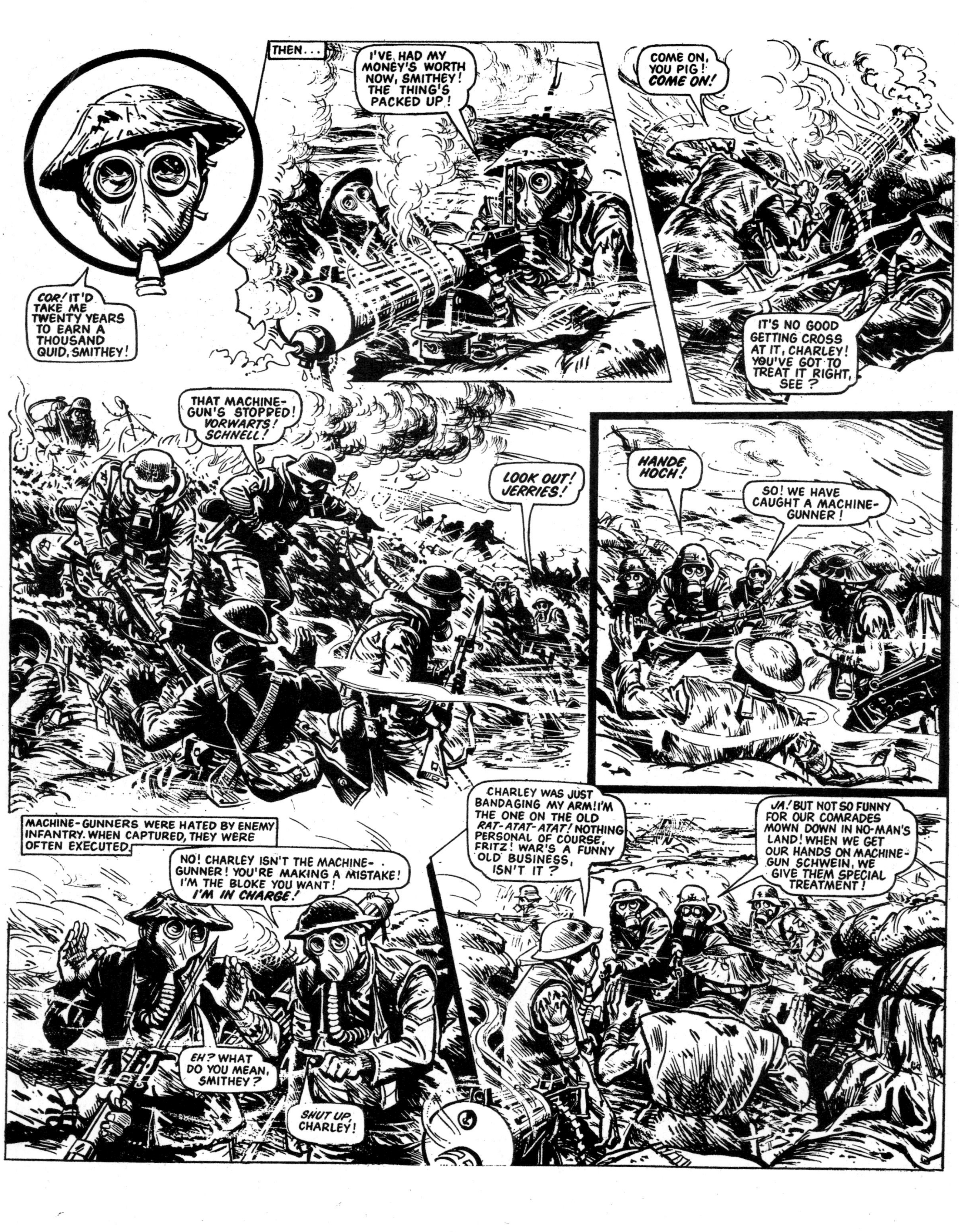
COR! IT'D TAKE ME TWENTY YEARS TO EARN A THOUSAND QUID, SMITHEY!
THEN...
I'VE HAD MY MONEY'S WORTH NOW, SMITHEY! THE THING'S PACKED UP!
COME ON, YOU PIG! COME ON!
IT'S NO GOOD GETTING CROSS AT IT, CHARLEY! YOU'VE GOT TO TREAT IT RIGHT, SEE?
THAT MACHINE-GUN'S STOPPED! VORWARTS! SCHNELL!
LOOK OUT! JERRIES!
HANDE HOCH!
SO! WE HAVE CAUGHT A MACHINE-GUNNER!
MACHINE-GUNNERS WERE HATED BY ENEMY INFANTRY. WHEN CAPTURED, THEY WERE OFTEN EXECUTED.
NO! CHARLEY ISN'T THE MACHINE-GUNNER! YOU'RE MAKING A MISTAKE! I'M THE BLOKE YOU WANT! I'M IN CHARGE!
EH? WHAT DO YOU MEAN, SMITHEY?
SHUT UP, CHARLEY!
CHARLEY WAS JUST BANDAGING MY ARM! I'M THE ONE ON THE OLD RAT-ATAT-ATAT! NOTHING PERSONAL OF COURSE, FRITZ! WAR'S A FUNNY OLD BUSINESS, ISN'T IT?
JA! BUT NOT SO FUNNY FOR OUR COMRADES MOWN DOWN IN NO-MAN'S LAND! WHEN WE GET OUR HANDS ON MACHINE-GUN SCHWEIN, WE GIVE THEM SPECIAL TREATMENT!

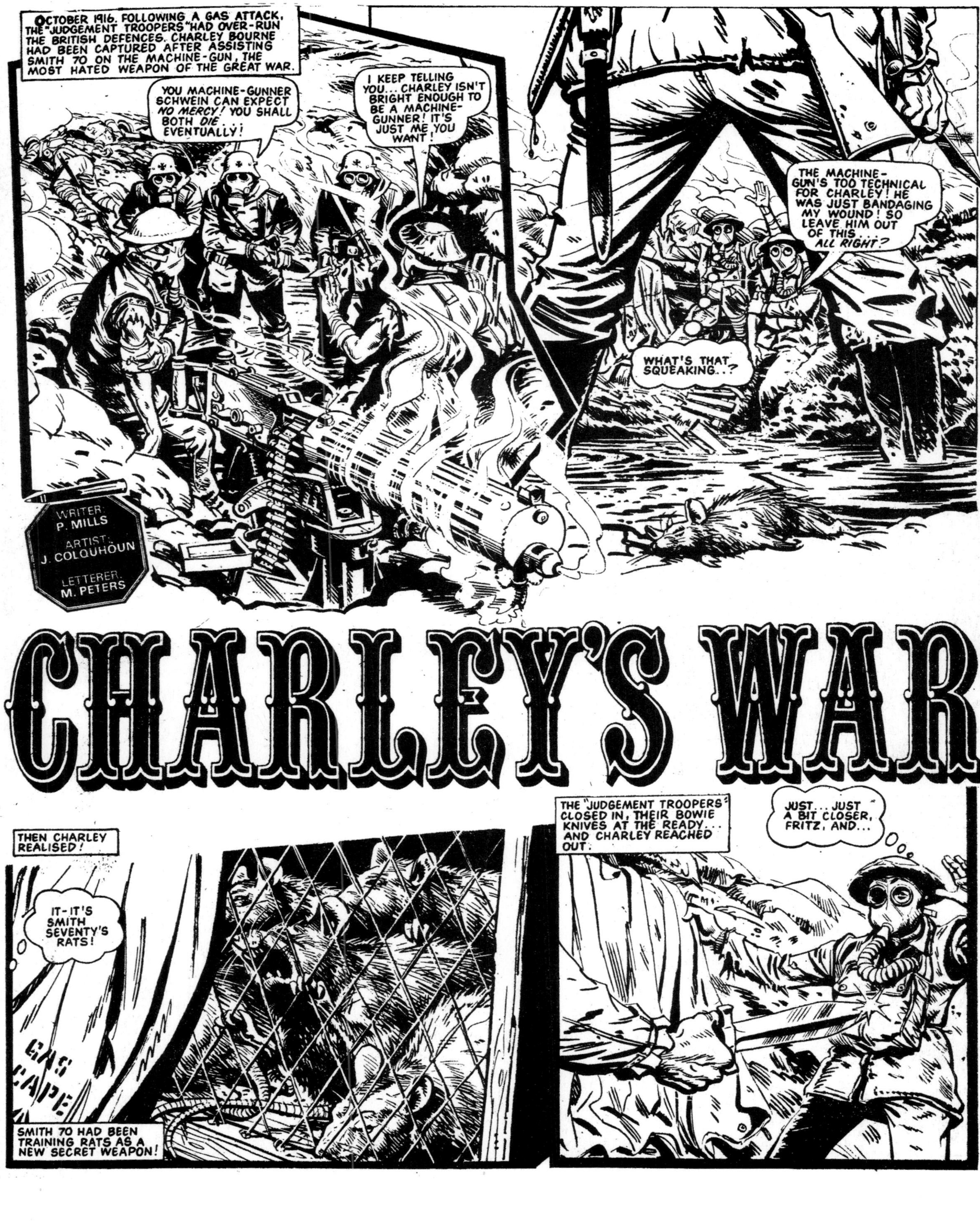
OCTOBER 1916. FOLLOWING A GAS ATTACK, THE "JUDGEMENT TROOPERS" HAD OVER-RUN THE BRITISH DEFENCES. CHARLEY BOURNE HAD BEEN CAPTURED AFTER ASSISTING SMITH 70 ON THE MACHINE-GUN, THE MOST HATED WEAPON OF THE GREAT WAR.
YOU MACHINE-GUNNER SCHWEIN CAN EXPECT NO MERCY! YOU SHALL BOTH DIE . . . EVENTUALLY!
I KEEP TELLING YOU... CHARLEY ISN'T BRIGHT ENOUGH TO BE A MACHINE-GUNNER! IT'S JUST ME YOU WANT!
THE MACHINE-GUN'S TOO TECHNICAL FOR CHARLEY! HE WAS JUST BANDAGING MY WOUND! SO LEAVE HIM OUT OF THIS . . . ALL RIGHT?
WHAT'S THAT SQUEAKING..?
WRITER: P. MILLS
ARTIST: J. COLQUHOUN
LETTERER: M. PETERS
CHARLEY'S WAR
THEN CHARLEY REALISED!
IT-IT'S SMITH SEVENTY'S RATS!
GAS CAPE
SMITH 70 HAD BEEN TRAINING RATS AS A NEW SECRET WEAPON!
THE "JUDGEMENT TROOPERS" CLOSED IN, THEIR BOWIE KNIVES AT THE READY... AND CHARLEY REACHED OUT.
JUST... JUST A BIT CLOSER, FRITZ, AND...

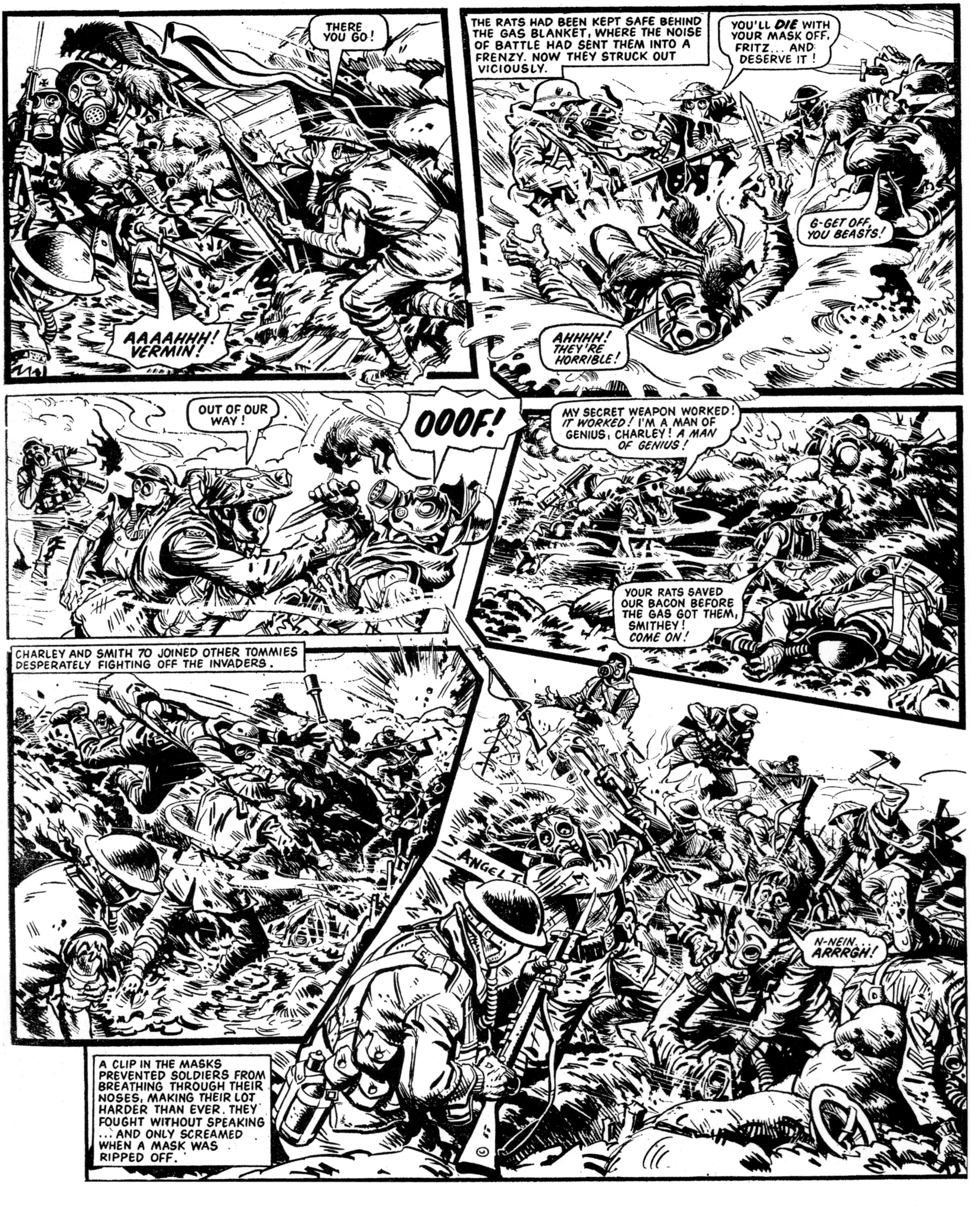

THERE YOU GO!
AAAAHHH! VERMIN!
THE RATS HAD BEEN KEPT SAFE BEHIND THE GAS BLANKET, WHERE THE NOISE OF BATTLE HAD SENT THEM INTO A FRENZY. NOW THEY STRUCK OUT VICIOUSLY.
YOU'LL DIE WITH YOUR MASK OFF, FRITZ... AND DESERVE IT!
G-GET OFF, YOU BEASTS!
AHHHH! THEY'RE HORRIBLE!
OUT OF OUR WAY!
OOOF!
MY SECRET WEAPON WORKED! IT WORKED! I'M A MAN OF GENIUS, CHARLEY! A MAN OF GENIUS!
YOUR RATS SAVED OUR BACON BEFORE THE GAS GOT THEM, SMITHEY! COME ON!
CHARLEY AND SMITH 70 JOINED OTHER TOMMIES DESPERATELY FIGHTING OFF THE INVADERS.
N-NEIN... ARRRGH!
A CLIP IN THE MASKS PREVENTED SOLDIERS FROM BREATHING THROUGH THEIR NOSES, MAKING THEIR LOT HARDER THAN EVER. THEY FOUGHT WITHOUT SPEAKING ... AND ONLY SCREAMED WHEN A MASK WAS RIPPED OFF.

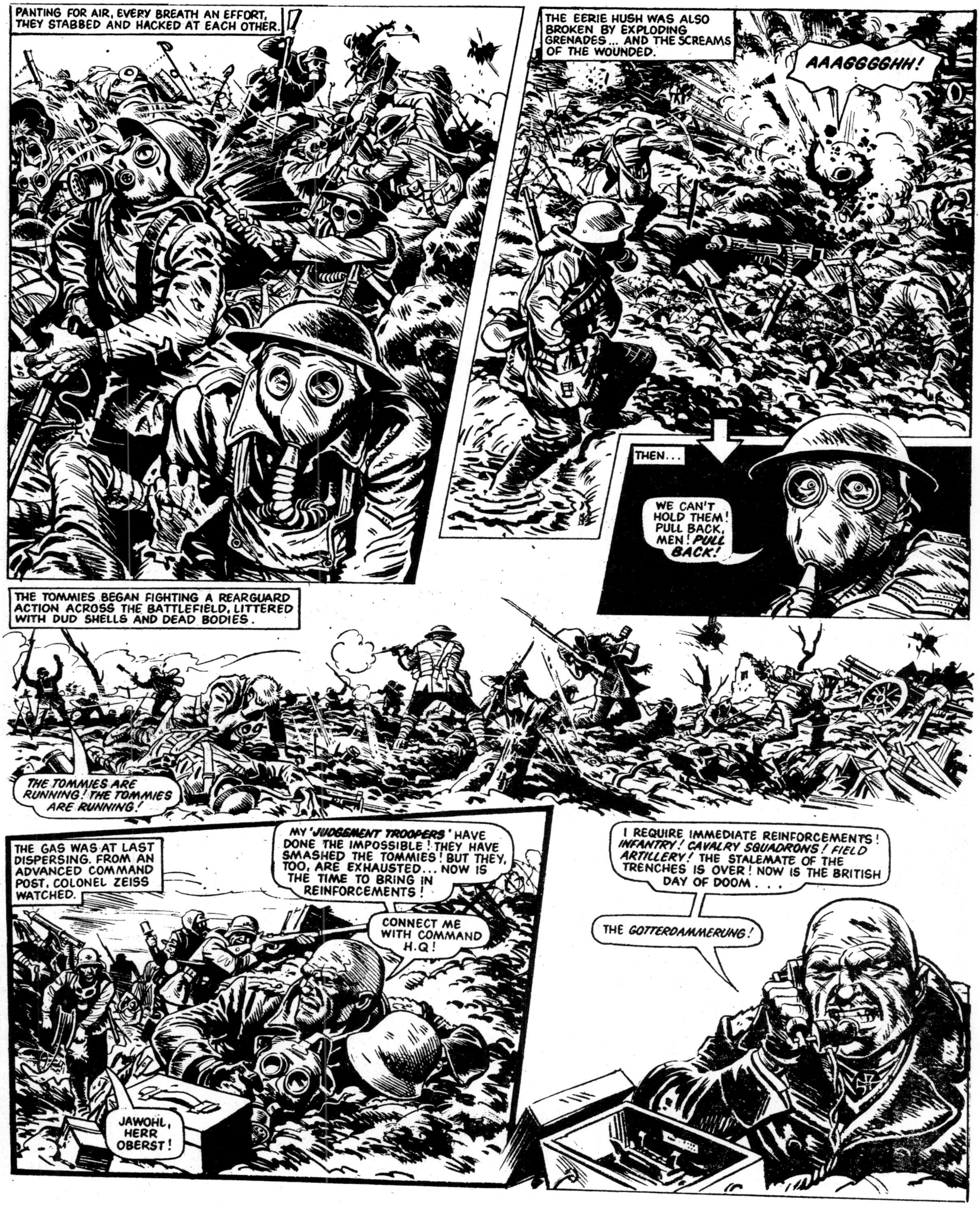
PANTING FOR AIR, EVERY BREATH AN EFFORT, THEY STABBED AND HACKED AT EACH OTHER.
THE EERIE HUSH WAS ALSO BROKEN BY EXPLODING GRENADES... AND THE SCREAMS OF THE WOUNDED.
AAAGGGGHH!
THEN...
WE CAN'T HOLD THEM! PULL BACK, MEN! PULL BACK!
THE TOMMIES BEGAN FIGHTING A REARGUARD ACTION ACROSS THE BATTLEFIELD, LITTERED WITH DUD SHELLS AND DEAD BODIES.
THE TOMMIES ARE RUNNING! THE TOMMIES ARE RUNNING!
THE GAS WAS AT LAST DISPERSING. FROM AN ADVANCED COMMAND POST, COLONEL ZEISS WATCHED.
MY 'JUDGEMENT TROOPERS' HAVE DONE THE IMPOSSIBLE! THEY HAVE SMASHED THE TOMMIES! BUT THEY, TOO, ARE EXHAUSTED... NOW IS THE TIME TO BRING IN REINFORCEMENTS!
CONNECT ME WITH COMMAND H.Q!
JAWOHL, HERR OBERST!
I REQUIRE IMMEDIATE REINFORCEMENTS! INFANTRY! CAVALRY SQUADRONS! FIELD ARTILLERY! THE STALEMATE OF THE TRENCHES IS OVER! NOW IS THE BRITISH DAY OF DOOM . . .
THE GOTTERDAMMERUNG!

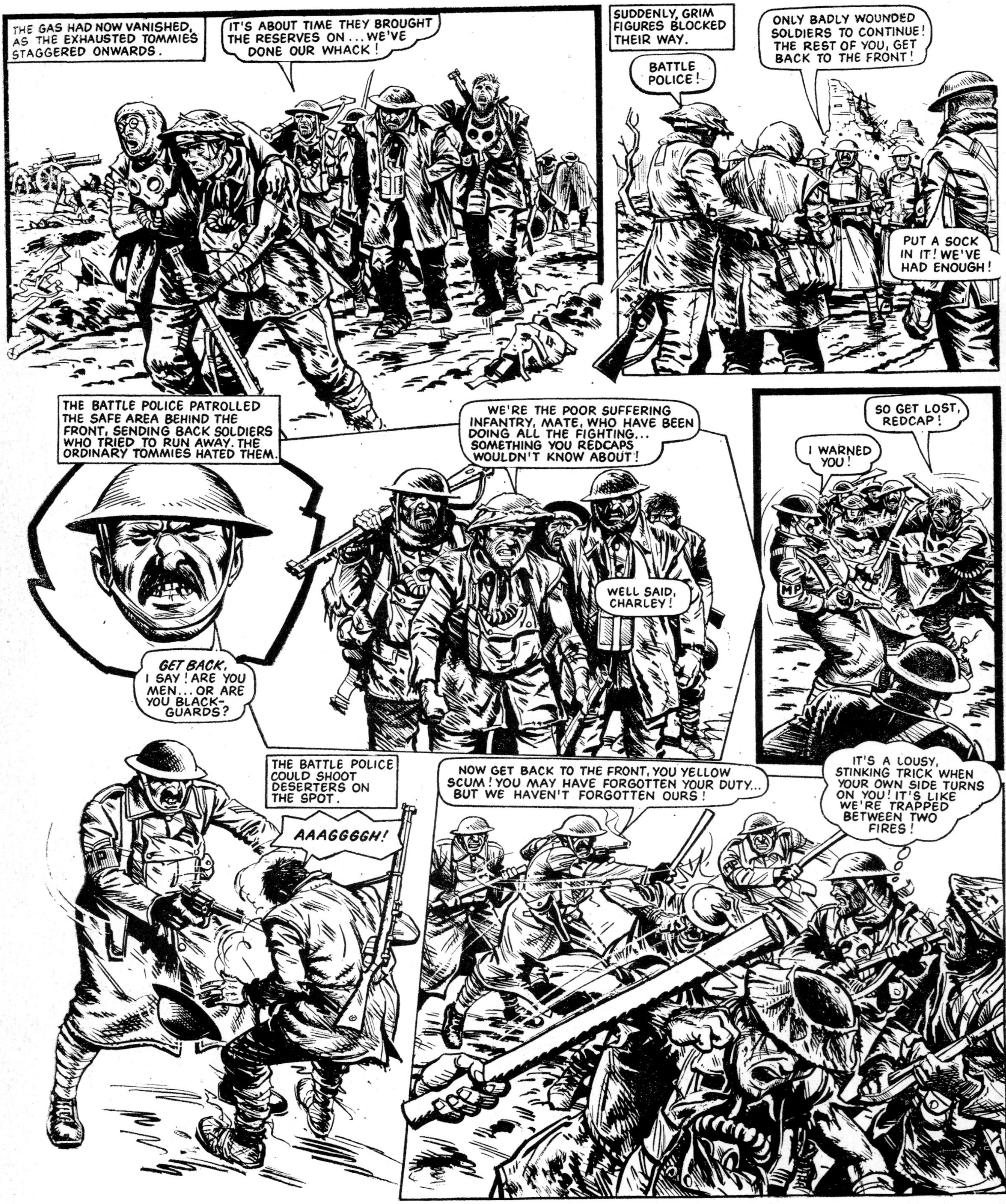
THE GAS HAD NOW VANISHED, AS THE EXHAUSTED TOMMIES STAGGERED ONWARDS.
IT'S ABOUT TIME THEY BROUGHT THE RESERVES ON... WE'VE DONE OUR WHACK!
SUDDENLY, GRIM FIGURES BLOCKED THEIR WAY.
BATTLE POLICE!
ONLY BADLY WOUNDED SOLDIERS TO CONTINUE! THE REST OF YOU, GET BACK TO THE FRONT!
PUT A SOCK IN IT! WE'VE HAD ENOUGH!
THE BATTLE POLICE PATROLLED THE SAFE AREA BEHIND THE FRONT, SENDING BACK SOLDIERS WHO TRIED TO RUN AWAY. THE ORDINARY TOMMIES HATED THEM.
GET BACK, I SAY! ARE YOU MEN... OR ARE YOU BLACK-GUARDS?
WE'RE THE POOR SUFFERING INFANTRY, MATE, WHO HAVE BEEN DOING ALL THE FIGHTING... SOMETHING YOU REDCAPS WOULDN'T KNOW ABOUT!
WELL SAID, CHARLEY!
I WARNED YOU!
SO GET LOST, REDCAP!
MP
THE BATTLE POLICE COULD SHOOT DESERTERS ON THE SPOT.
AAAGGGGH!
NOW GET BACK TO THE FRONT, YOU YELLOW SCUM! YOU MAY HAVE FORGOTTEN YOUR DUTY... BUT WE HAVEN'T FORGOTTEN OURS!
IT'S A LOUSY, STINKING TRICK WHEN YOUR OWN SIDE TURNS ON YOU! IT'S LIKE WE'RE TRAPPED BETWEEN TWO FIRES!

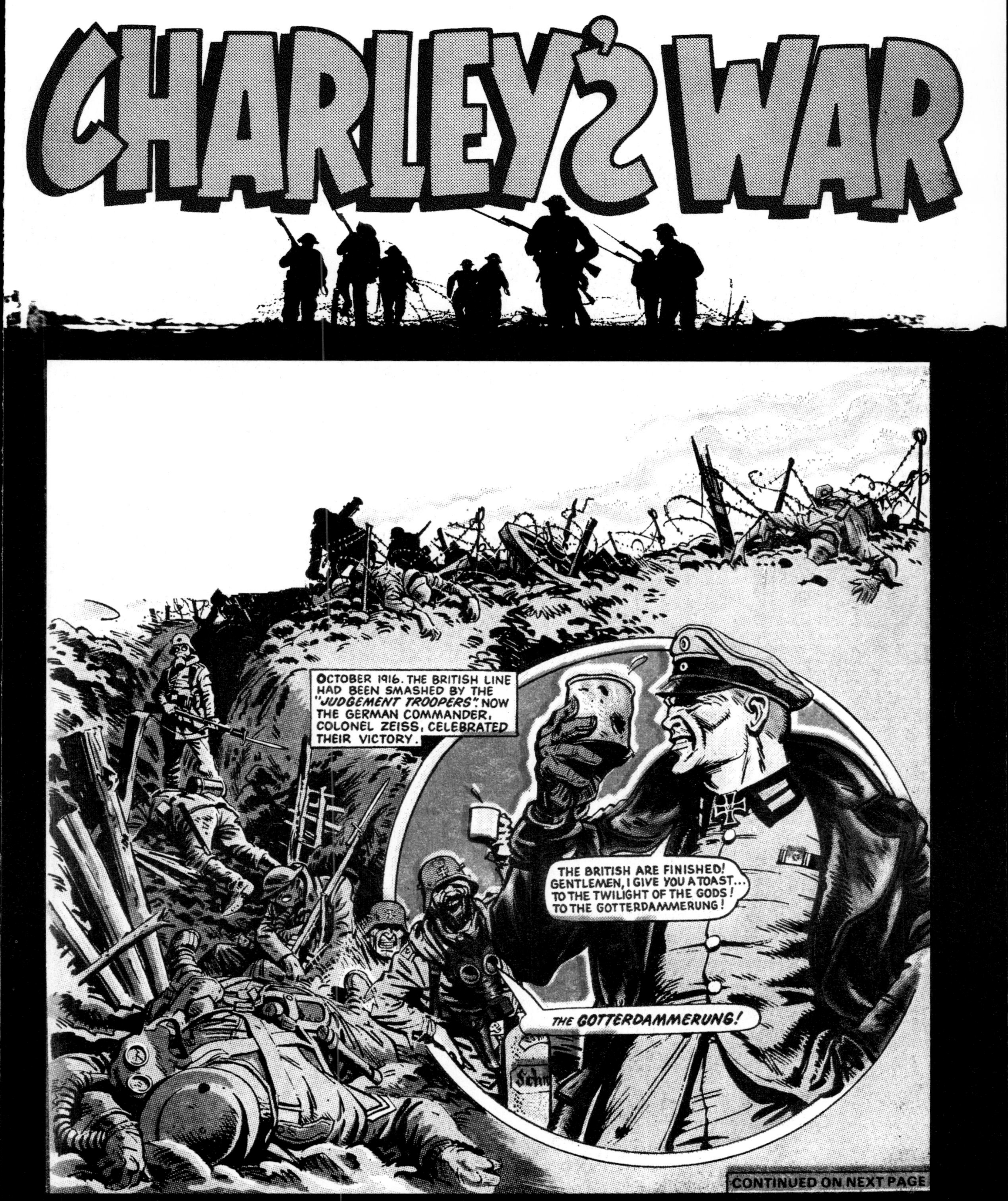

CHARLEY'S WAR
OCTOBER 1916. THE BRITISH LINE HAD BEEN SMASHED BY THE "JUDGEMENT TROOPERS". NOW THE GERMAN COMMANDER, COLONEL ZEISS, CELEBRATED THEIR VICTORY.
THE BRITISH ARE FINISHED! GENTLEMEN, I GIVE YOU A TOAST... TO THE TWILIGHT OF THE GODS! TO THE GOTTERDAMMERUNG!
THE GOTTERDAMMERUNG!

CONTINUED ON NEXT PAGE

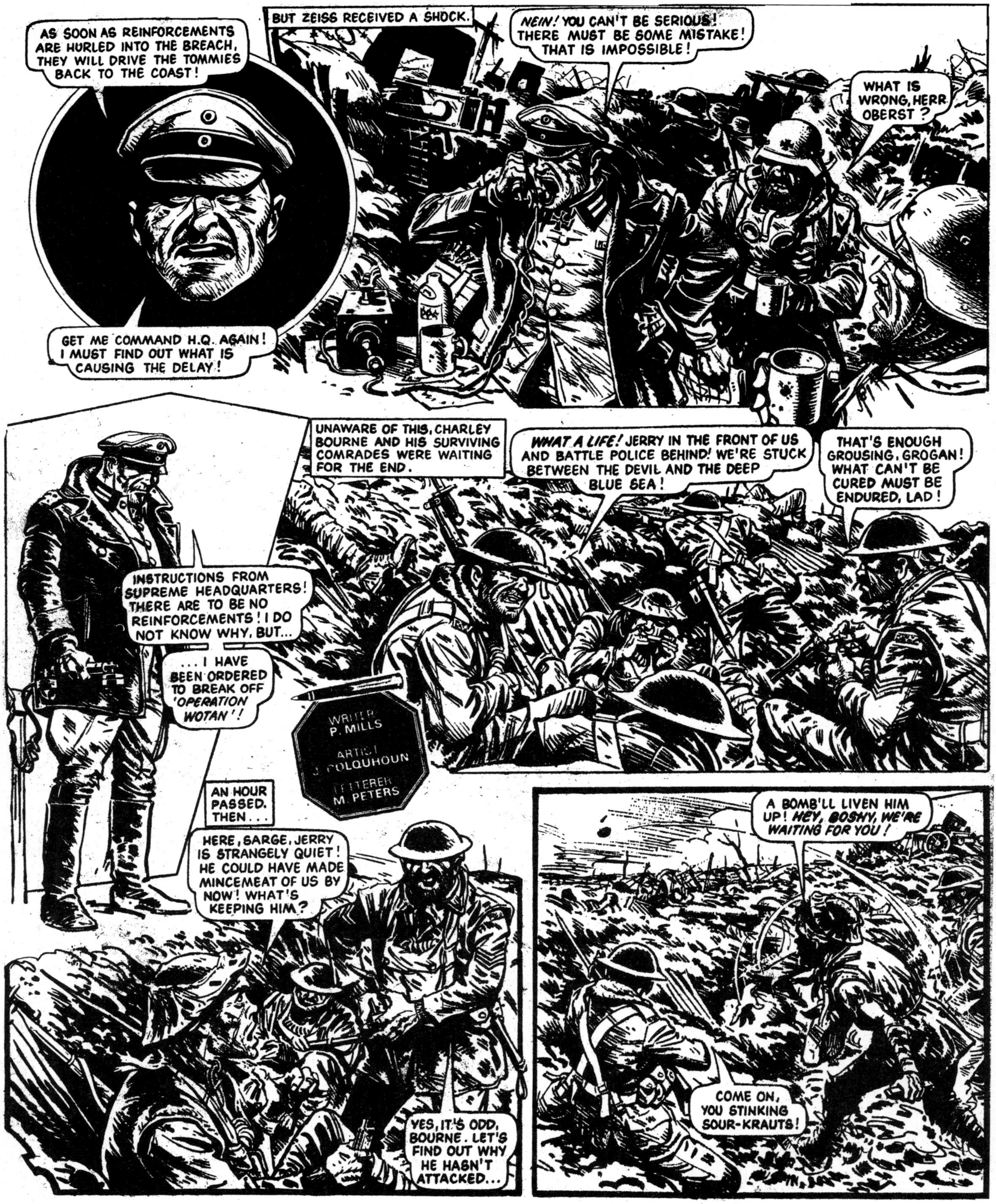
AS SOON AS REINFORCEMENTS ARE HURLED INTO THE BREACH, THEY WILL DRIVE THE TOMMIES BACK TO THE COAST!
GET ME COMMAND H.Q. AGAIN! I MUST FIND OUT WHAT IS CAUSING THE DELAY!
BUT ZEISS RECEIVED A SHOCK.
NEIN! YOU CAN'T BE SERIOUS! THERE MUST BE SOME MISTAKE! THAT IS IMPOSSIBLE!
WHAT IS WRONG, HERR OBERST?
INSTRUCTIONS FROM SUPREME HEADQUARTERS! THERE ARE TO BE NO REINFORCEMENTS! I DO NOT KNOW WHY, BUT...
...I HAVE BEEN ORDERED TO BREAK OFF 'OPERATION WOTAN'!
UNAWARE OF THIS, CHARLEY BOURNE AND HIS SURVIVING COMRADES WERE WAITING FOR THE END.
WHAT A LIFE! JERRY IN THE FRONT OF US AND BATTLE POLICE BEHIND! WE'RE STUCK BETWEEN THE DEVIL AND THE DEEP BLUE SEA!
THAT'S ENOUGH GROUSING, GROGAN! WHAT CAN'T BE CURED MUST BE ENDURED, LAD!
WRITER: P. MILLS
ARTIST: J. COLQUHOUN
LETTERER: M. PETERS
AN HOUR PASSED. THEN...
HERE, SARGE, JERRY IS STRANGELY QUIET! HE COULD HAVE MADE MINCEMEAT OF US BY NOW! WHAT'S KEEPING HIM?
YES, IT'S ODD, BOURNE. LET'S FIND OUT WHY HE HASN'T ATTACKED...
A BOMB'LL LIVEN HIM UP! HEY, BOSHY, WE'RE WAITING FOR YOU!
COME ON, YOU STINKING SOUR-KRAUTS!

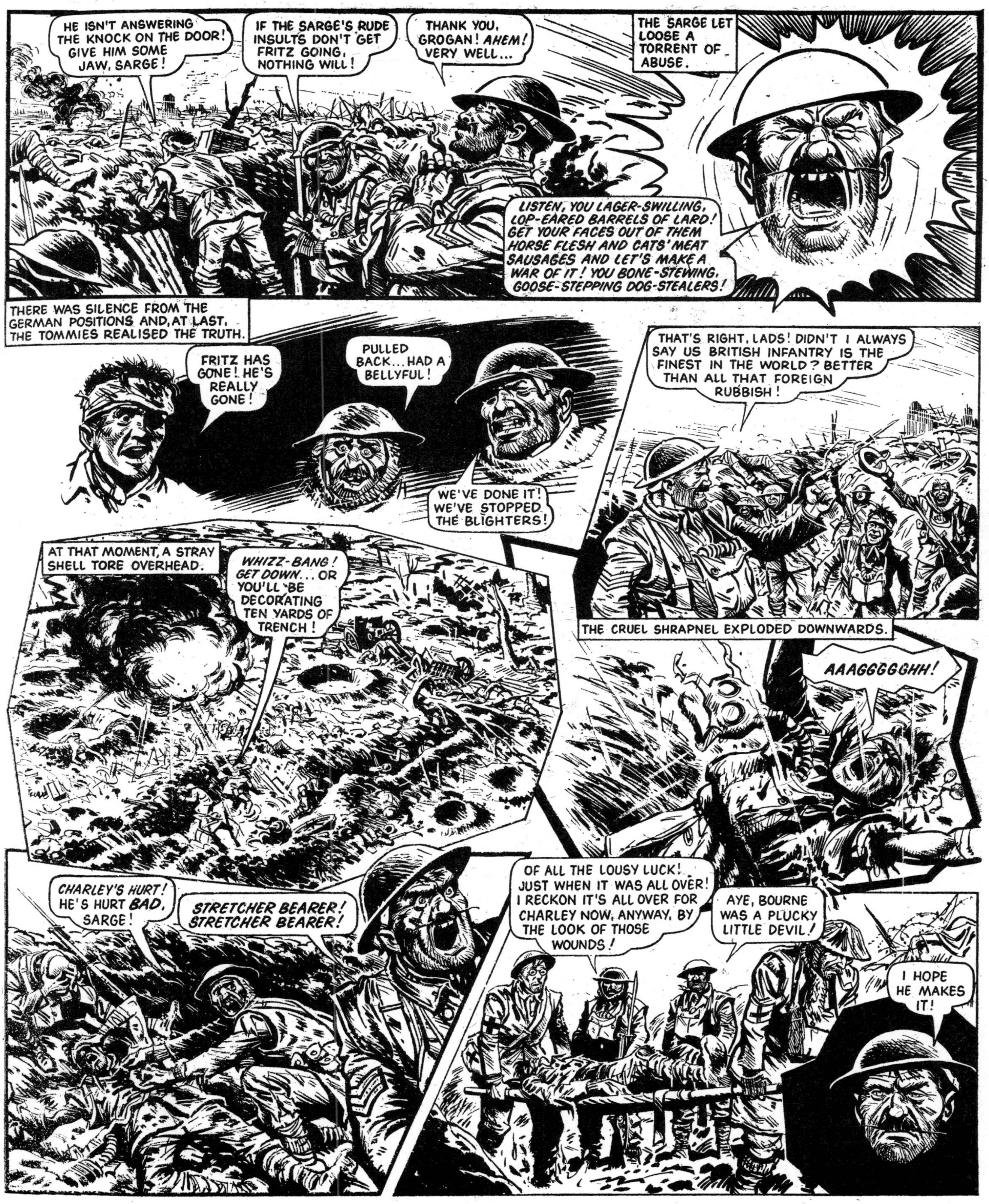
HE ISN'T ANSWERING THE KNOCK ON THE DOOR! GIVE HIM SOME JAW, SARGE!
IF THE SARGE'S RUDE INSULTS DON'T GET FRITZ GOING, NOTHING WILL!
THANK YOU, GROGAN! AHEM! VERY WELL...
THE SARGE LET LOOSE A TORRENT OF ABUSE.
LISTEN, YOU LAGER-SWILLING, LOP-EARED BARRELS OF LARD! GET YOUR FACES OUT OF THEM HORSE FLESH AND CATS' MEAT SAUSAGES AND LET'S MAKE A WAR OF IT! YOU BONE-STEWING, GOOSE-STEPPING DOG-STEALERS!
THERE WAS SILENCE FROM THE GERMAN POSITIONS AND, AT LAST, THE TOMMIES REALISED THE TRUTH.
FRITZ HAS GONE! HE'S REALLY GONE!
PULLED BACK... HAD A BELLYFUL!
WE'VE DONE IT! WE'VE STOPPED THE BLIGHTERS!
THAT'S RIGHT, LADS! DIDN'T I ALWAYS SAY US BRITISH INFANTRY IS THE FINEST IN THE WORLD? BETTER THAN ALL THAT FOREIGN RUBBISH!
AT THAT MOMENT, A STRAY SHELL TORE OVERHEAD.
WHIZZ-BANG! GET DOWN... OR YOU'LL BE DECORATING TEN YARDS OF TRENCH!
THE CRUEL SHRAPNEL EXPLODED DOWNWARDS.
AAAGGGGGHH!
CHARLEY'S HURT! HE'S HURT BAD, SARGE!
STRETCHER BEARER! STRETCHER BEARER!
OF ALL THE LOUSY LUCK! JUST WHEN IT WAS ALL OVER! I RECKON IT'S ALL OVER FOR CHARLEY NOW, ANYWAY, BY THE LOOK OF THOSE WOUNDS!
AYE, BOURNE WAS A PLUCKY LITTLE DEVIL!
I HOPE HE MAKES IT!

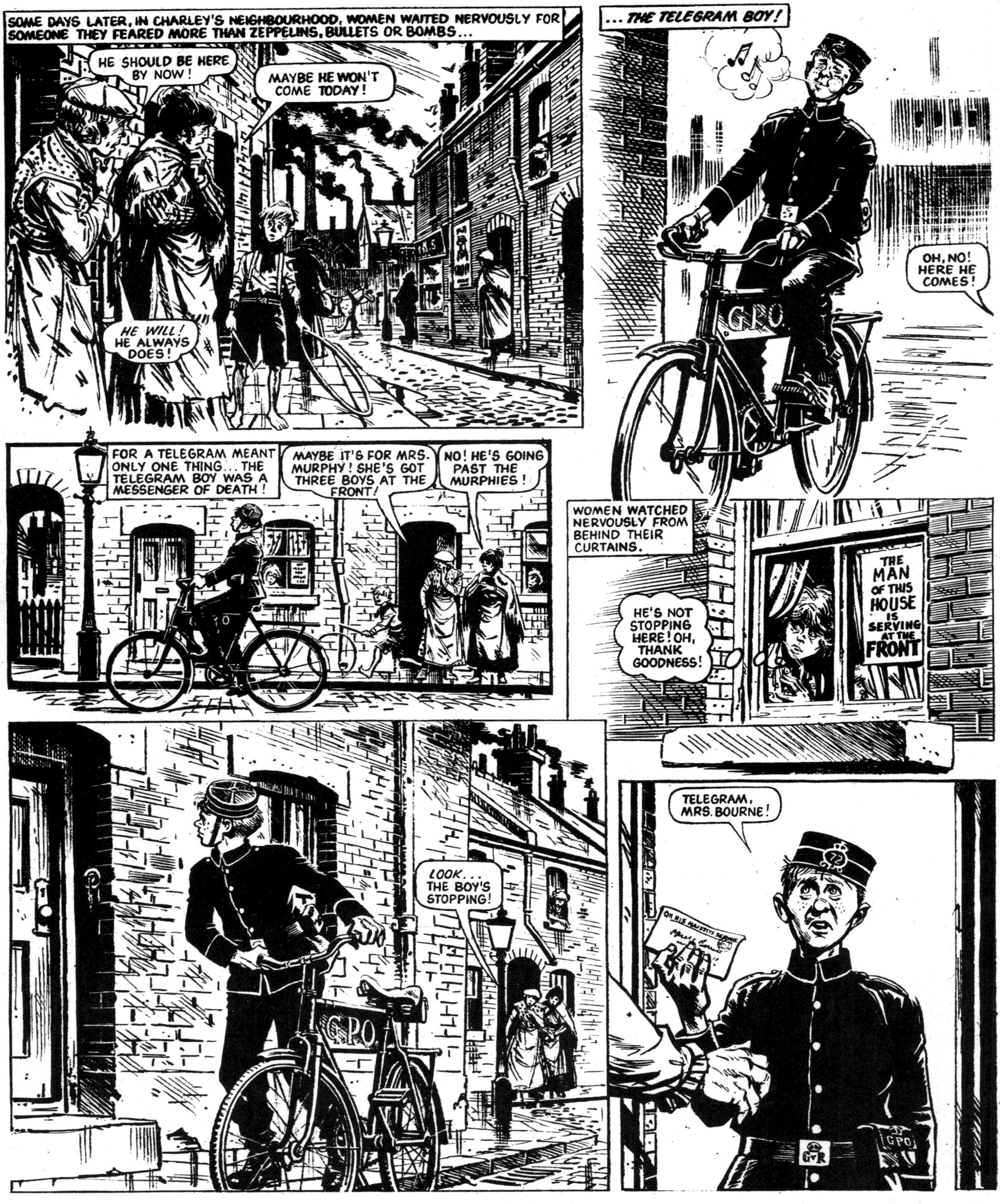

SOME DAYS LATER, IN CHARLEY'S NEIGHBOURHOOD, WOMEN WAITED NERVOUSLY FOR SOMEONE THEY FEARED MORE THAN ZEPPELINS, BULLETS OR BOMBS...
HE SHOULD BE HERE BY NOW!
MAYBE HE WON'T COME TODAY!
HE WILL! HE ALWAYS DOES!
... THE TELEGRAM BOY!
OH, NO! HERE HE COMES!
GPO
FOR A TELEGRAM MEANT ONLY ONE THING... THE TELEGRAM BOY WAS A MESSENGER OF DEATH!
MAYBE IT'S FOR MRS. MURPHY! SHE'S GOT THREE BOYS AT THE FRONT!
NO! HE'S GOING PAST THE MURPHIES!
WOMEN WATCHED NERVOUSLY FROM BEHIND THEIR CURTAINS.
HE'S NOT STOPPING HERE! OH, THANK GOODNESS!
THE MAN OF THIS HOUSE IS SERVING AT THE FRONT
LOOK... THE BOY'S STOPPING!
GPO
TELEGRAM, MRS. BOURNE!
GPO

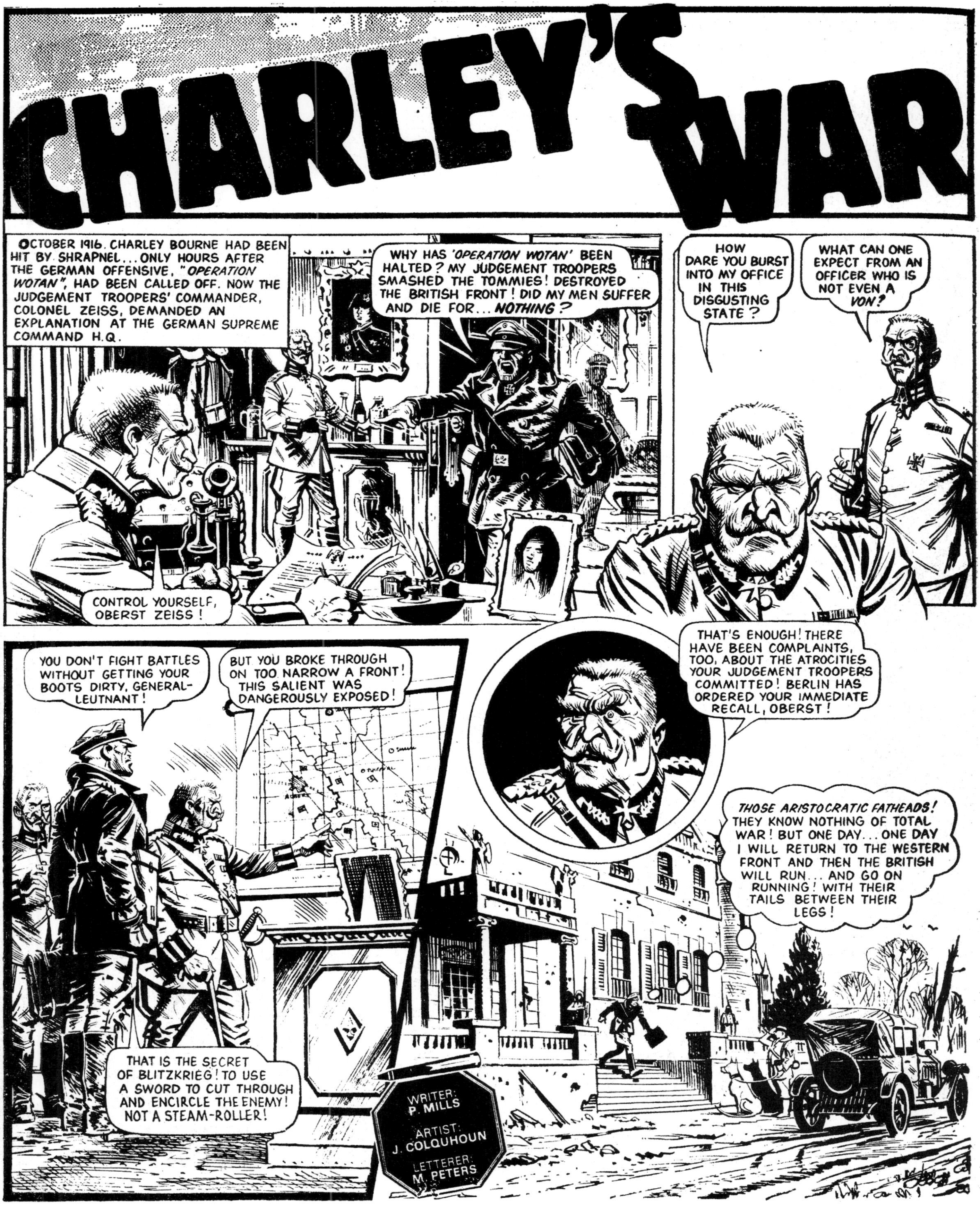
CHARLEY'S WAR
OCTOBER 1916. CHARLEY BOURNE HAD BEEN HIT BY SHRAPNEL... ONLY HOURS AFTER THE GERMAN OFFENSIVE, "OPERATION WOTAN", HAD BEEN CALLED OFF. NOW THE JUDGEMENT TROOPERS' COMMANDER, COLONEL ZEISS, DEMANDED AN EXPLANATION AT THE GERMAN SUPREME COMMAND H.Q.
WHY HAS 'OPERATION WOTAN' BEEN HALTED? MY JUDGEMENT TROOPERS SMASHED THE TOMMIES! DESTROYED THE BRITISH FRONT! DID MY MEN SUFFER AND DIE FOR... NOTHING?
CONTROL YOURSELF, OBERST ZEISS!
HOW DARE YOU BURST INTO MY OFFICE IN THIS DISGUSTING STATE?
WHAT CAN ONE EXPECT FROM AN OFFICER WHO IS NOT EVEN A VON?
YOU DON'T FIGHT BATTLES WITHOUT GETTING YOUR BOOTS DIRTY, GENERAL-LEUTNANT!
BUT YOU BROKE THROUGH ON TOO NARROW A FRONT! THIS SALIENT WAS DANGEROUSLY EXPOSED!
THAT IS THE SECRET OF BLITZKRIEG! TO USE A SWORD TO CUT THROUGH AND ENCIRCLE THE ENEMY! NOT A STEAM-ROLLER!
THAT'S ENOUGH! THERE HAVE BEEN COMPLAINTS, TOO, ABOUT THE ATROCITIES YOUR JUDGEMENT TROOPERS COMMITTED! BERLIN HAS ORDERED YOUR IMMEDIATE RECALL, OBERST!
THOSE ARISTOCRATIC FATHEADS! THEY KNOW NOTHING OF TOTAL WAR! BUT ONE DAY... ONE DAY I WILL RETURN TO THE WESTERN FRONT AND THEN THE BRITISH WILL RUN... AND GO ON RUNNING! WITH THEIR TAILS BETWEEN THEIR LEGS!
WRITER: P. MILLS
ARTIST: J. COLQUHOUN
LETTERER: M. PETERS

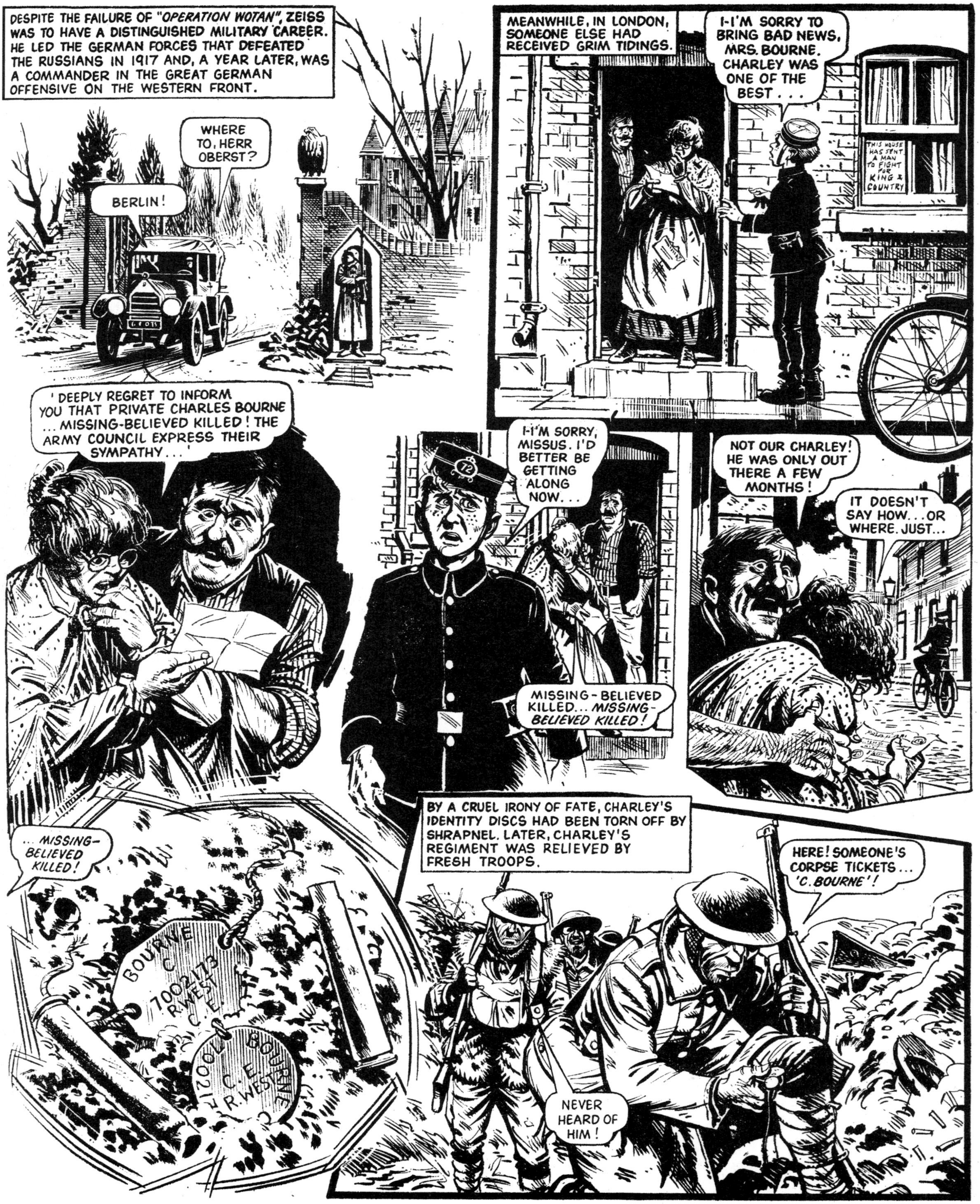
DESPITE THE FAILURE OF "OPERATION WOTAN", ZEISS WAS TO HAVE A DISTINGUISHED MILITARY CAREER. HE LED THE GERMAN FORCES THAT DEFEATED THE RUSSIANS IN 1917 AND, A YEAR LATER, WAS A COMMANDER IN THE GREAT GERMAN OFFENSIVE ON THE WESTERN FRONT.
WHERE TO, HERR OBERST?
BERLIN!
MEANWHILE, IN LONDON, SOMEONE ELSE HAD RECEIVED GRIM TIDINGS.
I-I'M SORRY TO BRING BAD NEWS, MRS. BOURNE. CHARLEY WAS ONE OF THE BEST . . .
THIS HOUSE HAS SENT A MAN TO FIGHT FOR KING & COUNTRY
'DEEPLY REGRET TO INFORM YOU THAT PRIVATE CHARLES BOURNE ... MISSING-BELIEVED KILLED! THE ARMY COUNCIL EXPRESS THEIR SYMPATHY . . .'
I-I'M SORRY, MISSUS. I'D BETTER BE GETTING ALONG NOW. . .
MISSING - BELIEVED KILLED... MISSING - BELIEVED KILLED!
NOT OUR CHARLEY! HE WAS ONLY OUT THERE A FEW MONTHS!
IT DOESN'T SAY HOW...OR WHERE. JUST...
... MISSING - BELIEVED KILLED!
BOURNE C 7002173 R.WEST C.E.
BY A CRUEL IRONY OF FATE, CHARLEY'S IDENTITY DISCS HAD BEEN TORN OFF BY SHRAPNEL. LATER, CHARLEY'S REGIMENT WAS RELIEVED BY FRESH TROOPS.
HERE! SOMEONE'S CORPSE TICKETS ... 'C. BOURNE'!
NEVER HEARD OF HIM!

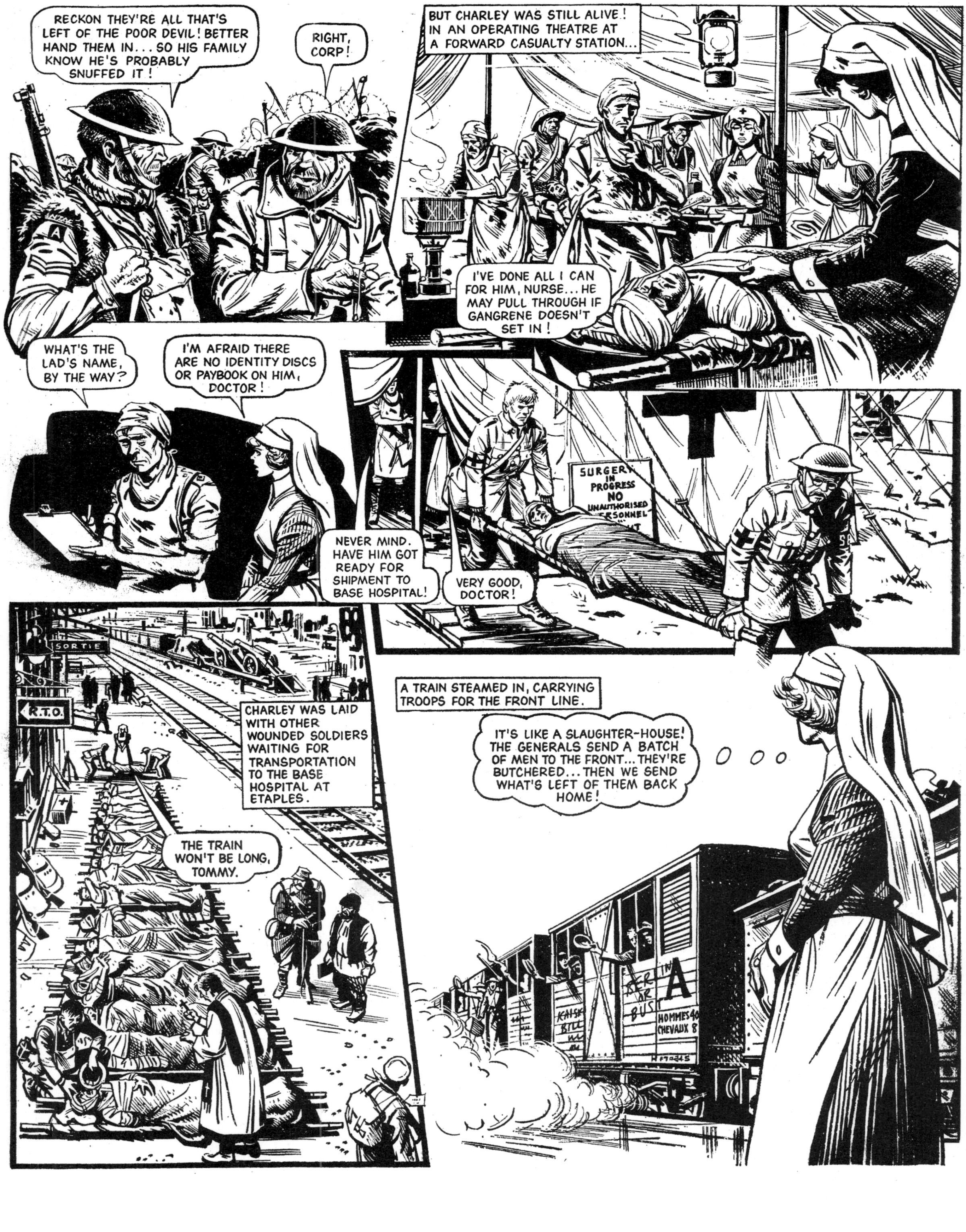
RECKON THEY'RE ALL THAT'S LEFT OF THE POOR DEVIL! BETTER HAND THEM IN... SO HIS FAMILY KNOW HE'S PROBABLY SNUFFED IT!
RIGHT, CORP!
BUT CHARLEY WAS STILL ALIVE! IN AN OPERATING THEATRE AT A FORWARD CASUALTY STATION...
I'VE DONE ALL I CAN FOR HIM, NURSE... HE MAY PULL THROUGH IF GANGRENE DOESN'T SET IN!
WHAT'S THE LAD'S NAME, BY THE WAY?
I'M AFRAID THERE ARE NO IDENTITY DISCS OR PAYBOOK ON HIM, DOCTOR!
NEVER MIND. HAVE HIM GOT READY FOR SHIPMENT TO BASE HOSPITAL!
VERY GOOD, DOCTOR!
SURGERY IN PROGRESS NO UNAUTHORISED
SORTIE
R.T.O.
CHARLEY WAS LAID WITH OTHER WOUNDED SOLDIERS WAITING FOR TRANSPORTATION TO THE BASE HOSPITAL AT ETAPLES.
THE TRAIN WON'T BE LONG, TOMMY.
A TRAIN STEAMED IN, CARRYING TROOPS FOR THE FRONT LINE.
IT'S LIKE A SLAUGHTER-HOUSE! THE GENERALS SEND A BATCH OF MEN TO THE FRONT... THEY'RE BUTCHERED... THEN WE SEND WHAT'S LEFT OF THEM BACK HOME!
HOMMES 40 CHEVAUX 8

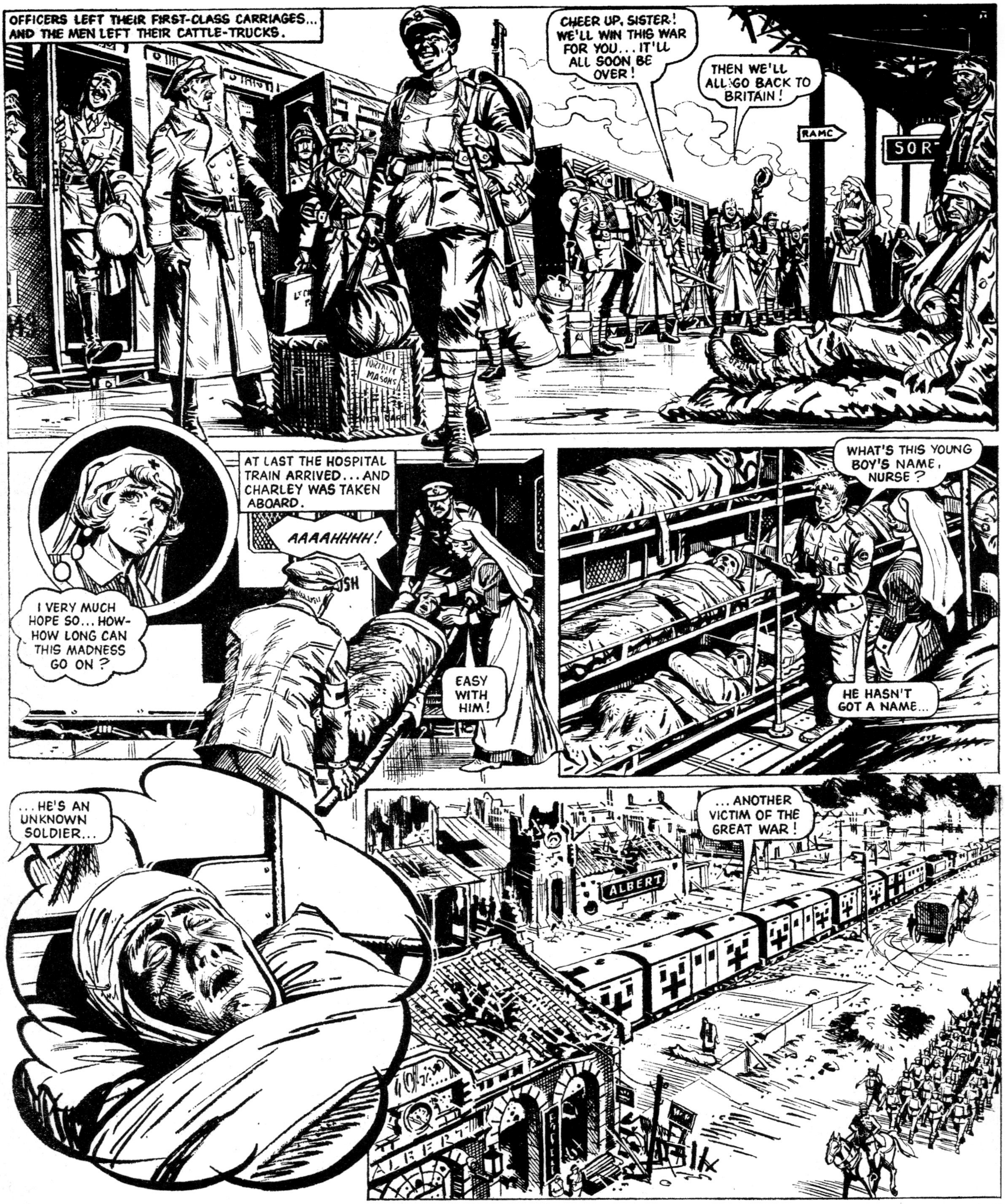
OFFICERS LEFT THEIR FIRST-CLASS CARRIAGES... AND THE MEN LEFT THEIR CATTLE-TRUCKS.
CHEER UP, SISTER! WE'LL WIN THIS WAR FOR YOU... IT'LL ALL SOON BE OVER!
THEN WE'LL ALL GO BACK TO BRITAIN!
RAMC
I VERY MUCH HOPE SO... HOW-HOW LONG CAN THIS MADNESS GO ON?
AT LAST THE HOSPITAL TRAIN ARRIVED... AND CHARLEY WAS TAKEN ABOARD.
AAAAHHHH!
EASY WITH HIM!
WHAT'S THIS YOUNG BOY'S NAME, NURSE?
HE HASN'T GOT A NAME...
...HE'S AN UNKNOWN SOLDIER...
...ANOTHER VICTIM OF THE GREAT WAR!
ALBERT

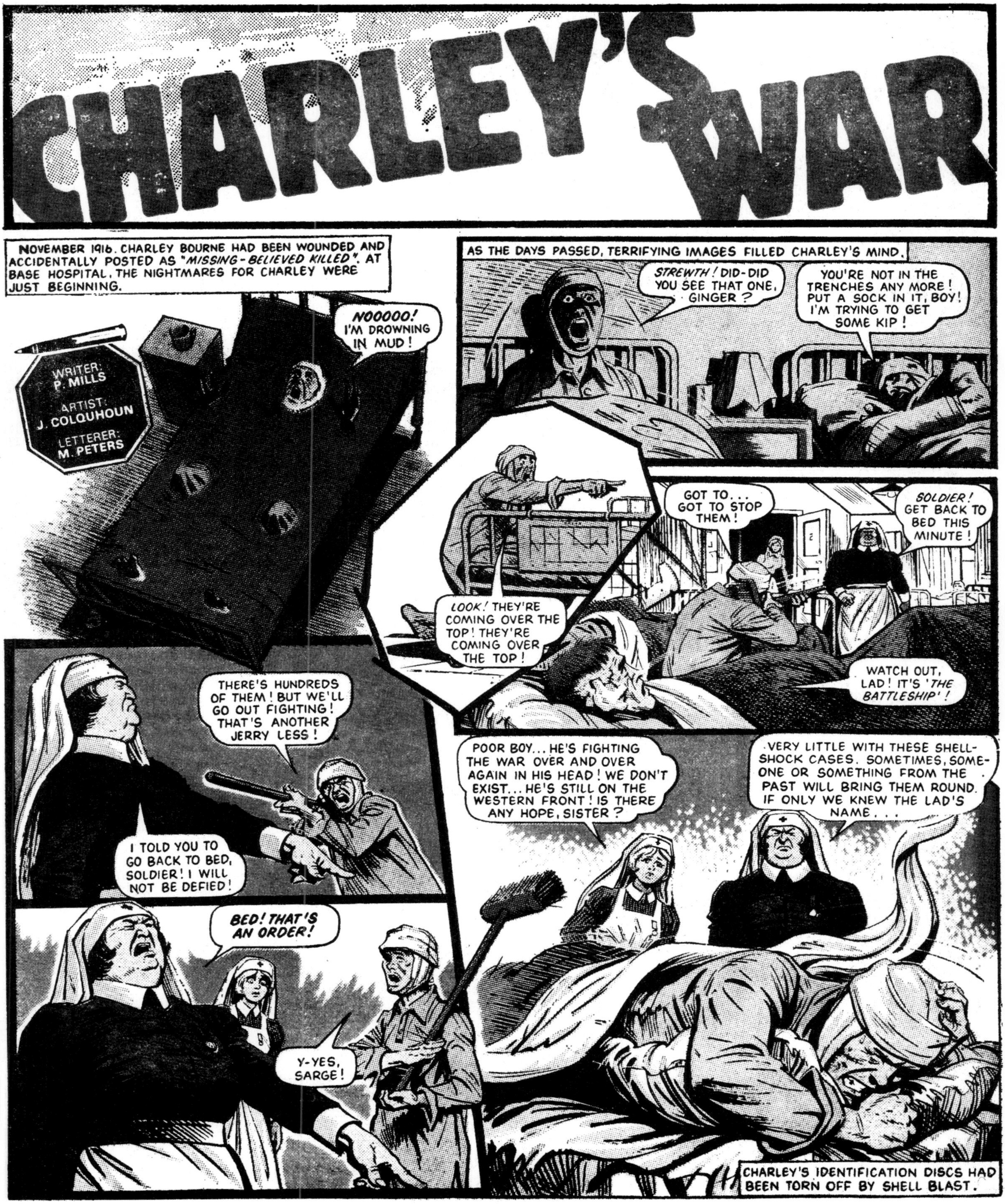
CHARLEY'S WAR
NOVEMBER 1916. CHARLEY BOURNE HAD BEEN WOUNDED AND ACCIDENTALLY POSTED AS "MISSING-BELIEVED KILLED". AT BASE HOSPITAL, THE NIGHTMARES FOR CHARLEY WERE JUST BEGINNING.
WRITER: P. MILLS
ARTIST: J. COLQUHOUN
LETTERER: M. PETERS
NOOOOO! I'M DROWNING IN MUD!
AS THE DAYS PASSED, TERRIFYING IMAGES FILLED CHARLEY'S MIND.
STREWTH! DID-DID YOU SEE THAT ONE, GINGER?
YOU'RE NOT IN THE TRENCHES ANY MORE! PUT A SOCK IN IT, BOY! I'M TRYING TO GET SOME KIP!
LOOK! THEY'RE COMING OVER THE TOP! THEY'RE COMING OVER THE TOP!
GOT TO... GOT TO STOP THEM!
SOLDIER! GET BACK TO BED THIS MINUTE!
WATCH OUT, LAD! IT'S 'THE BATTLESHIP'!
THERE'S HUNDREDS OF THEM! BUT WE'LL GO OUT FIGHTING! THAT'S ANOTHER JERRY LESS!
I TOLD YOU TO GO BACK TO BED, SOLDIER! I WILL NOT BE DEFIED!
BED! THAT'S AN ORDER!
Y-YES, SARGE!
POOR BOY... HE'S FIGHTING THE WAR OVER AND OVER AGAIN IN HIS HEAD! WE DON'T EXIST... HE'S STILL ON THE WESTERN FRONT! IS THERE ANY HOPE, SISTER?
VERY LITTLE WITH THESE SHELL-SHOCK CASES. SOMETIMES, SOMEONE OR SOMETHING FROM THE PAST WILL BRING THEM ROUND. IF ONLY WE KNEW THE LAD'S NAME...
CHARLEY'S IDENTIFICATION DISCS HAD BEEN TORN OFF BY SHELL BLAST.

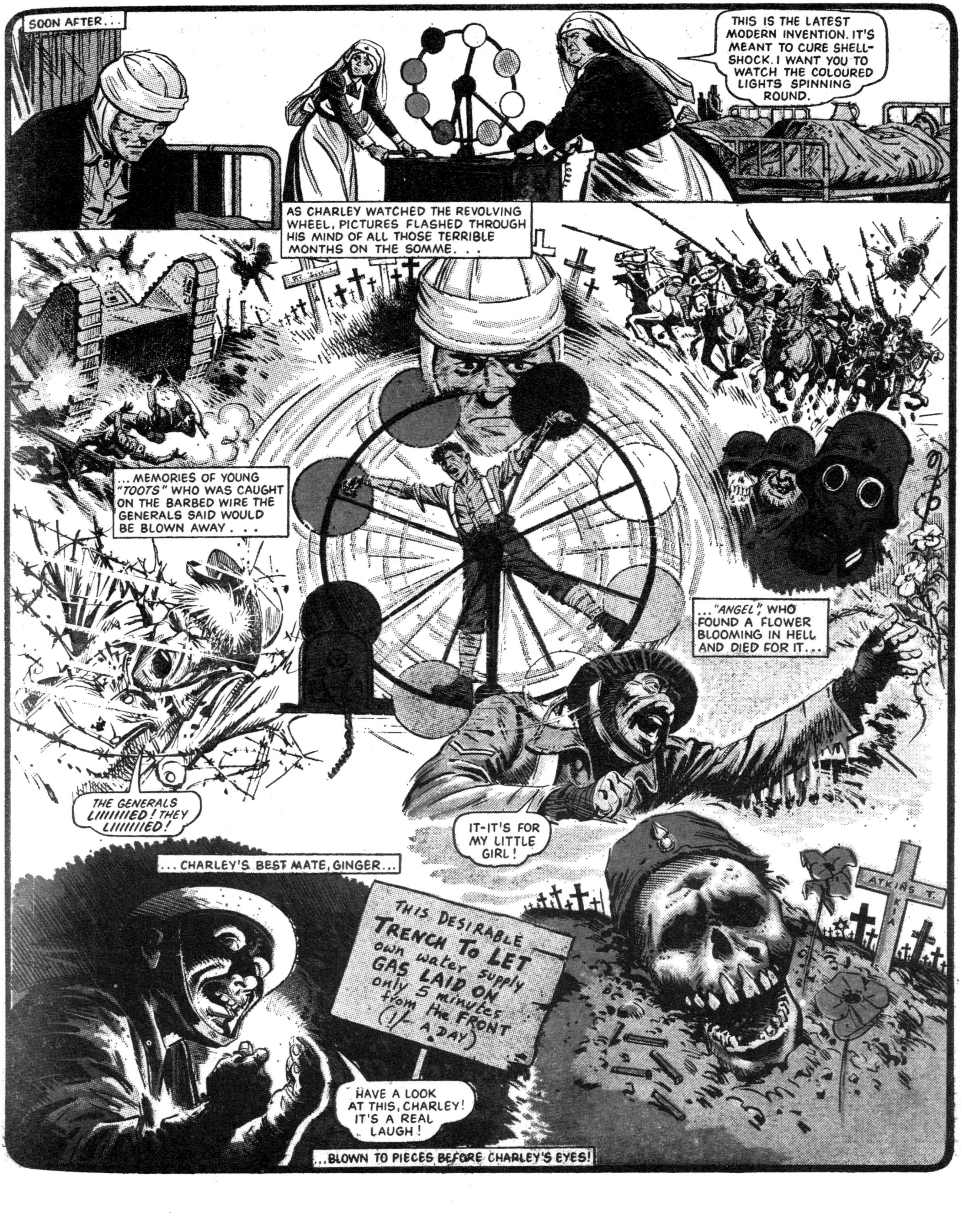
SOON AFTER...
THIS IS THE LATEST MODERN INVENTION. IT'S MEANT TO CURE SHELL-SHOCK. I WANT YOU TO WATCH THE COLOURED LIGHTS SPINNING ROUND.
AS CHARLEY WATCHED THE REVOLVING WHEEL, PICTURES FLASHED THROUGH HIS MIND OF ALL THOSE TERRIBLE MONTHS ON THE SOMME. . .
...MEMORIES OF YOUNG "TOOTS" WHO WAS CAUGHT ON THE BARBED WIRE THE GENERALS SAID WOULD BE BLOWN AWAY . . .
THE GENERALS LIIIIIIED! THEY LIIIIIIED!
..."ANGEL", WHO FOUND A FLOWER BLOOMING IN HELL AND DIED FOR IT...
IT-IT'S FOR MY LITTLE GIRL!
...CHARLEY'S BEST MATE, GINGER...
THIS DESIRABLE TRENCH TO LET own water supply GAS LAID ON only 5 minutes from the FRONT (1/- A DAY)
HAVE A LOOK AT THIS, CHARLEY! IT'S A REAL LAUGH!
ATKINS T.
...BLOWN TO PIECES BEFORE CHARLEY'S EYES!

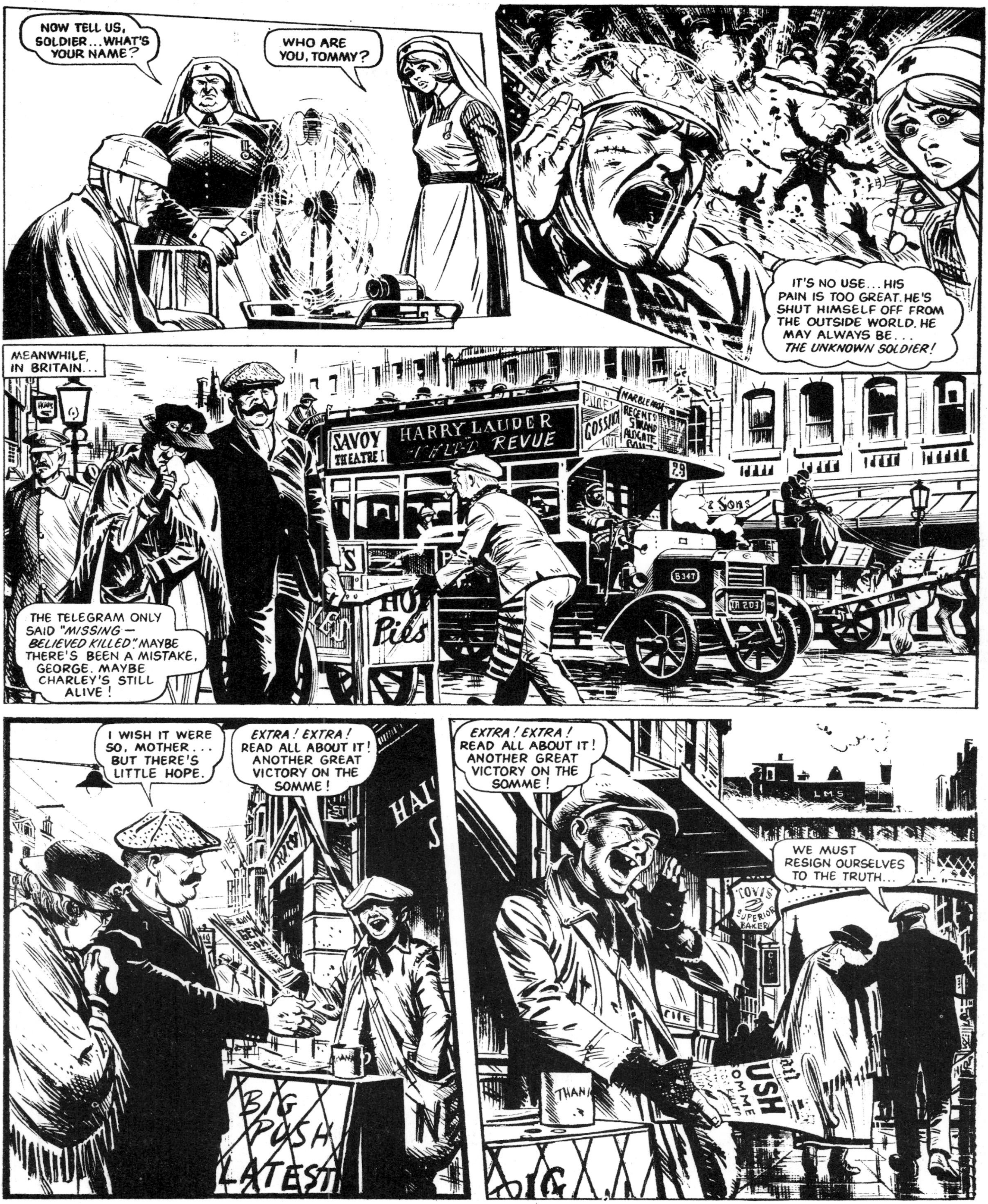
NOW TELL US, SOLDIER... WHAT'S YOUR NAME?
WHO ARE YOU, TOMMY?
IT'S NO USE... HIS PAIN IS TOO GREAT. HE'S SHUT HIMSELF OFF FROM THE OUTSIDE WORLD. HE MAY ALWAYS BE... THE UNKNOWN SOLDIER!
MEANWHILE, IN BRITAIN...
SAVOY THEATRE
HARRY LAUDER
REVUE
THE TELEGRAM ONLY SAID "MISSING — BELIEVED KILLED". MAYBE THERE'S BEEN A MISTAKE, GEORGE. MAYBE CHARLEY'S STILL ALIVE!
I WISH IT WERE SO, MOTHER... BUT THERE'S LITTLE HOPE.
EXTRA! EXTRA! READ ALL ABOUT IT! ANOTHER GREAT VICTORY ON THE SOMME!
BIG PUSH LATEST
EXTRA! EXTRA! READ ALL ABOUT IT! ANOTHER GREAT VICTORY ON THE SOMME!
WE MUST RESIGN OURSELVES TO THE TRUTH...

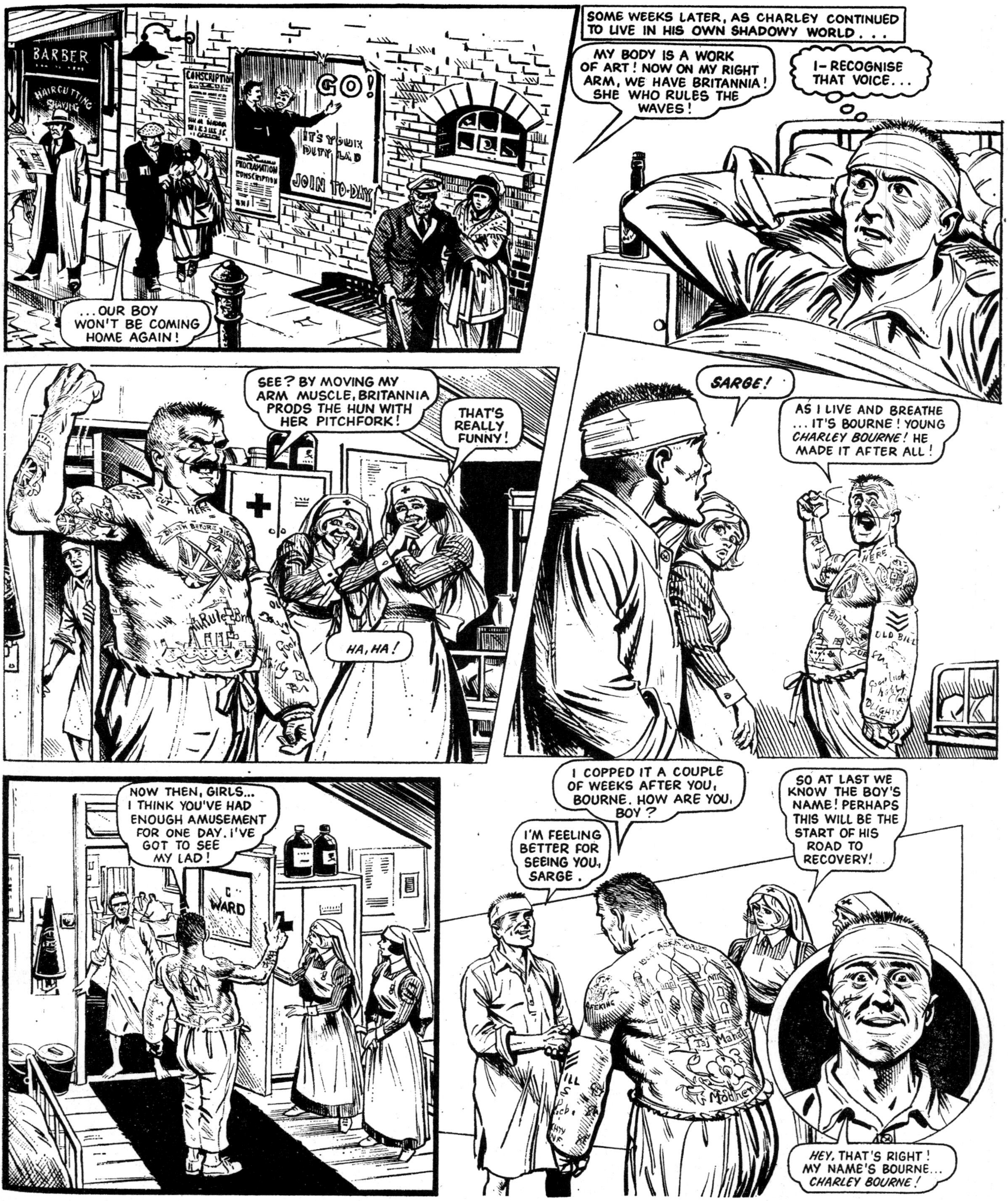
BARBER
HAIRCUTTING SHAVING
CONSCRIPTION
PROCLAMATION CONSCRIPTION
GO!
IT'S YOUR DUTY LAD
JOIN TO-DAY
...OUR BOY WON'T BE COMING HOME AGAIN!
SOME WEEKS LATER, AS CHARLEY CONTINUED TO LIVE IN HIS OWN SHADOWY WORLD...
MY BODY IS A WORK OF ART! NOW ON MY RIGHT ARM, WE HAVE BRITANNIA! SHE WHO RULES THE WAVES!
I- RECOGNISE THAT VOICE...
SEE? BY MOVING MY ARM MUSCLE, BRITANNIA PRODS THE HUN WITH HER PITCHFORK!
THAT'S REALLY FUNNY!
HA, HA!
SARGE!
AS I LIVE AND BREATHE ... IT'S BOURNE! YOUNG CHARLEY BOURNE! HE MADE IT AFTER ALL!
NOW THEN, GIRLS... I THINK YOU'VE HAD ENOUGH AMUSEMENT FOR ONE DAY. I'VE GOT TO SEE MY LAD!
WARD
I COPPED IT A COUPLE OF WEEKS AFTER YOU, BOURNE. HOW ARE YOU, BOY?
I'M FEELING BETTER FOR SEEING YOU, SARGE.
SO AT LAST WE KNOW THE BOY'S NAME! PERHAPS THIS WILL BE THE START OF HIS ROAD TO RECOVERY!
Taj Mahal
Mother
HEY, THAT'S RIGHT! MY NAME'S BOURNE... CHARLEY BOURNE!

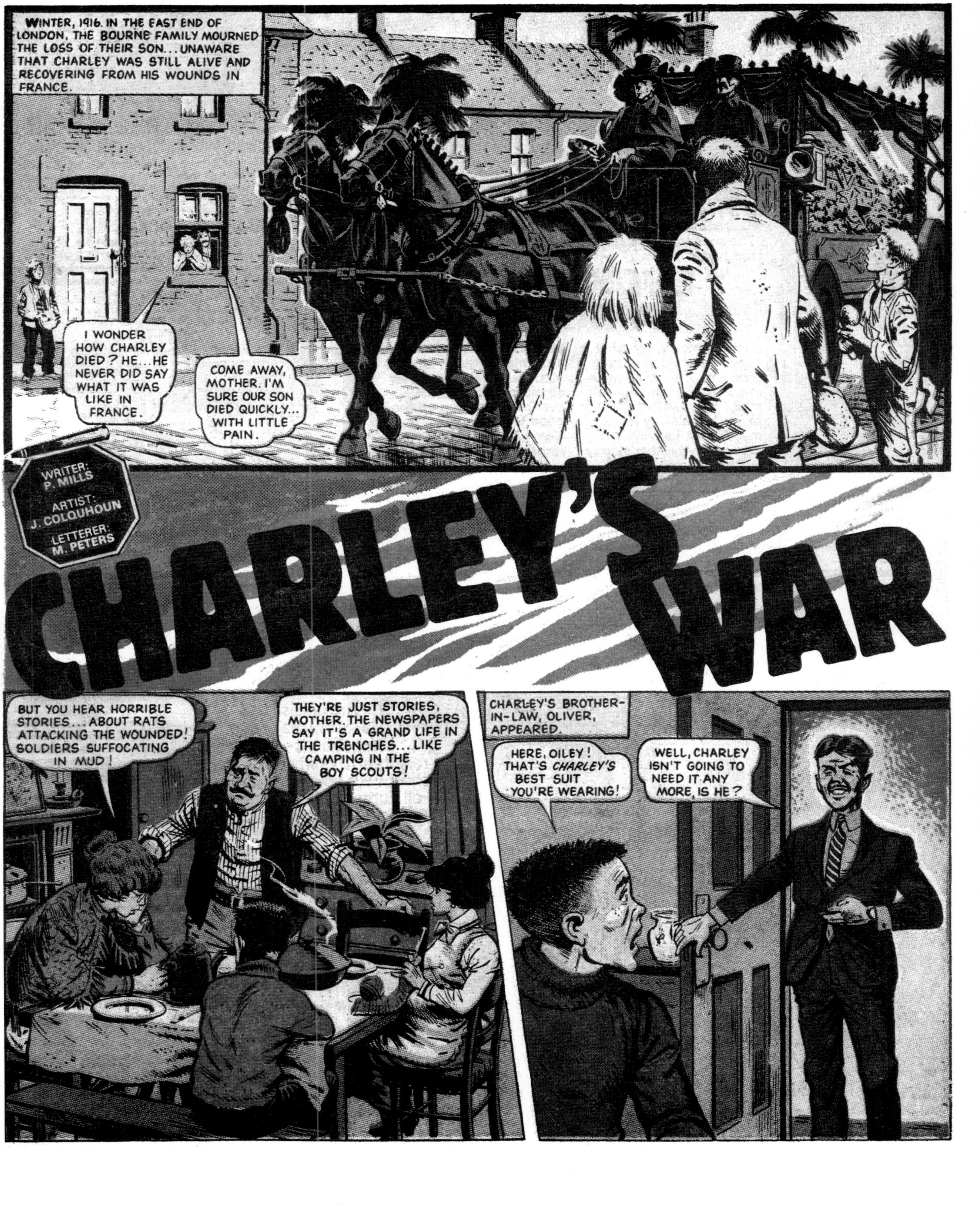
WINTER, 1916. IN THE EAST END OF LONDON, THE BOURNE FAMILY MOURNED THE LOSS OF THEIR SON... UNAWARE THAT CHARLEY WAS STILL ALIVE AND RECOVERING FROM HIS WOUNDS IN FRANCE.
I WONDER HOW CHARLEY DIED? HE... HE NEVER DID SAY WHAT IT WAS LIKE IN FRANCE.
COME AWAY, MOTHER. I'M SURE OUR SON DIED QUICKLY... WITH LITTLE PAIN.
WRITER: P. MILLS
ARTIST: J. COLQUHOUN
LETTERER: M. PETERS
CHARLEY'S WAR
BUT YOU HEAR HORRIBLE STORIES... ABOUT RATS ATTACKING THE WOUNDED! SOLDIERS SUFFOCATING IN MUD!
THEY'RE JUST STORIES, MOTHER. THE NEWSPAPERS SAY IT'S A GRAND LIFE IN THE TRENCHES... LIKE CAMPING IN THE BOY SCOUTS!
CHARLEY'S BROTHER-IN-LAW, OLIVER, APPEARED.
HERE, OILEY! THAT'S CHARLEY'S BEST SUIT YOU'RE WEARING!
WELL, CHARLEY ISN'T GOING TO NEED IT ANY MORE, IS HE?

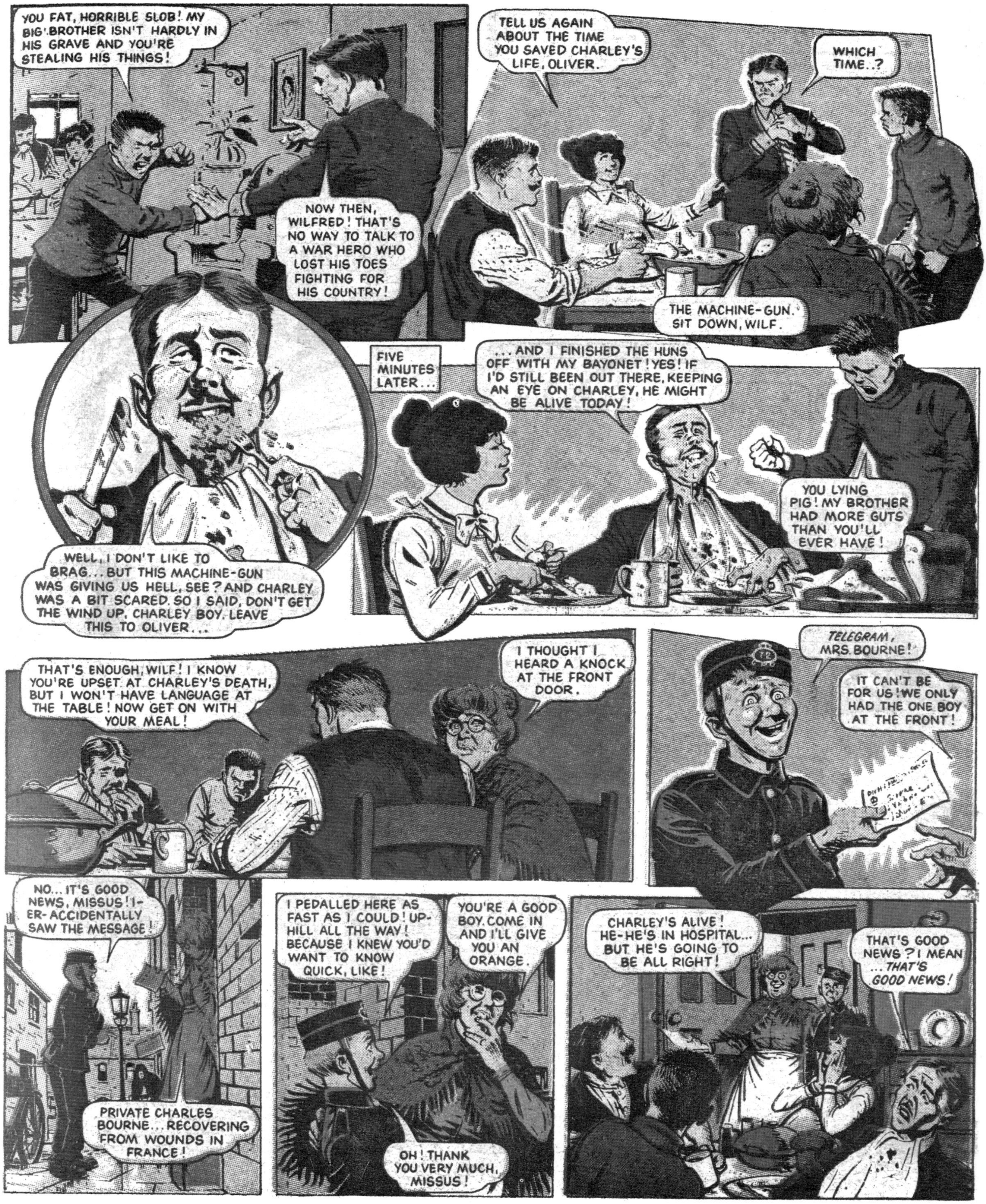
YOU FAT, HORRIBLE SLOB! MY BIG BROTHER ISN'T HARDLY IN HIS GRAVE AND YOU'RE STEALING HIS THINGS!
NOW THEN, WILFRED! THAT'S NO WAY TO TALK TO A WAR HERO WHO LOST HIS TOES FIGHTING FOR HIS COUNTRY!
TELL US AGAIN ABOUT THE TIME YOU SAVED CHARLEY'S LIFE, OLIVER.
WHICH TIME..?
THE MACHINE-GUN. SIT DOWN, WILF.
WELL, I DON'T LIKE TO BRAG... BUT THIS MACHINE-GUN WAS GIVING US HELL, SEE? AND CHARLEY WAS A BIT SCARED. SO I SAID, DON'T GET THE WIND UP, CHARLEY BOY. LEAVE THIS TO OLIVER...
FIVE MINUTES LATER...
...AND I FINISHED THE HUNS OFF WITH MY BAYONET! YES! IF I'D STILL BEEN OUT THERE, KEEPING AN EYE ON CHARLEY, HE MIGHT BE ALIVE TODAY!
YOU LYING PIG! MY BROTHER HAD MORE GUTS THAN YOU'LL EVER HAVE!
THAT'S ENOUGH, WILF! I KNOW YOU'RE UPSET AT CHARLEY'S DEATH, BUT I WON'T HAVE LANGUAGE AT THE TABLE! NOW GET ON WITH YOUR MEAL!
I THOUGHT I HEARD A KNOCK AT THE FRONT DOOR.
TELEGRAM, MRS. BOURNE!
IT CAN'T BE FOR US! WE ONLY HAD THE ONE BOY AT THE FRONT!
NO... IT'S GOOD NEWS, MISSUS! I-ER-ACCIDENTALLY SAW THE MESSAGE!
PRIVATE CHARLES BOURNE... RECOVERING FROM WOUNDS IN FRANCE!
I PEDALLED HERE AS FAST AS I COULD! UP-HILL ALL THE WAY! BECAUSE I KNEW YOU'D WANT TO KNOW QUICK, LIKE!
YOU'RE A GOOD BOY. COME IN AND I'LL GIVE YOU AN ORANGE.
OH! THANK YOU VERY MUCH, MISSUS!
CHARLEY'S ALIVE! HE-HE'S IN HOSPITAL... BUT HE'S GOING TO BE ALL RIGHT!
THAT'S GOOD NEWS? I MEAN ...THAT'S GOOD NEWS!

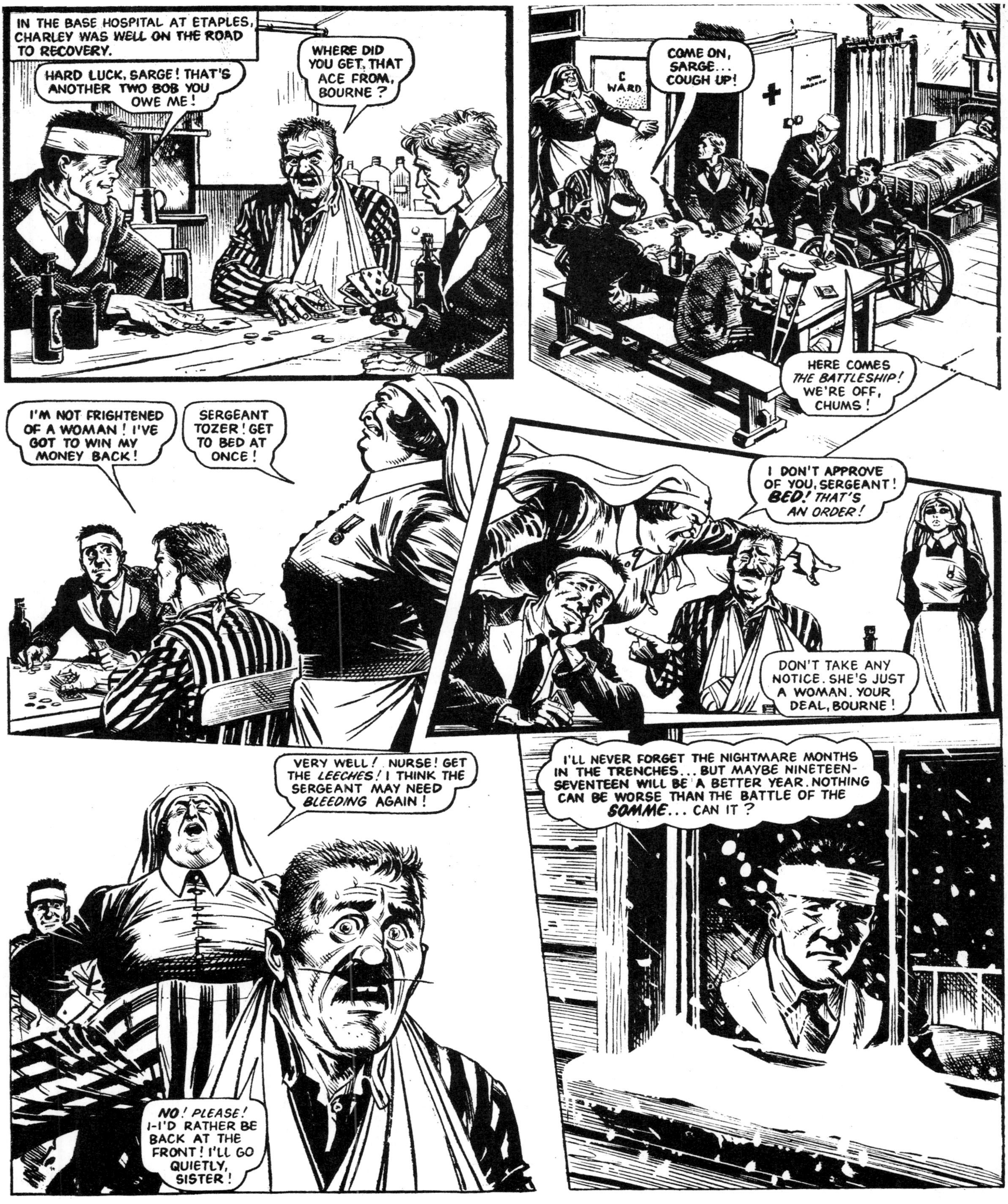
IN THE BASE HOSPITAL AT ETAPLES, CHARLEY WAS WELL ON THE ROAD TO RECOVERY.
HARD LUCK, SARGE! THAT'S ANOTHER TWO BOB YOU OWE ME!
WHERE DID YOU GET THAT ACE FROM, BOURNE?
COME ON, SARGE... COUGH UP!
C WARD
HERE COMES THE BATTLESHIP! WE'RE OFF, CHUMS!
I'M NOT FRIGHTENED OF A WOMAN! I'VE GOT TO WIN MY MONEY BACK!
SERGEANT TOZER! GET TO BED AT ONCE!
I DON'T APPROVE OF YOU, SERGEANT! BED! THAT'S AN ORDER!
DON'T TAKE ANY NOTICE. SHE'S JUST A WOMAN. YOUR DEAL, BOURNE!
VERY WELL! NURSE! GET THE LEECHES! I THINK THE SERGEANT MAY NEED BLEEDING AGAIN!
NO! PLEASE! I-I'D RATHER BE BACK AT THE FRONT! I'LL GO QUIETLY, SISTER!
I'LL NEVER FORGET THE NIGHTMARE MONTHS IN THE TRENCHES... BUT MAYBE NINETEEN-SEVENTEEN WILL BE A BETTER YEAR. NOTHING CAN BE WORSE THAN THE BATTLE OF THE SOMME... CAN IT?

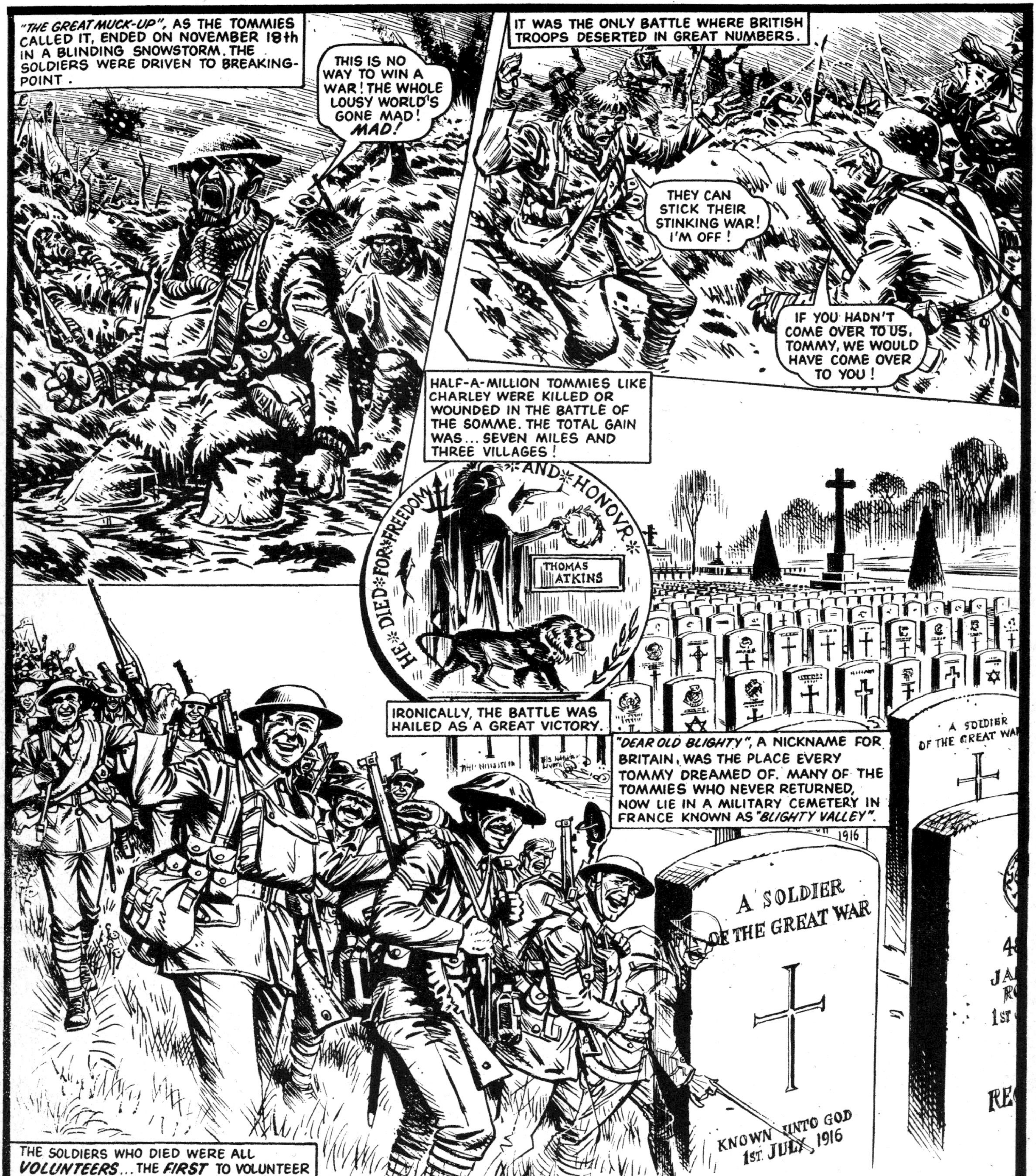
"THE GREAT MUCK-UP", AS THE TOMMIES CALLED IT, ENDED ON NOVEMBER 18th IN A BLINDING SNOWSTORM. THE SOLDIERS WERE DRIVEN TO BREAKING-POINT.
THIS IS NO WAY TO WIN A WAR! THE WHOLE LOUSY WORLD'S GONE MAD! MAD!
IT WAS THE ONLY BATTLE WHERE BRITISH TROOPS DESERTED IN GREAT NUMBERS.
THEY CAN STICK THEIR STINKING WAR! I'M OFF!
IF YOU HADN'T COME OVER TO US, TOMMY, WE WOULD HAVE COME OVER TO YOU!
HALF-A-MILLION TOMMIES LIKE CHARLEY WERE KILLED OR WOUNDED IN THE BATTLE OF THE SOMME. THE TOTAL GAIN WAS... SEVEN MILES AND THREE VILLAGES!
HE DIED FOR FREEDOM AND HONOVR
THOMAS ATKINS
IRONICALLY, THE BATTLE WAS HAILED AS A GREAT VICTORY.
"DEAR OLD BLIGHTY", A NICKNAME FOR BRITAIN, WAS THE PLACE EVERY TOMMY DREAMED OF. MANY OF THE TOMMIES WHO NEVER RETURNED, NOW LIE IN A MILITARY CEMETERY IN FRANCE KNOWN AS "BLIGHTY VALLEY".
A SOLDIER OF THE GREAT WAR
A SOLDIER OF THE GREAT WAR
KNOWN UNTO GOD 1ST. JULY, 1916
THE SOLDIERS WHO DIED WERE ALL VOLUNTEERS... THE FIRST TO VOLUNTEER ... LADS EAGER TO SERVE THEIR COUNTRY. THEY WERE YOUNG, HEALTHY AND BRAVE ... THE "BEST OF BRITISH".
THE BATTLE OF THE SOMME WIPED THEM OUT!

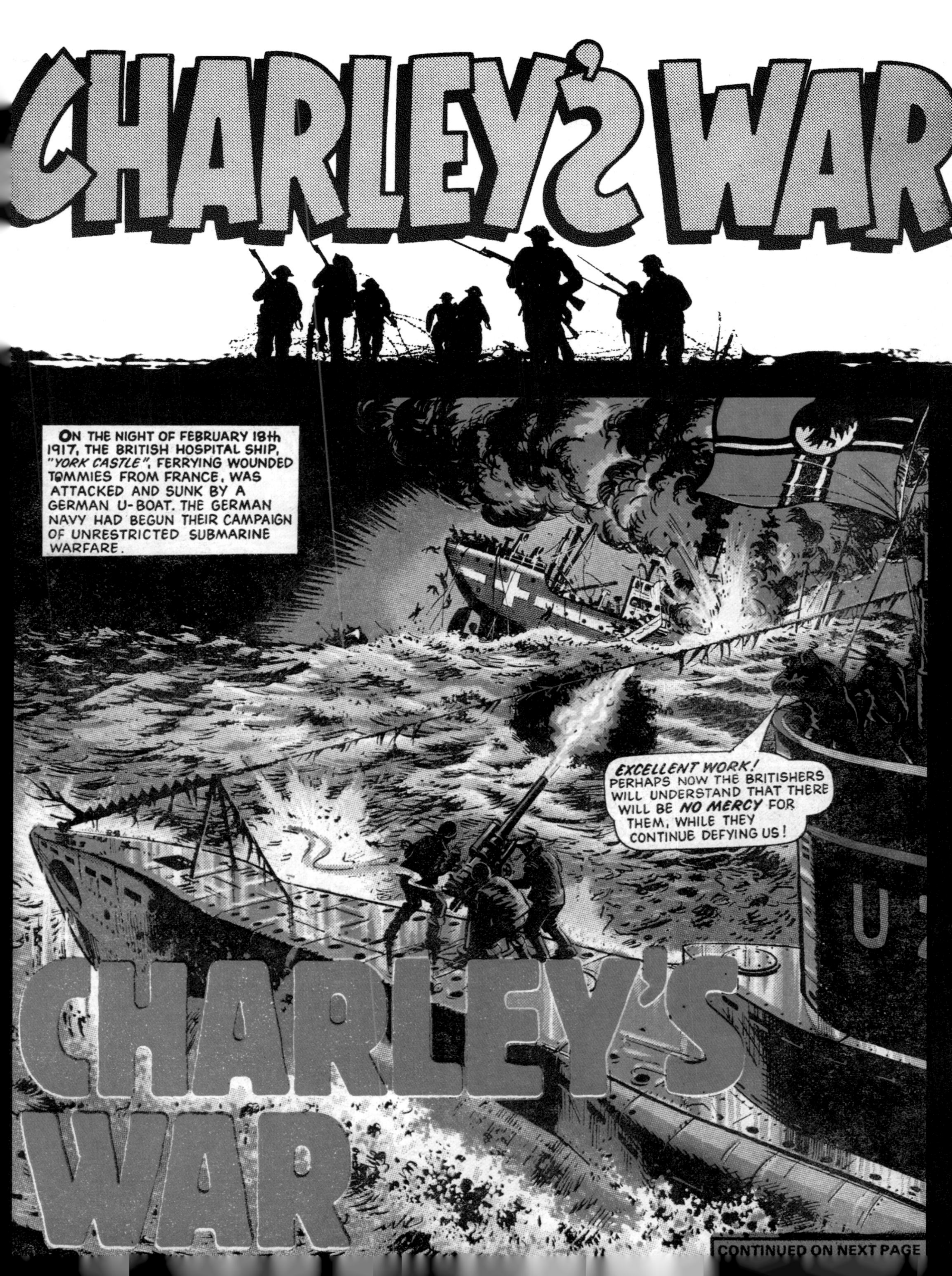
CHARLEY'S WAR
ON THE NIGHT OF FEBRUARY 18th 1917, THE BRITISH HOSPITAL SHIP, "YORK CASTLE", FERRYING WOUNDED TOMMIES FROM FRANCE, WAS ATTACKED AND SUNK BY A GERMAN U-BOAT. THE GERMAN NAVY HAD BEGUN THEIR CAMPAIGN OF UNRESTRICTED SUBMARINE WARFARE.
EXCELLENT WORK! PERHAPS NOW THE BRITISHERS WILL UNDERSTAND THAT THERE WILL BE NO MERCY FOR THEM, WHILE THEY CONTINUE DEFYING US!
CHARLEY'S WAR
CONTINUED ON NEXT PAGE

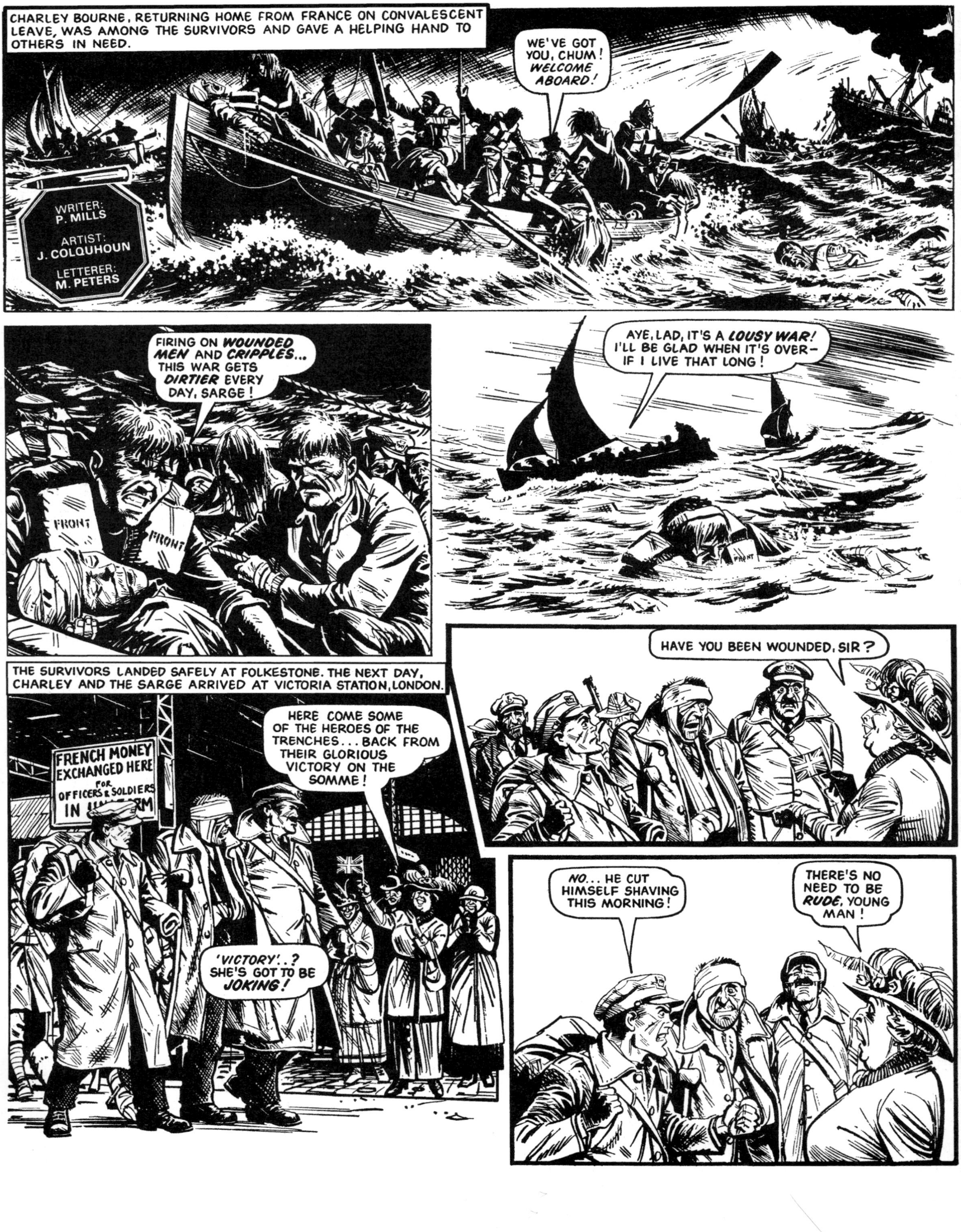
CHARLEY BOURNE, RETURNING HOME FROM FRANCE ON CONVALESCENT LEAVE, WAS AMONG THE SURVIVORS AND GAVE A HELPING HAND TO OTHERS IN NEED.
WE'VE GOT YOU, CHUM! WELCOME ABOARD!
WRITER: P. MILLS
ARTIST: J. COLQUHOUN
LETTERER: M. PETERS
FIRING ON WOUNDED MEN AND CRIPPLES... THIS WAR GETS DIRTIER EVERY DAY, SARGE!
FRONT
FRONT
AYE, LAD, IT'S A LOUSY WAR! I'LL BE GLAD WHEN IT'S OVER-- IF I LIVE THAT LONG!
THE SURVIVORS LANDED SAFELY AT FOLKESTONE. THE NEXT DAY, CHARLEY AND THE SARGE ARRIVED AT VICTORIA STATION, LONDON.
FRENCH MONEY EXCHANGED HERE FOR OFFICERS & SOLDIERS IN UNIFORM
HERE COME SOME OF THE HEROES OF THE TRENCHES... BACK FROM THEIR GLORIOUS VICTORY ON THE SOMME!
'VICTORY'..? SHE'S GOT TO BE JOKING!
HAVE YOU BEEN WOUNDED, SIR?
NO... HE CUT HIMSELF SHAVING THIS MORNING!
THERE'S NO NEED TO BE RUDE, YOUNG MAN!

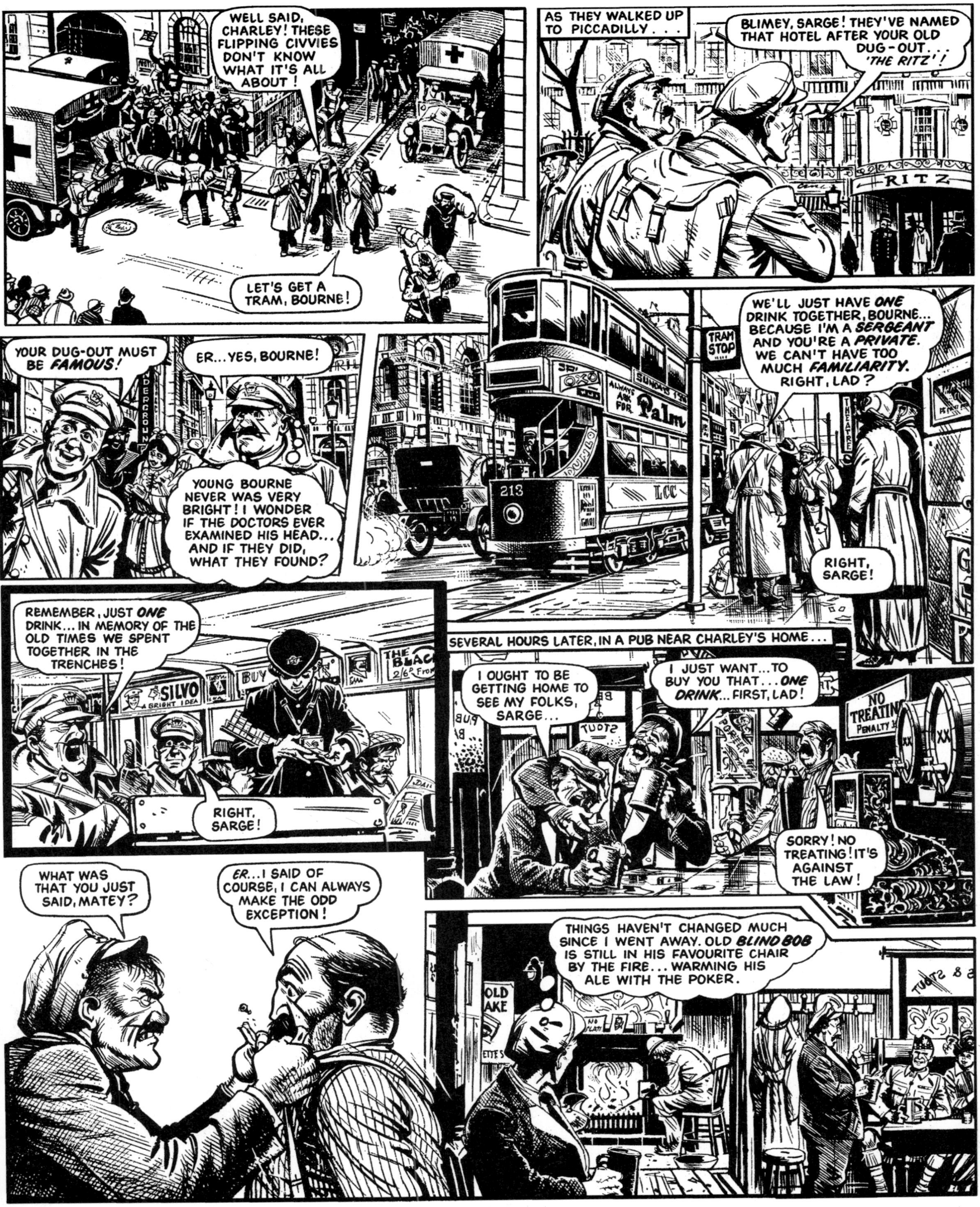
WELL SAID, CHARLEY! THESE FLIPPING CIVVIES DON'T KNOW WHAT IT'S ALL ABOUT!
LET'S GET A TRAM, BOURNE!
AS THEY WALKED UP TO PICCADILLY . . .
BLIMEY, SARGE! THEY'VE NAMED THAT HOTEL AFTER YOUR OLD DUG-OUT... 'THE RITZ'!
RITZ
YOUR DUG-OUT MUST BE FAMOUS!
ER... YES, BOURNE!
YOUNG BOURNE NEVER WAS VERY BRIGHT! I WONDER IF THE DOCTORS EVER EXAMINED HIS HEAD... AND IF THEY DID, WHAT THEY FOUND?
TRAM STOP
WE'LL JUST HAVE ONE DRINK TOGETHER, BOURNE... BECAUSE I'M A SERGEANT AND YOU'RE A PRIVATE. WE CAN'T HAVE TOO MUCH FAMILIARITY. RIGHT, LAD?
RIGHT, SARGE!
REMEMBER, JUST ONE DRINK... IN MEMORY OF THE OLD TIMES WE SPENT TOGETHER IN THE TRENCHES!
SILVO
RIGHT, SARGE!
SEVERAL HOURS LATER, IN A PUB NEAR CHARLEY'S HOME...
I OUGHT TO BE GETTING HOME TO SEE MY FOLKS, SARGE...
I JUST WANT... TO BUY YOU THAT... ONE DRINK... FIRST, LAD!
NO TREATING
SORRY! NO TREATING! IT'S AGAINST THE LAW!
WHAT WAS THAT YOU JUST SAID, MATEY?
ER... I SAID OF COURSE, I CAN ALWAYS MAKE THE ODD EXCEPTION!
THINGS HAVEN'T CHANGED MUCH SINCE I WENT AWAY. OLD BLIND BOB IS STILL IN HIS FAVOURITE CHAIR BY THE FIRE... WARMING HIS ALE WITH THE POKER.

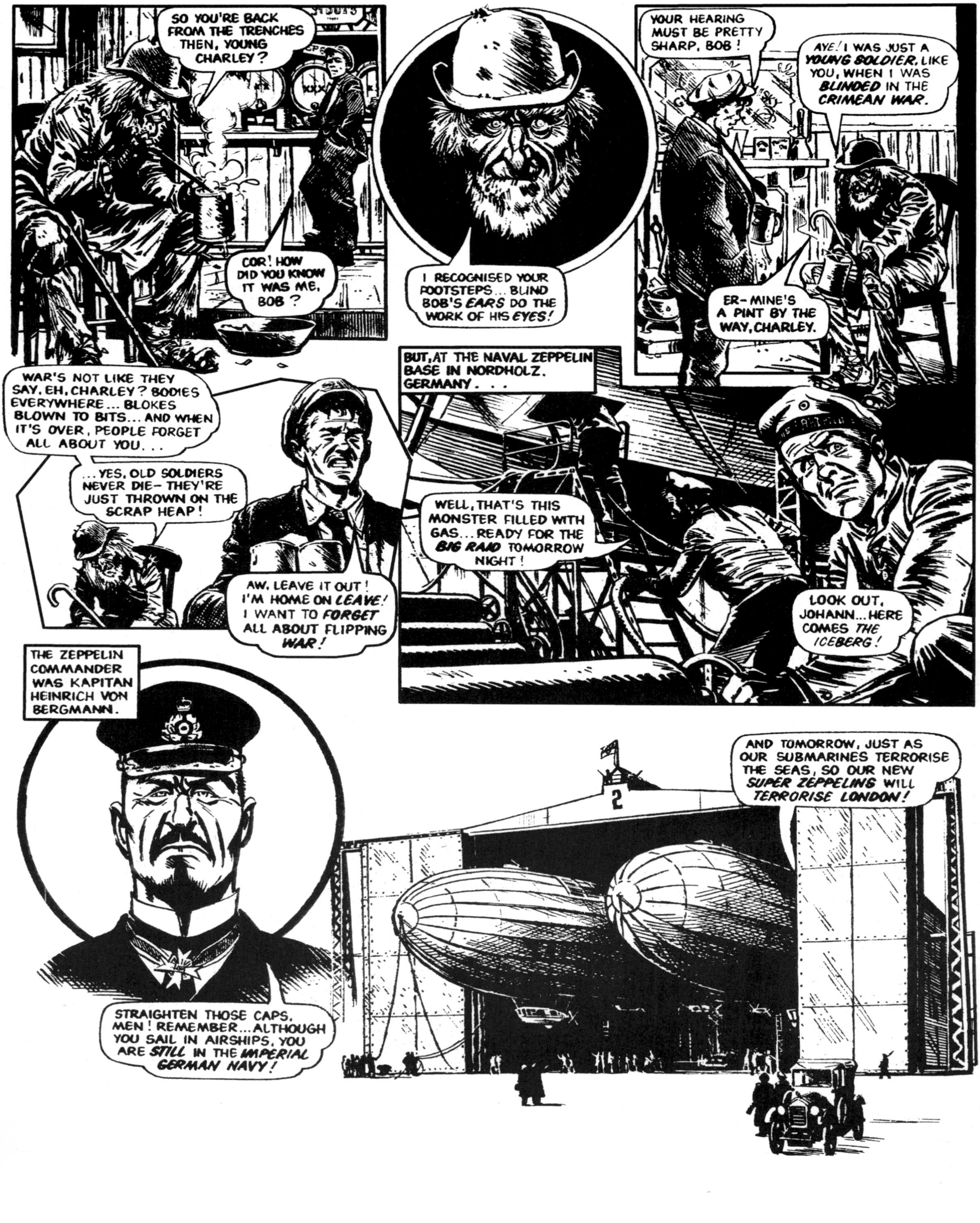

SO YOU'RE BACK FROM THE TRENCHES THEN, YOUNG CHARLEY?
COR! HOW DID YOU KNOW IT WAS ME, BOB?
I RECOGNISED YOUR FOOTSTEPS... BLIND BOB'S EARS DO THE WORK OF HIS EYES!
YOUR HEARING MUST BE PRETTY SHARP, BOB!
AYE! I WAS JUST A YOUNG SOLDIER, LIKE YOU, WHEN I WAS BLINDED IN THE CRIMEAN WAR.
ER-MINE'S A PINT BY THE WAY, CHARLEY.
WAR'S NOT LIKE THEY SAY, EH, CHARLEY? BODIES EVERYWHERE... BLOKES BLOWN TO BITS... AND WHEN IT'S OVER, PEOPLE FORGET ALL ABOUT YOU...
...YES, OLD SOLDIERS NEVER DIE- THEY'RE JUST THROWN ON THE SCRAP HEAP!
AW, LEAVE IT OUT! I'M HOME ON LEAVE! I WANT TO FORGET ALL ABOUT FLIPPING WAR!
BUT, AT THE NAVAL ZEPPELIN BASE IN NORDHOLZ, GERMANY...
WELL, THAT'S THIS MONSTER FILLED WITH GAS... READY FOR THE BIG RAID TOMORROW NIGHT!
LOOK OUT, JOHANN... HERE COMES THE ICEBERG!
THE ZEPPELIN COMMANDER WAS KAPITAN HEINRICH VON BERGMANN.
STRAIGHTEN THOSE CAPS, MEN! REMEMBER... ALTHOUGH YOU SAIL IN AIRSHIPS, YOU ARE STILL IN THE IMPERIAL GERMAN NAVY!
AND TOMORROW, JUST AS OUR SUBMARINES TERRORISE THE SEAS, SO OUR NEW SUPER ZEPPELING WILL TERRORISE LONDON!

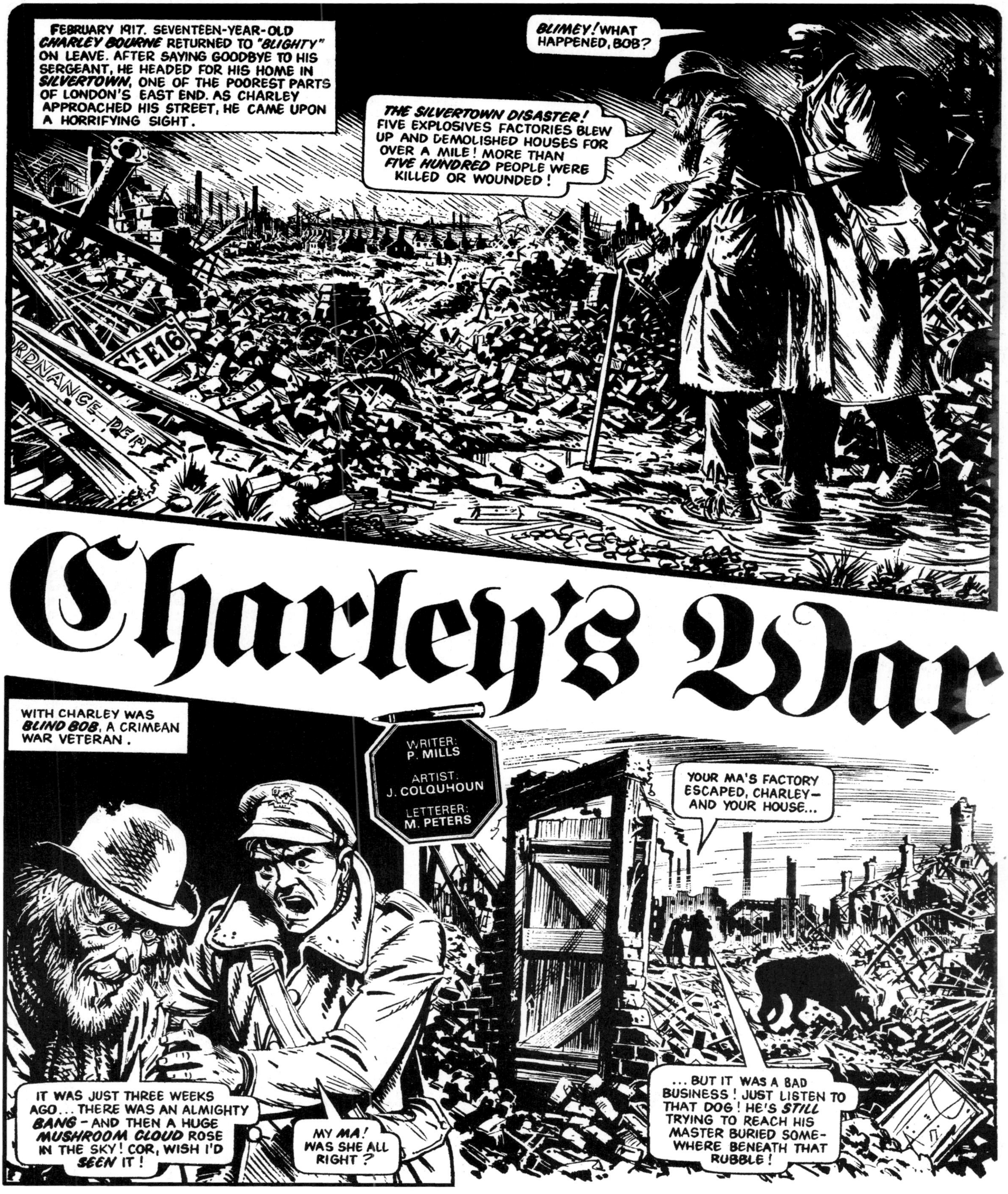
FEBRUARY 1917. SEVENTEEN-YEAR-OLD CHARLEY BOURNE RETURNED TO "BLIGHTY" ON LEAVE. AFTER SAYING GOODBYE TO HIS SERGEANT, HE HEADED FOR HIS HOME IN SILVERTOWN, ONE OF THE POOREST PARTS OF LONDON'S EAST END. AS CHARLEY APPROACHED HIS STREET, HE CAME UPON A HORRIFYING SIGHT.
BLIMEY! WHAT HAPPENED, BOB?
THE SILVERTOWN DISASTER! FIVE EXPLOSIVES FACTORIES BLEW UP AND DEMOLISHED HOUSES FOR OVER A MILE! MORE THAN FIVE HUNDRED PEOPLE WERE KILLED OR WOUNDED!
Charley's War
WITH CHARLEY WAS BLIND BOB, A CRIMEAN WAR VETERAN.
WRITER: P. MILLS
ARTIST: J. COLQUHOUN
LETTERER: M. PETERS
IT WAS JUST THREE WEEKS AGO... THERE WAS AN ALMIGHTY BANG - AND THEN A HUGE MUSHROOM CLOUD ROSE IN THE SKY! COR, WISH I'D SEEN IT!
MY MA! WAS SHE ALL RIGHT?
YOUR MA'S FACTORY ESCAPED, CHARLEY— AND YOUR HOUSE...
... BUT IT WAS A BAD BUSINESS! JUST LISTEN TO THAT DOG! HE'S STILL TRYING TO REACH HIS MASTER BURIED SOMEWHERE BENEATH THAT RUBBLE!

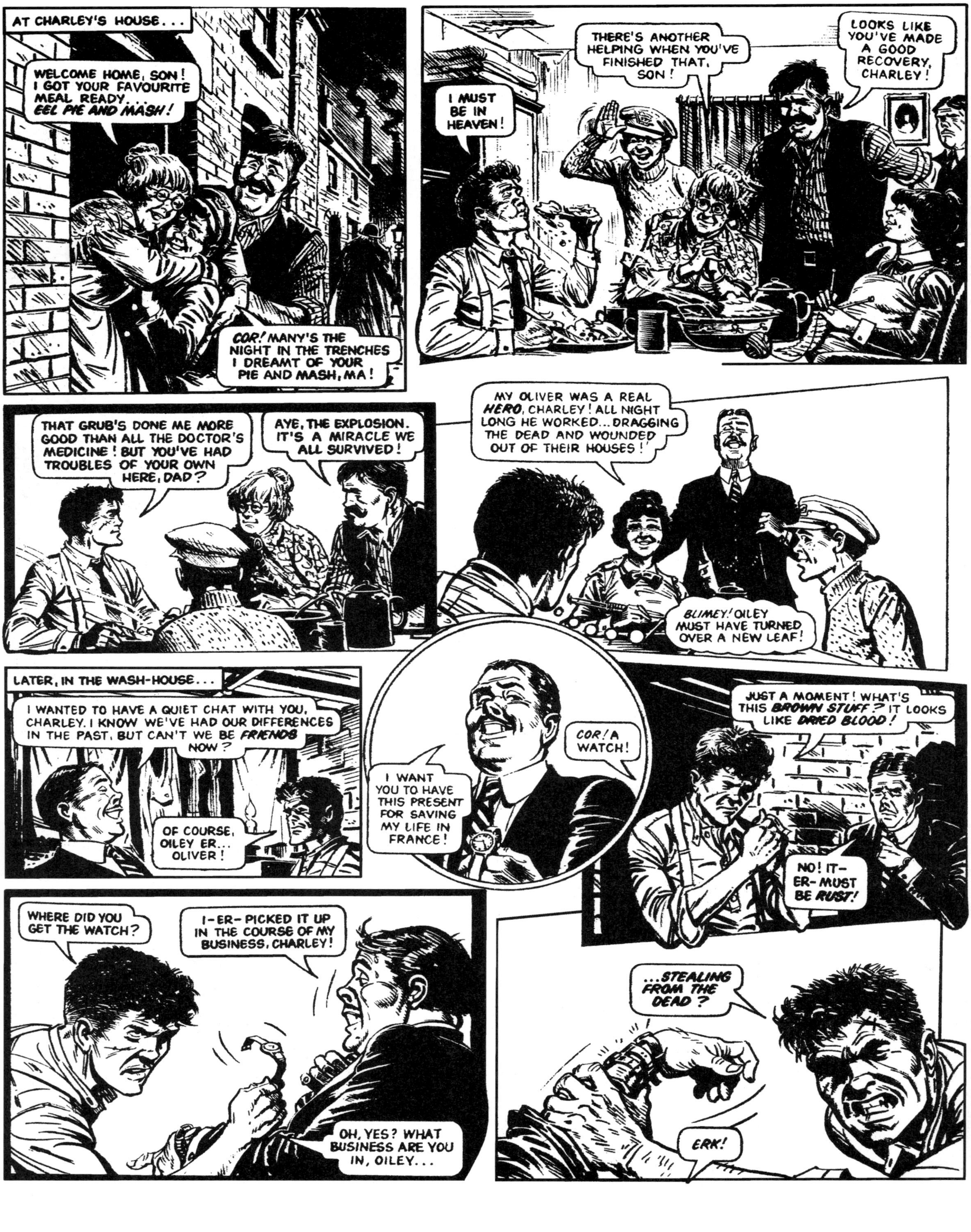
AT CHARLEY'S HOUSE...
WELCOME HOME, SON! I GOT YOUR FAVOURITE MEAL READY... EEL PIE AND MASH!
COR! MANY'S THE NIGHT IN THE TRENCHES I DREAMT OF YOUR PIE AND MASH, MA!
I MUST BE IN HEAVEN!
THERE'S ANOTHER HELPING WHEN YOU'VE FINISHED THAT, SON!
LOOKS LIKE YOU'VE MADE A GOOD RECOVERY, CHARLEY!
THAT GRUB'S DONE ME MORE GOOD THAN ALL THE DOCTOR'S MEDICINE! BUT YOU'VE HAD TROUBLES OF YOUR OWN HERE, DAD?
AYE, THE EXPLOSION. IT'S A MIRACLE WE ALL SURVIVED!
MY OLIVER WAS A REAL HERO, CHARLEY! ALL NIGHT LONG HE WORKED... DRAGGING THE DEAD AND WOUNDED OUT OF THEIR HOUSES!
BLIMEY! OILEY MUST HAVE TURNED OVER A NEW LEAF!
LATER, IN THE WASH-HOUSE...
I WANTED TO HAVE A QUIET CHAT WITH YOU, CHARLEY. I KNOW WE'VE HAD OUR DIFFERENCES IN THE PAST, BUT CAN'T WE BE FRIENDS NOW?
OF COURSE, OILEY ER... OLIVER!
I WANT YOU TO HAVE THIS PRESENT FOR SAVING MY LIFE IN FRANCE!
COR! A WATCH!
JUST A MOMENT! WHAT'S THIS BROWN STUFF? IT LOOKS LIKE DRIED BLOOD!
NO! IT- ER- MUST BE RUST!
WHERE DID YOU GET THE WATCH?
I-ER-PICKED IT UP IN THE COURSE OF MY BUSINESS, CHARLEY!
OH, YES? WHAT BUSINESS ARE YOU IN, OILEY...
...STEALING FROM THE DEAD?
ERK!

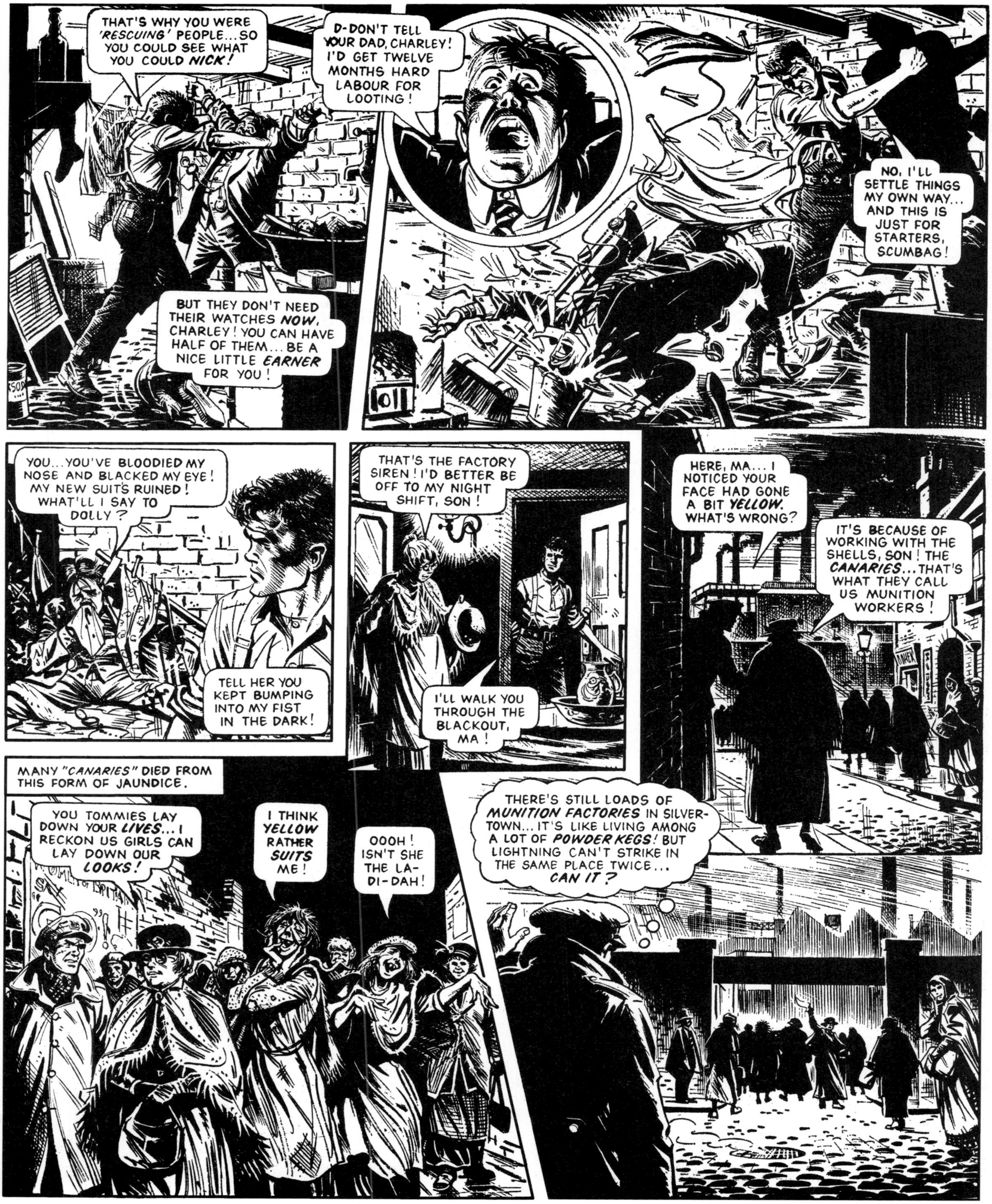

THAT'S WHY YOU WERE 'RESCUING' PEOPLE... SO YOU COULD SEE WHAT YOU COULD NICK!
BUT THEY DON'T NEED THEIR WATCHES NOW, CHARLEY! YOU CAN HAVE HALF OF THEM... BE A NICE LITTLE EARNER FOR YOU!
D-DON'T TELL YOUR DAD, CHARLEY! I'D GET TWELVE MONTHS HARD LABOUR FOR LOOTING!
NO, I'LL SETTLE THINGS MY OWN WAY... AND THIS IS JUST FOR STARTERS, SCUMBAG!
YOU... YOU'VE BLOODIED MY NOSE AND BLACKED MY EYE! MY NEW SUIT'S RUINED! WHAT'LL I SAY TO DOLLY?
TELL HER YOU KEPT BUMPING INTO MY FIST IN THE DARK!
THAT'S THE FACTORY SIREN! I'D BETTER BE OFF TO MY NIGHT SHIFT, SON!
I'LL WALK YOU THROUGH THE BLACKOUT, MA!
HERE, MA... I NOTICED YOUR FACE HAD GONE A BIT YELLOW. WHAT'S WRONG?
IT'S BECAUSE OF WORKING WITH THE SHELLS, SON! THE CANARIES... THAT'S WHAT THEY CALL US MUNITION WORKERS!
MANY "CANARIES" DIED FROM THIS FORM OF JAUNDICE.
YOU TOMMIES LAY DOWN YOUR LIVES... I RECKON US GIRLS CAN LAY DOWN OUR LOOKS!
I THINK YELLOW RATHER SUITS ME!
OOOH! ISN'T SHE THE LA-DI-DAH!
THERE'S STILL LOADS OF MUNITION FACTORIES IN SILVERTOWN... IT'S LIKE LIVING AMONG A LOT OF POWDER KEGS! BUT LIGHTNING CAN'T STRIKE IN THE SAME PLACE TWICE... CAN IT?

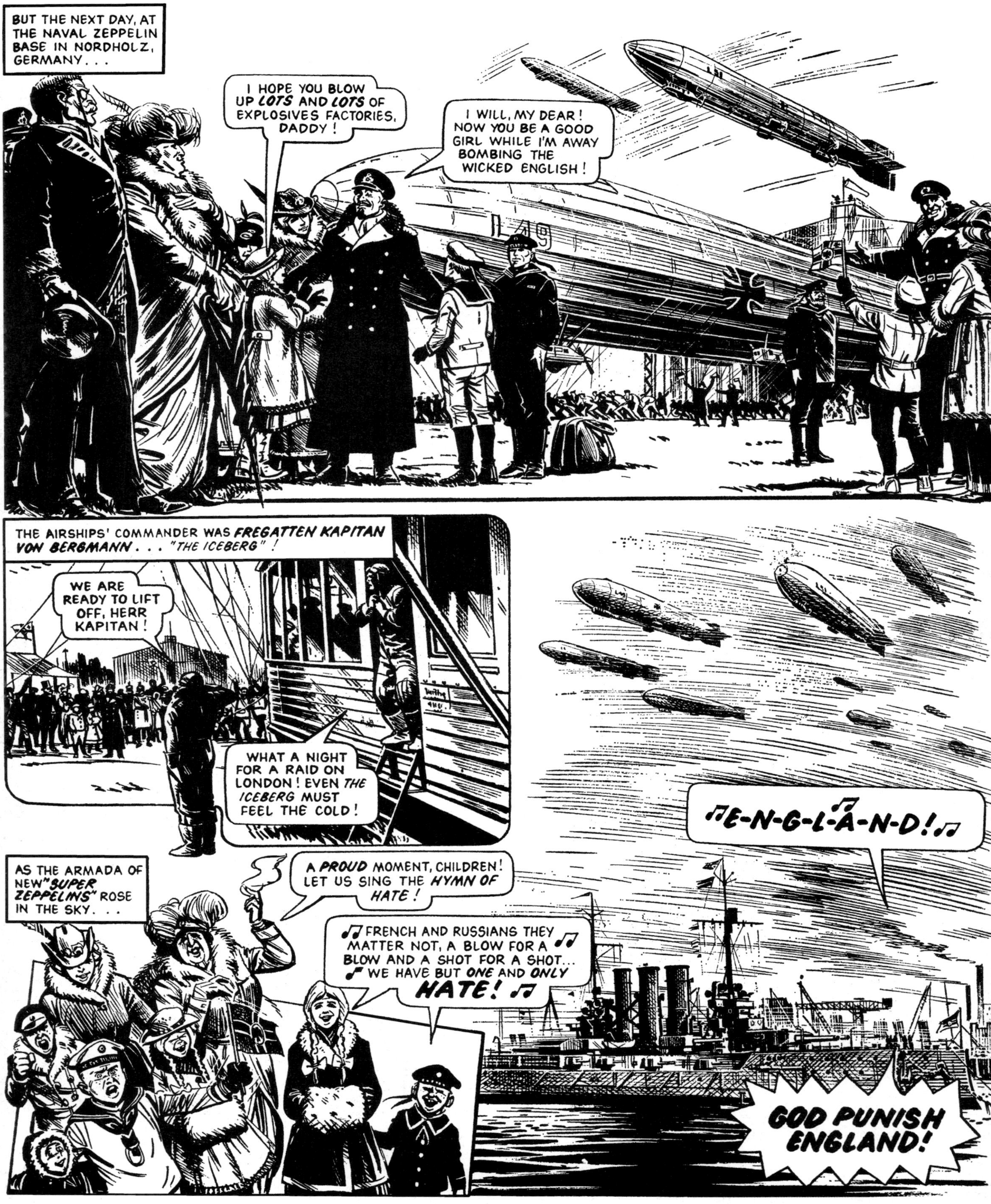

BUT THE NEXT DAY, AT THE NAVAL ZEPPELIN BASE IN NORDHOLZ, GERMANY . . .
I HOPE YOU BLOW UP LOTS AND LOTS OF EXPLOSIVES FACTORIES, DADDY!
I WILL, MY DEAR! NOW YOU BE A GOOD GIRL WHILE I'M AWAY BOMBING THE WICKED ENGLISH!
THE AIRSHIPS' COMMANDER WAS FREGATTEN KAPITAN VON BERGMANN . . . "THE ICEBERG"!
WE ARE READY TO LIFT OFF, HERR KAPITAN!
WHAT A NIGHT FOR A RAID ON LONDON! EVEN THE ICEBERG MUST FEEL THE COLD!
♫E-N-G-L-A-N-D!♫
AS THE ARMADA OF NEW "SUPER ZEPPELINS" ROSE IN THE SKY. . .
A PROUD MOMENT, CHILDREN! LET US SING THE HYMN OF HATE!
♫ FRENCH AND RUSSIANS THEY MATTER NOT, A BLOW FOR A BLOW AND A SHOT FOR A SHOT... WE HAVE BUT ONE AND ONLY HATE! ♫
GOD PUNISH ENGLAND!

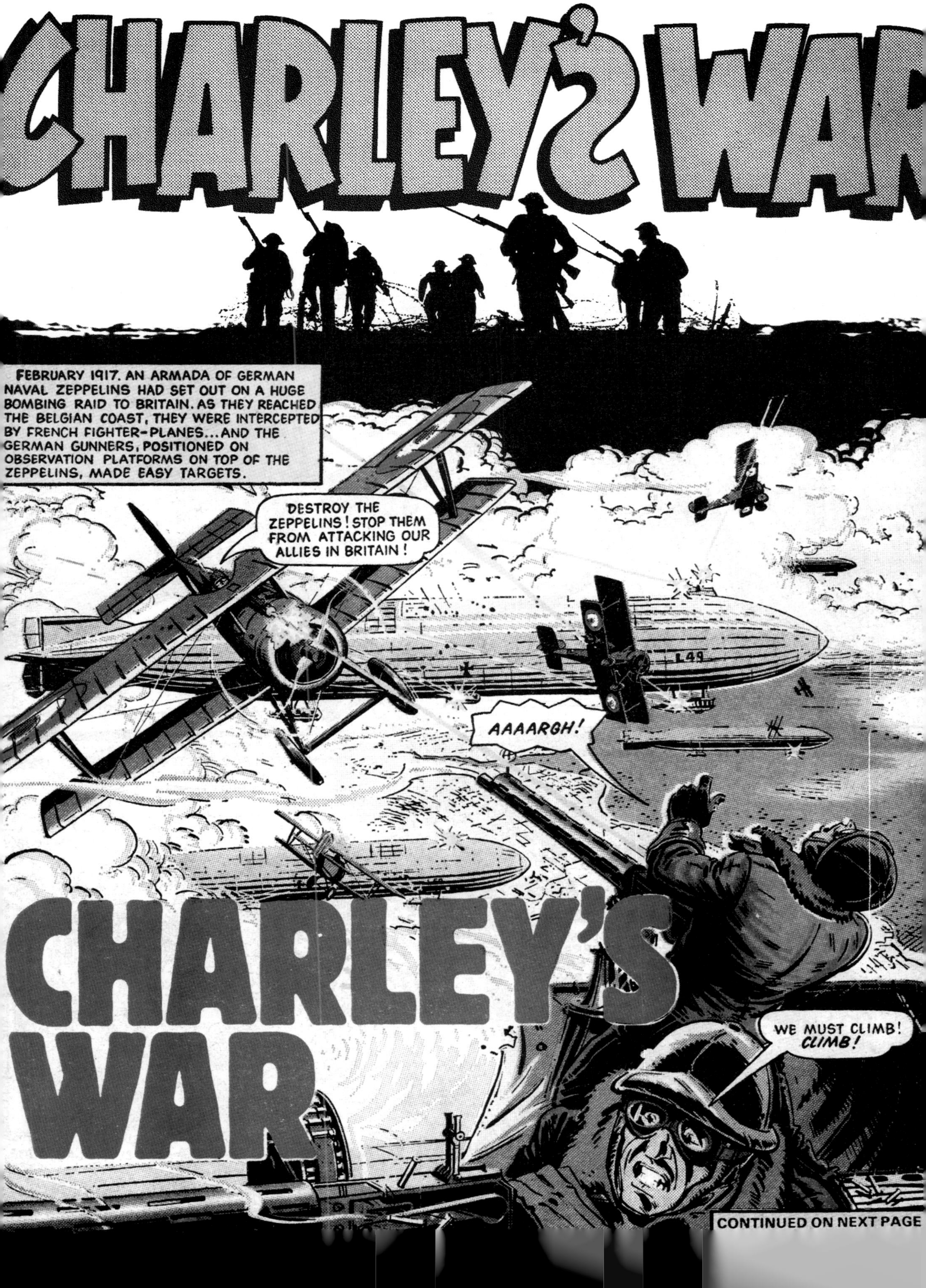
CHARLEY'S WAR
FEBRUARY 1917. AN ARMADA OF GERMAN NAVAL ZEPPELINS HAD SET OUT ON A HUGE BOMBING RAID TO BRITAIN. AS THEY REACHED THE BELGIAN COAST, THEY WERE INTERCEPTED BY FRENCH FIGHTER-PLANES... AND THE GERMAN GUNNERS, POSITIONED ON OBSERVATION PLATFORMS ON TOP OF THE ZEPPELINS, MADE EASY TARGETS.
DESTROY THE ZEPPELINS! STOP THEM FROM ATTACKING OUR ALLIES IN BRITAIN!
L49
AAAARGH!
CHARLEY'S WAR
WE MUST CLIMB! CLIMB!

CONTINUED ON NEXT PAGE

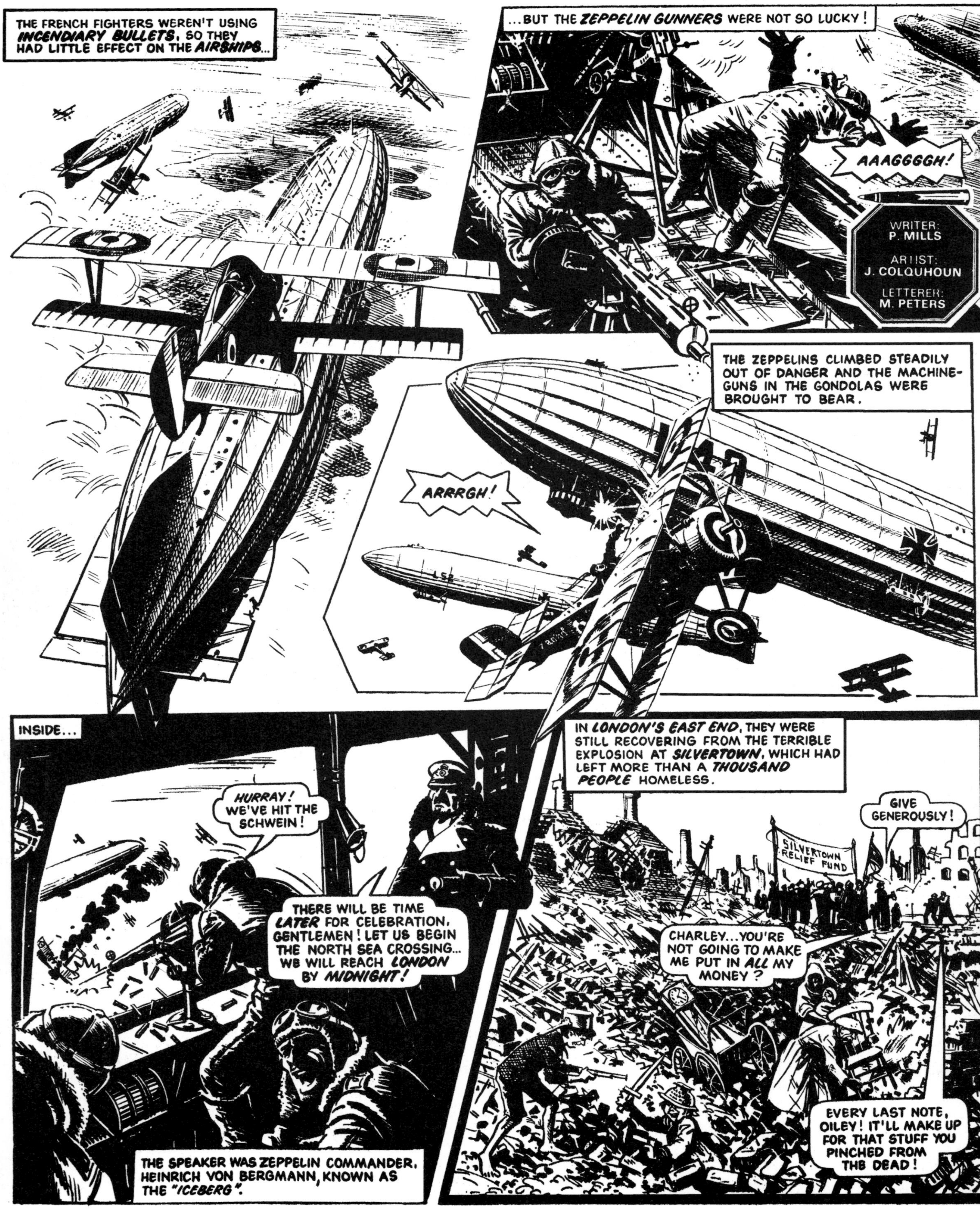

THE FRENCH FIGHTERS WEREN'T USING INCENDIARY BULLETS, SO THEY HAD LITTLE EFFECT ON THE AIRSHIPS...
...BUT THE ZEPPELIN GUNNERS WERE NOT SO LUCKY!
AAAGGGGH!
WRITER: P. MILLS
ARTIST: J. COLQUHOUN
LETTERER: M. PETERS
THE ZEPPELINS CLIMBED STEADILY OUT OF DANGER AND THE MACHINE-GUNS IN THE GONDOLAS WERE BROUGHT TO BEAR.
ARRRGH!
INSIDE...
HURRAY! WE'VE HIT THE SCHWEIN!
THERE WILL BE TIME LATER FOR CELEBRATION, GENTLEMEN! LET US BEGIN THE NORTH SEA CROSSING... WE WILL REACH LONDON BY MIDNIGHT!
THE SPEAKER WAS ZEPPELIN COMMANDER, HEINRICH VON BERGMANN, KNOWN AS THE "ICEBERG".
IN LONDON'S EAST END, THEY WERE STILL RECOVERING FROM THE TERRIBLE EXPLOSION AT SILVERTOWN, WHICH HAD LEFT MORE THAN A THOUSAND PEOPLE HOMELESS.
GIVE GENEROUSLY!
SILVERTOWN RELIEF FUND
CHARLEY... YOU'RE NOT GOING TO MAKE ME PUT IN ALL MY MONEY?
EVERY LAST NOTE, OILEY! IT'LL MAKE UP FOR THAT STUFF YOU PINCHED FROM THE DEAD!

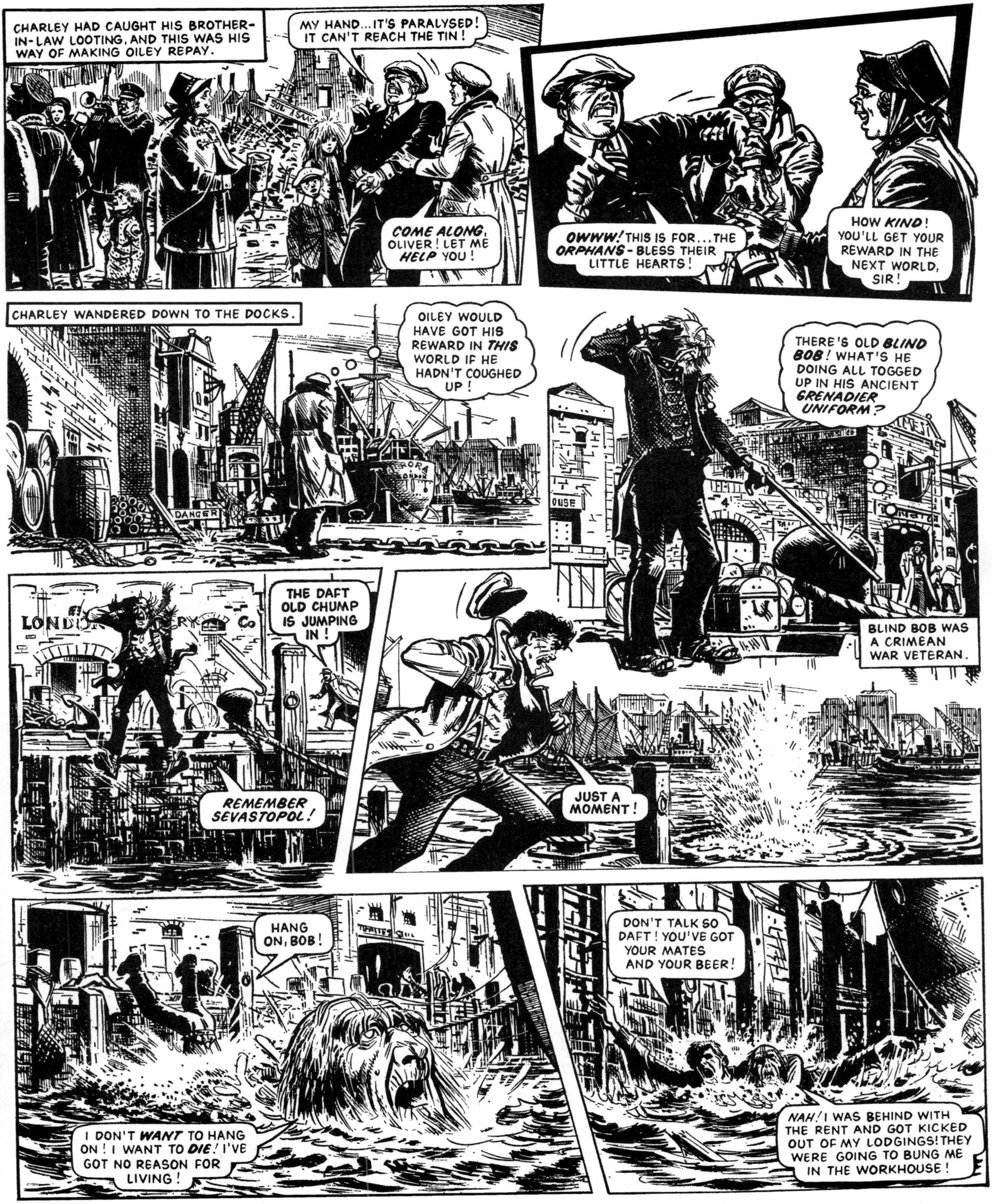

CHARLEY HAD CAUGHT HIS BROTHER-IN-LAW LOOTING, AND THIS WAS HIS WAY OF MAKING OILEY REPAY.
MY HAND... IT'S PARALYSED! IT CAN'T REACH THE TIN!
COME ALONG, OLIVER! LET ME HELP YOU!
OWWW! THIS IS FOR... THE ORPHANS - BLESS THEIR LITTLE HEARTS!
HOW KIND! YOU'LL GET YOUR REWARD IN THE NEXT WORLD, SIR!
CHARLEY WANDERED DOWN TO THE DOCKS.
OILEY WOULD HAVE GOT HIS REWARD IN THIS WORLD IF HE HADN'T COUGHED UP!
DANGER
THERE'S OLD BLIND BOB! WHAT'S HE DOING ALL TOGGED UP IN HIS ANCIENT GRENADIER UNIFORM?
BLIND BOB WAS A CRIMEAN WAR VETERAN.
THE DAFT OLD CHUMP IS JUMPING IN!
REMEMBER SEVASTOPOL!
JUST A MOMENT!
HANG ON, BOB!
I DON'T WANT TO HANG ON! I WANT TO DIE! I'VE GOT NO REASON FOR LIVING!
DON'T TALK SO DAFT! YOU'VE GOT YOUR MATES AND YOUR BEER!
NAH! I WAS BEHIND WITH THE RENT AND GOT KICKED OUT OF MY LODGINGS! THEY WERE GOING TO BUNG ME IN THE WORKHOUSE!

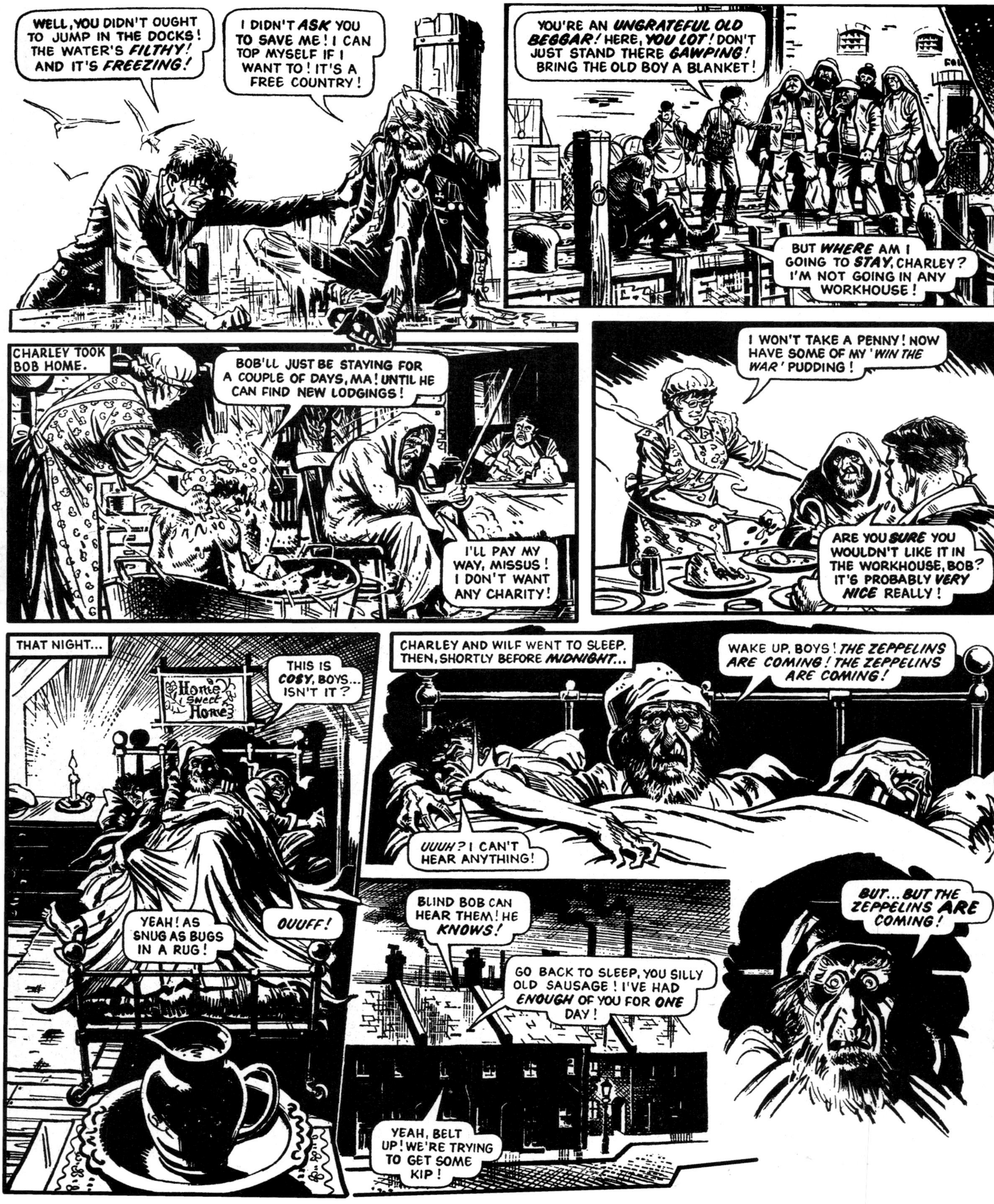
WELL, YOU DIDN'T OUGHT TO JUMP IN THE DOCKS! THE WATER'S FILTHY! AND IT'S FREEZING!
I DIDN'T ASK YOU TO SAVE ME! I CAN TOP MYSELF IF I WANT TO! IT'S A FREE COUNTRY!
YOU'RE AN UNGRATEFUL OLD BEGGAR! HERE, YOU LOT! DON'T JUST STAND THERE GAWPING! BRING THE OLD BOY A BLANKET!
BUT WHERE AM I GOING TO STAY, CHARLEY? I'M NOT GOING IN ANY WORKHOUSE!
CHARLEY TOOK BOB HOME.
BOB'LL JUST BE STAYING FOR A COUPLE OF DAYS, MA! UNTIL HE CAN FIND NEW LODGINGS!
I'LL PAY MY WAY, MISSUS! I DON'T WANT ANY CHARITY!
I WON'T TAKE A PENNY! NOW HAVE SOME OF MY 'WIN THE WAR' PUDDING!
ARE YOU SURE YOU WOULDN'T LIKE IT IN THE WORKHOUSE, BOB? IT'S PROBABLY VERY NICE REALLY!
THAT NIGHT...
Home Sweet Home
THIS IS COSY, BOYS... ISN'T IT?
YEAH! AS SNUG AS BUGS IN A RUG!
OUUFF!
CHARLEY AND WILF WENT TO SLEEP. THEN, SHORTLY BEFORE MIDNIGHT...
WAKE UP, BOYS! THE ZEPPELINS ARE COMING! THE ZEPPELINS ARE COMING!
UUUH? I CAN'T HEAR ANYTHING!
BLIND BOB CAN HEAR THEM! HE KNOWS!
GO BACK TO SLEEP, YOU SILLY OLD SAUSAGE! I'VE HAD ENOUGH OF YOU FOR ONE DAY!
YEAH, BELT UP! WE'RE TRYING TO GET SOME KIP!
BUT... BUT THE ZEPPELINS ARE COMING!

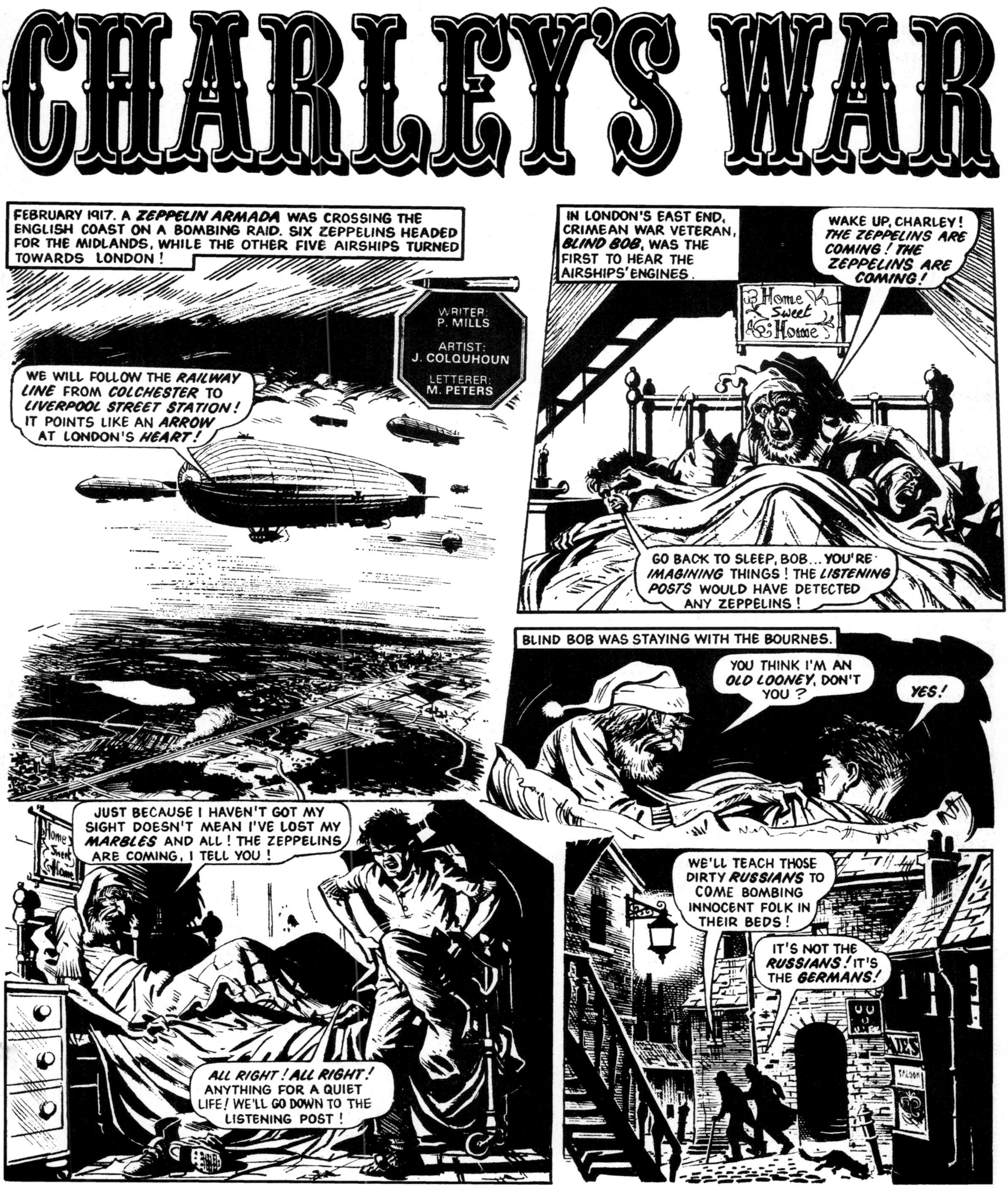
CHARLEY'S WAR
FEBRUARY 1917. A ZEPPELIN ARMADA WAS CROSSING THE ENGLISH COAST ON A BOMBING RAID. SIX ZEPPELINS HEADED FOR THE MIDLANDS, WHILE THE OTHER FIVE AIRSHIPS TURNED TOWARDS LONDON!
WRITER: P. MILLS
ARTIST: J. COLQUHOUN
LETTERER: M. PETERS
WE WILL FOLLOW THE RAILWAY LINE FROM COLCHESTER TO LIVERPOOL STREET STATION! IT POINTS LIKE AN ARROW AT LONDON'S HEART!
IN LONDON'S EAST END, CRIMEAN WAR VETERAN, BLIND BOB, WAS THE FIRST TO HEAR THE AIRSHIPS' ENGINES.
WAKE UP, CHARLEY! THE ZEPPELINS ARE COMING! THE ZEPPELINS ARE COMING!
Home Sweet Home
GO BACK TO SLEEP, BOB... YOU'RE IMAGINING THINGS! THE LISTENING POSTS WOULD HAVE DETECTED ANY ZEPPELINS!
BLIND BOB WAS STAYING WITH THE BOURNES.
YOU THINK I'M AN OLD LOONEY, DON'T YOU?
YES!
JUST BECAUSE I HAVEN'T GOT MY SIGHT DOESN'T MEAN I'VE LOST MY MARBLES AND ALL! THE ZEPPELINS ARE COMING, I TELL YOU!
ALL RIGHT! ALL RIGHT! ANYTHING FOR A QUIET LIFE! WE'LL GO DOWN TO THE LISTENING POST!
WE'LL TEACH THOSE DIRTY RUSSIANS TO COME BOMBING INNOCENT FOLK IN THEIR BEDS!
IT'S NOT THE RUSSIANS! IT'S THE GERMANS!
SALOON

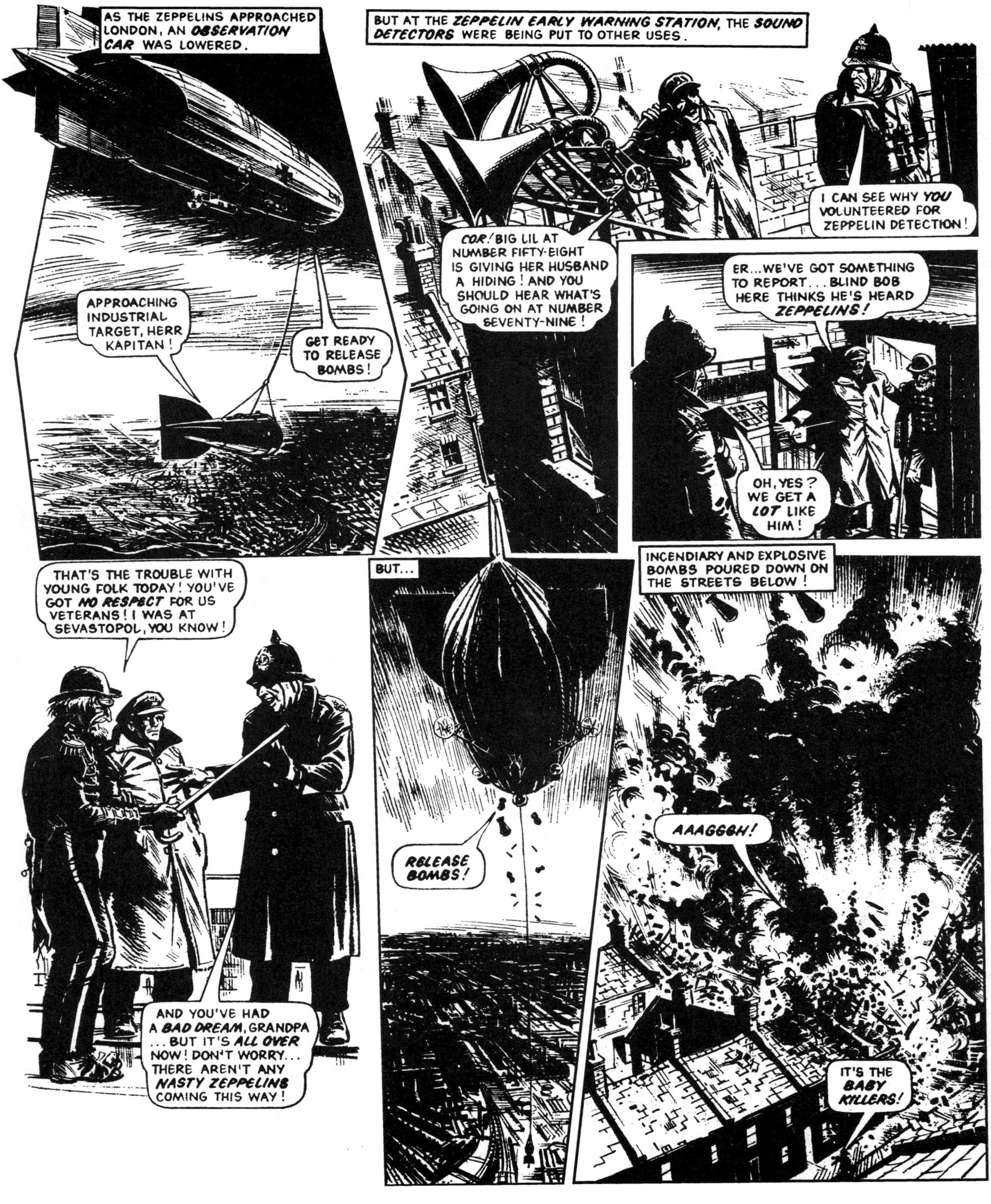
AS THE ZEPPELINS APPROACHED LONDON, AN OBSERVATION CAR WAS LOWERED.
APPROACHING INDUSTRIAL TARGET, HERR KAPITAN!
GET READY TO RELEASE BOMBS!
BUT AT THE ZEPPELIN EARLY WARNING STATION, THE SOUND DETECTORS WERE BEING PUT TO OTHER USES.
COR! BIG LIL AT NUMBER FIFTY-EIGHT IS GIVING HER HUSBAND A HIDING! AND YOU SHOULD HEAR WHAT'S GOING ON AT NUMBER SEVENTY-NINE!
I CAN SEE WHY YOU VOLUNTEERED FOR ZEPPELIN DETECTION!
ER...WE'VE GOT SOMETHING TO REPORT... BLIND BOB HERE THINKS HE'S HEARD ZEPPELINS!
OH, YES? WE GET A LOT LIKE HIM!
THAT'S THE TROUBLE WITH YOUNG FOLK TODAY! YOU'VE GOT NO RESPECT FOR US VETERANS! I WAS AT SEVASTOPOL, YOU KNOW!
AND YOU'VE HAD A BAD DREAM, GRANDPA ...BUT IT'S ALL OVER NOW! DON'T WORRY... THERE AREN'T ANY NASTY ZEPPELINS COMING THIS WAY!
BUT...
RELEASE BOMBS!
INCENDIARY AND EXPLOSIVE BOMBS POURED DOWN ON THE STREETS BELOW!
AAAGGGH!
IT'S THE BABY KILLERS!

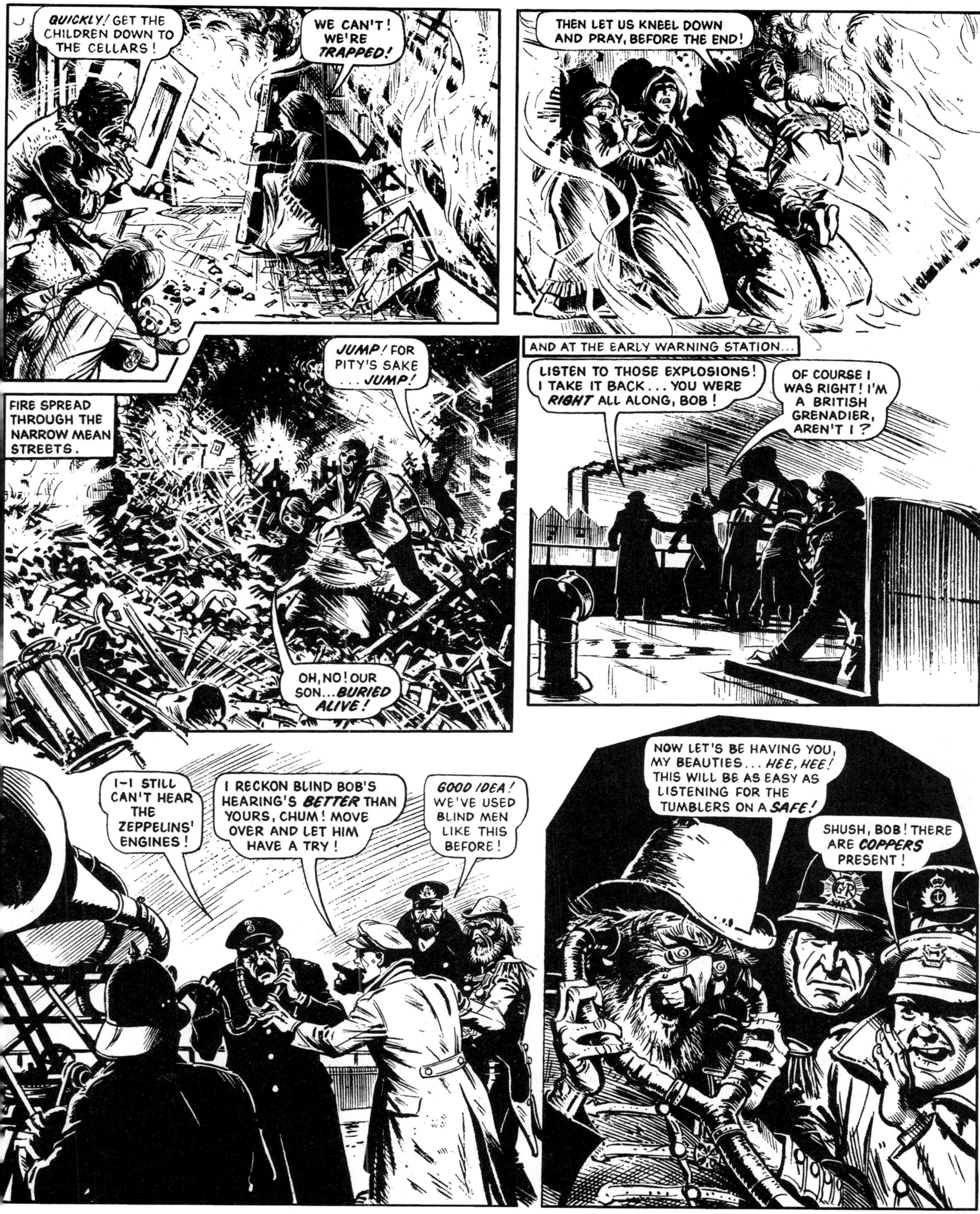

QUICKLY! GET THE CHILDREN DOWN TO THE CELLARS!
WE CAN'T! WE'RE TRAPPED!
THEN LET US KNEEL DOWN AND PRAY, BEFORE THE END!
FIRE SPREAD THROUGH THE NARROW MEAN STREETS.
JUMP! FOR PITY'S SAKE ... JUMP!
OH, NO! OUR SON... BURIED ALIVE!
AND AT THE EARLY WARNING STATION...
LISTEN TO THOSE EXPLOSIONS! I TAKE IT BACK... YOU WERE RIGHT ALL ALONG, BOB!
OF COURSE I WAS RIGHT! I'M A BRITISH GRENADIER, AREN'T I?
I-I STILL CAN'T HEAR THE ZEPPELINS' ENGINES!
I RECKON BLIND BOB'S HEARING'S BETTER THAN YOURS, CHUM! MOVE OVER AND LET HIM HAVE A TRY!
GOOD IDEA! WE'VE USED BLIND MEN LIKE THIS BEFORE!
NOW LET'S BE HAVING YOU, MY BEAUTIES... HEE, HEE! THIS WILL BE AS EASY AS LISTENING FOR THE TUMBLERS ON A SAFE!
SHUSH, BOB! THERE ARE COPPERS PRESENT!

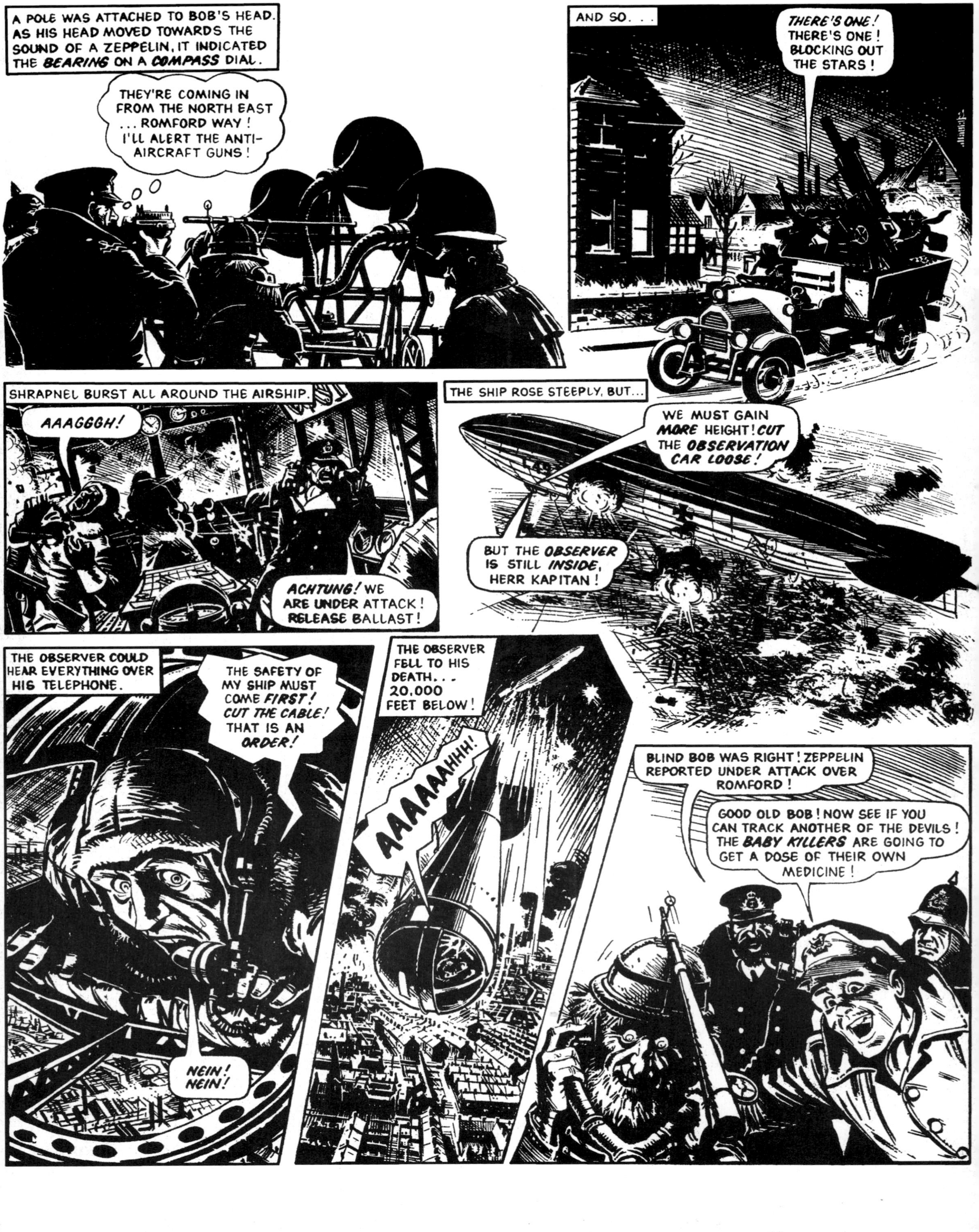
A POLE WAS ATTACHED TO BOB'S HEAD. AS HIS HEAD MOVED TOWARDS THE SOUND OF A ZEPPELIN, IT INDICATED THE BEARING ON A COMPASS DIAL.
THEY'RE COMING IN FROM THE NORTH EAST ... ROMFORD WAY! I'LL ALERT THE ANTI-AIRCRAFT GUNS!
AND SO. . .
THERE'S ONE! THERE'S ONE! BLOCKING OUT THE STARS!
SHRAPNEL BURST ALL AROUND THE AIRSHIP.
AAAGGGH!
ACHTUNG! WE ARE UNDER ATTACK! RELEASE BALLAST!
THE SHIP ROSE STEEPLY, BUT...
WE MUST GAIN MORE HEIGHT! CUT THE OBSERVATION CAR LOOSE!
BUT THE OBSERVER IS STILL INSIDE, HERR KAPITAN!
THE OBSERVER COULD HEAR EVERYTHING OVER HIS TELEPHONE.
THE SAFETY OF MY SHIP MUST COME FIRST! CUT THE CABLE! THAT IS AN ORDER!
NEIN! NEIN!
THE OBSERVER FELL TO HIS DEATH. . . 20,000 FEET BELOW!
AAAAAAAHHH!
BLIND BOB WAS RIGHT! ZEPPELIN REPORTED UNDER ATTACK OVER ROMFORD!
GOOD OLD BOB! NOW SEE IF YOU CAN TRACK ANOTHER OF THE DEVILS! THE BABY KILLERS ARE GOING TO GET A DOSE OF THEIR OWN MEDICINE!

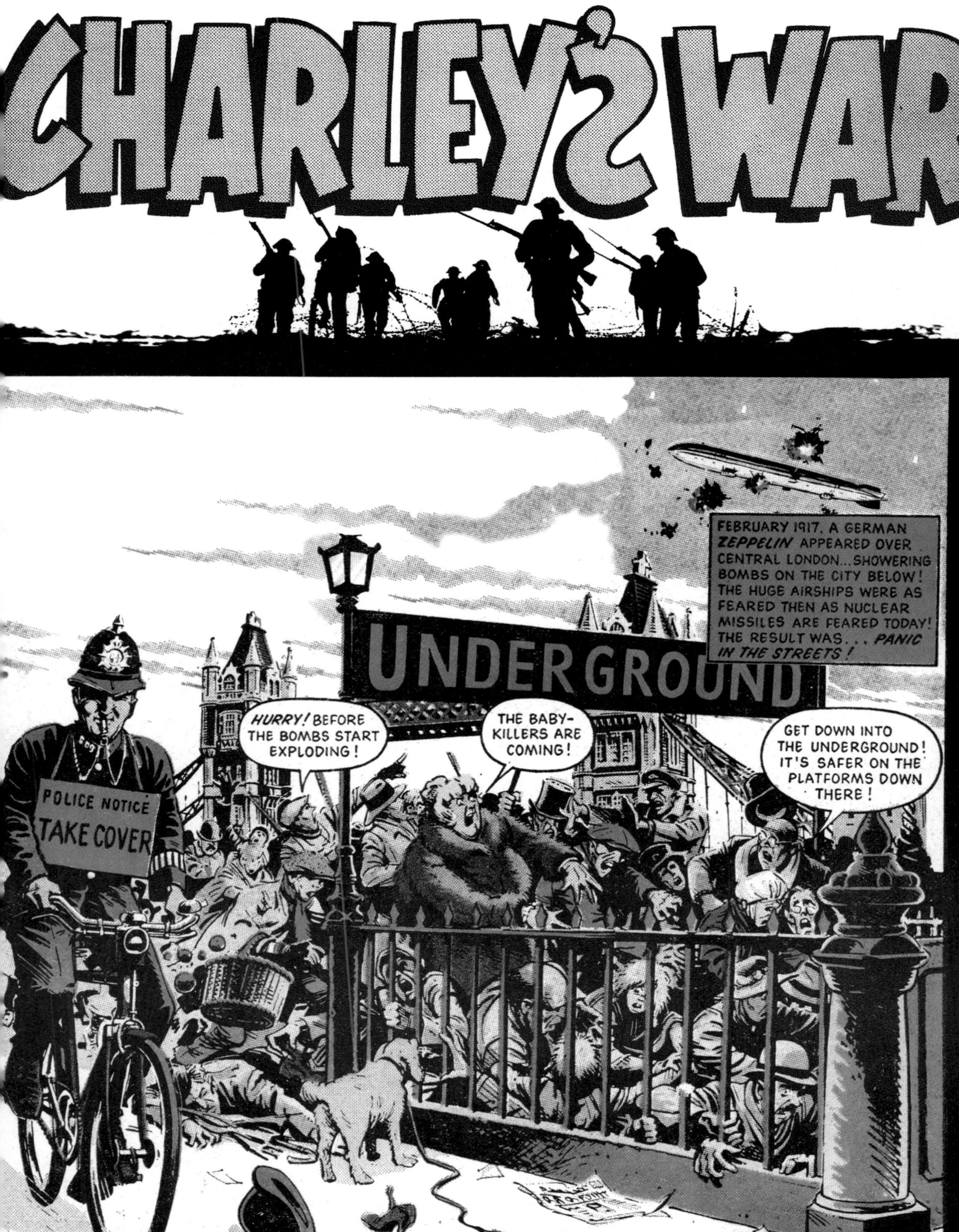
CHARLEY'S WAR
FEBRUARY 1917. A GERMAN ZEPPELIN APPEARED OVER CENTRAL LONDON...SHOWERING BOMBS ON THE CITY BELOW! THE HUGE AIRSHIPS WERE AS FEARED THEN AS NUCLEAR MISSILES ARE FEARED TODAY! THE RESULT WAS... PANIC IN THE STREETS!
UNDERGROUND
POLICE NOTICE
TAKE COVER
HURRY! BEFORE THE BOMBS START EXPLODING!
THE BABY-KILLERS ARE COMING!
GET DOWN INTO THE UNDERGROUND! IT'S SAFER ON THE PLATFORMS DOWN THERE!

CONTINUED ON NEXT PAGE

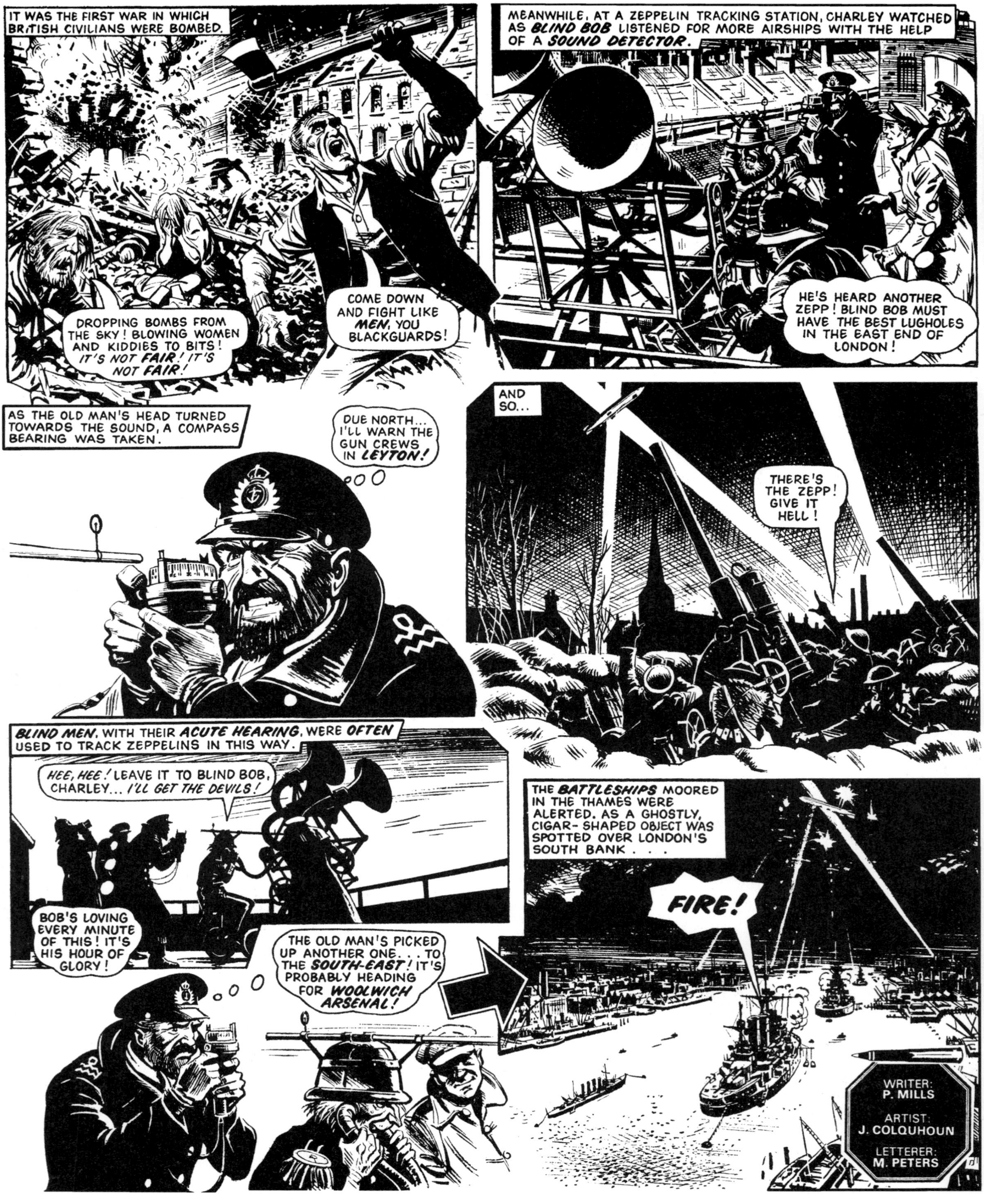
IT WAS THE FIRST WAR IN WHICH BRITISH CIVILIANS WERE BOMBED.
DROPPING BOMBS FROM THE SKY! BLOWING WOMEN AND KIDDIES TO BITS! IT'S NOT FAIR! IT'S NOT FAIR!
COME DOWN AND FIGHT LIKE MEN, YOU BLACKGUARDS!
MEANWHILE, AT A ZEPPELIN TRACKING STATION, CHARLEY WATCHED AS BLIND BOB LISTENED FOR MORE AIRSHIPS WITH THE HELP OF A SOUND DETECTOR.
HE'S HEARD ANOTHER ZEPP! BLIND BOB MUST HAVE THE BEST LUGHOLES IN THE EAST END OF LONDON!
AS THE OLD MAN'S HEAD TURNED TOWARDS THE SOUND, A COMPASS BEARING WAS TAKEN.
DUE NORTH... I'LL WARN THE GUN CREWS IN LEYTON!
AND SO...
THERE'S THE ZEPP! GIVE IT HELL!
BLIND MEN, WITH THEIR ACUTE HEARING, WERE OFTEN USED TO TRACK ZEPPELINS IN THIS WAY.
HEE, HEE! LEAVE IT TO BLIND BOB, CHARLEY... I'LL GET THE DEVILS!
BOB'S LOVING EVERY MINUTE OF THIS! IT'S HIS HOUR OF GLORY!
THE OLD MAN'S PICKED UP ANOTHER ONE. . . TO THE SOUTH-EAST! IT'S PROBABLY HEADING FOR WOOLWICH ARSENAL!
THE BATTLESHIPS MOORED IN THE THAMES WERE ALERTED, AS A GHOSTLY, CIGAR-SHAPED OBJECT WAS SPOTTED OVER LONDON'S SOUTH BANK . . .
FIRE!
WRITER: P. MILLS
ARTIST: J. COLQUHOUN
LETTERER: M. PETERS

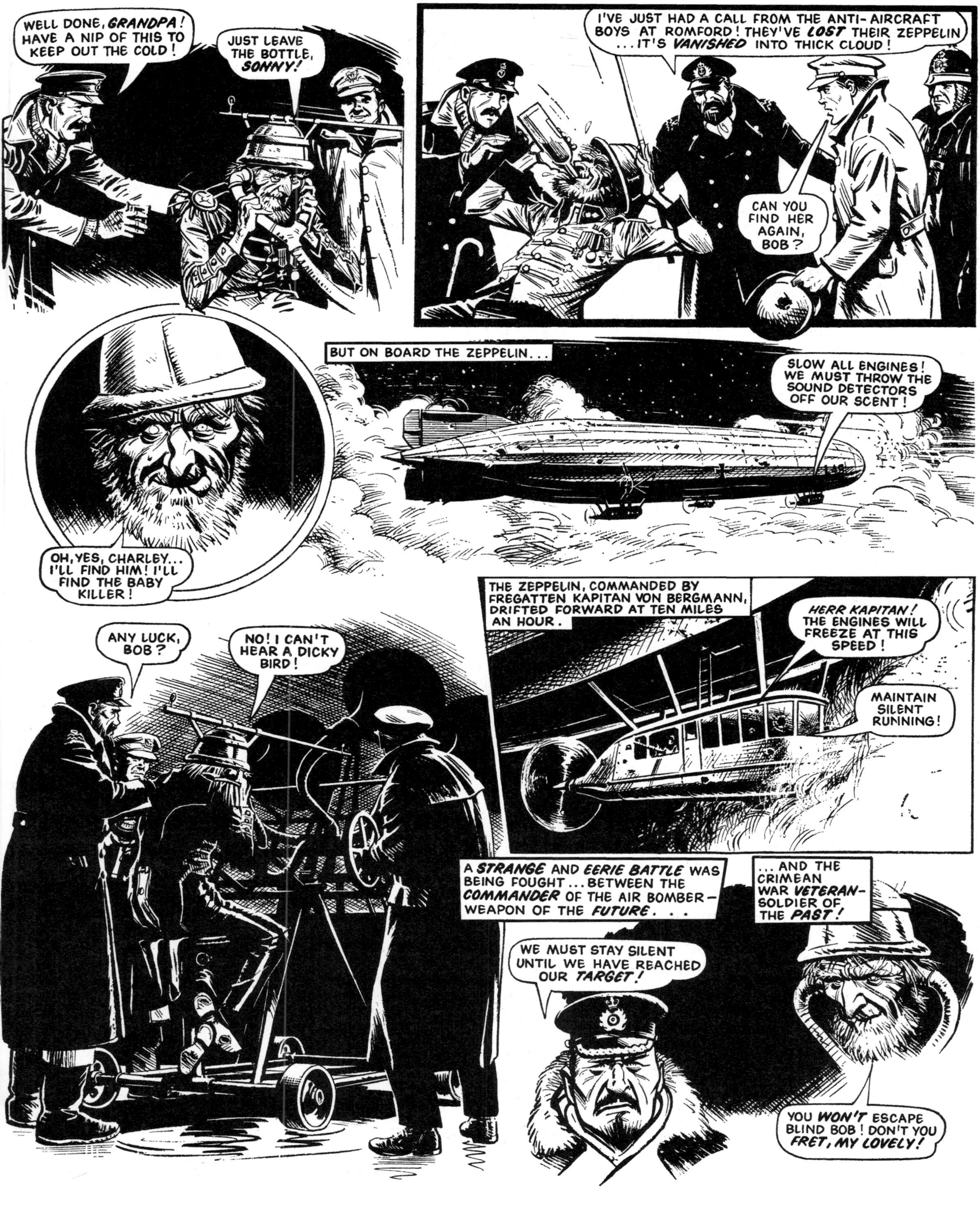
WELL DONE, GRANDPA! HAVE A NIP OF THIS TO KEEP OUT THE COLD!
JUST LEAVE THE BOTTLE, SONNY!
I'VE JUST HAD A CALL FROM THE ANTI-AIRCRAFT BOYS AT ROMFORD! THEY'VE LOST THEIR ZEPPELIN ... IT'S VANISHED INTO THICK CLOUD!
CAN YOU FIND HER AGAIN, BOB?
OH, YES, CHARLEY... I'LL FIND HIM! I'LL FIND THE BABY KILLER!
BUT ON BOARD THE ZEPPELIN...
SLOW ALL ENGINES! WE MUST THROW THE SOUND DETECTORS OFF OUR SCENT!
ANY LUCK, BOB?
NO! I CAN'T HEAR A DICKY BIRD!
THE ZEPPELIN, COMMANDED BY FREGATTEN KAPITAN VON BERGMANN, DRIFTED FORWARD AT TEN MILES AN HOUR.
HERR KAPITAN! THE ENGINES WILL FREEZE AT THIS SPEED!
MAINTAIN SILENT RUNNING!
A STRANGE AND EERIE BATTLE WAS BEING FOUGHT ... BETWEEN THE COMMANDER OF THE AIR BOMBER - WEAPON OF THE FUTURE . . .
... AND THE CRIMEAN WAR VETERAN - SOLDIER OF THE PAST!
WE MUST STAY SILENT UNTIL WE HAVE REACHED OUR TARGET!
YOU WON'T ESCAPE BLIND BOB! DON'T YOU FRET, MY LOVELY!

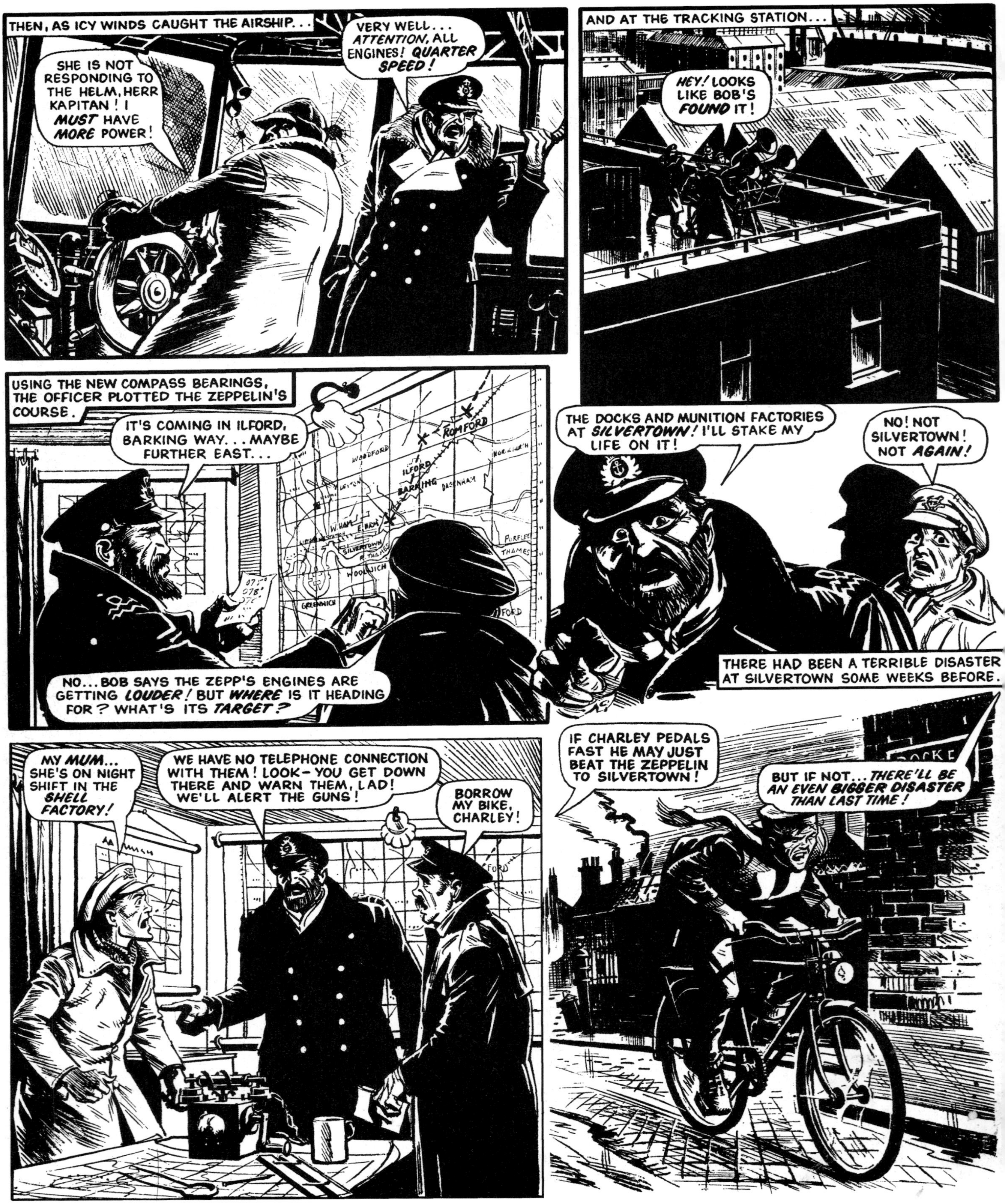

THEN, AS ICY WINDS CAUGHT THE AIRSHIP...
SHE IS NOT RESPONDING TO THE HELM, HERR KAPITAN! I MUST HAVE MORE POWER!
VERY WELL... ATTENTION, ALL ENGINES! QUARTER SPEED!
AND AT THE TRACKING STATION...
HEY! LOOKS LIKE BOB'S FOUND IT!
USING THE NEW COMPASS BEARINGS, THE OFFICER PLOTTED THE ZEPPELIN'S COURSE.
IT'S COMING IN ILFORD, BARKING WAY... MAYBE FURTHER EAST...
ROMFORD
ILFORD
BARKING
NO... BOB SAYS THE ZEPP'S ENGINES ARE GETTING LOUDER! BUT WHERE IS IT HEADING FOR? WHAT'S ITS TARGET?
THE DOCKS AND MUNITION FACTORIES AT SILVERTOWN! I'LL STAKE MY LIFE ON IT!
NO! NOT SILVERTOWN! NOT AGAIN!
THERE HAD BEEN A TERRIBLE DISASTER AT SILVERTOWN SOME WEEKS BEFORE.
MY MUM... SHE'S ON NIGHT SHIFT IN THE SHELL FACTORY!
WE HAVE NO TELEPHONE CONNECTION WITH THEM! LOOK— YOU GET DOWN THERE AND WARN THEM, LAD! WE'LL ALERT THE GUNS!
BORROW MY BIKE, CHARLEY!
IF CHARLEY PEDALS FAST HE MAY JUST BEAT THE ZEPPELIN TO SILVERTOWN!
BUT IF NOT... THERE'LL BE AN EVEN BIGGER DISASTER THAN LAST TIME!

Charley's War

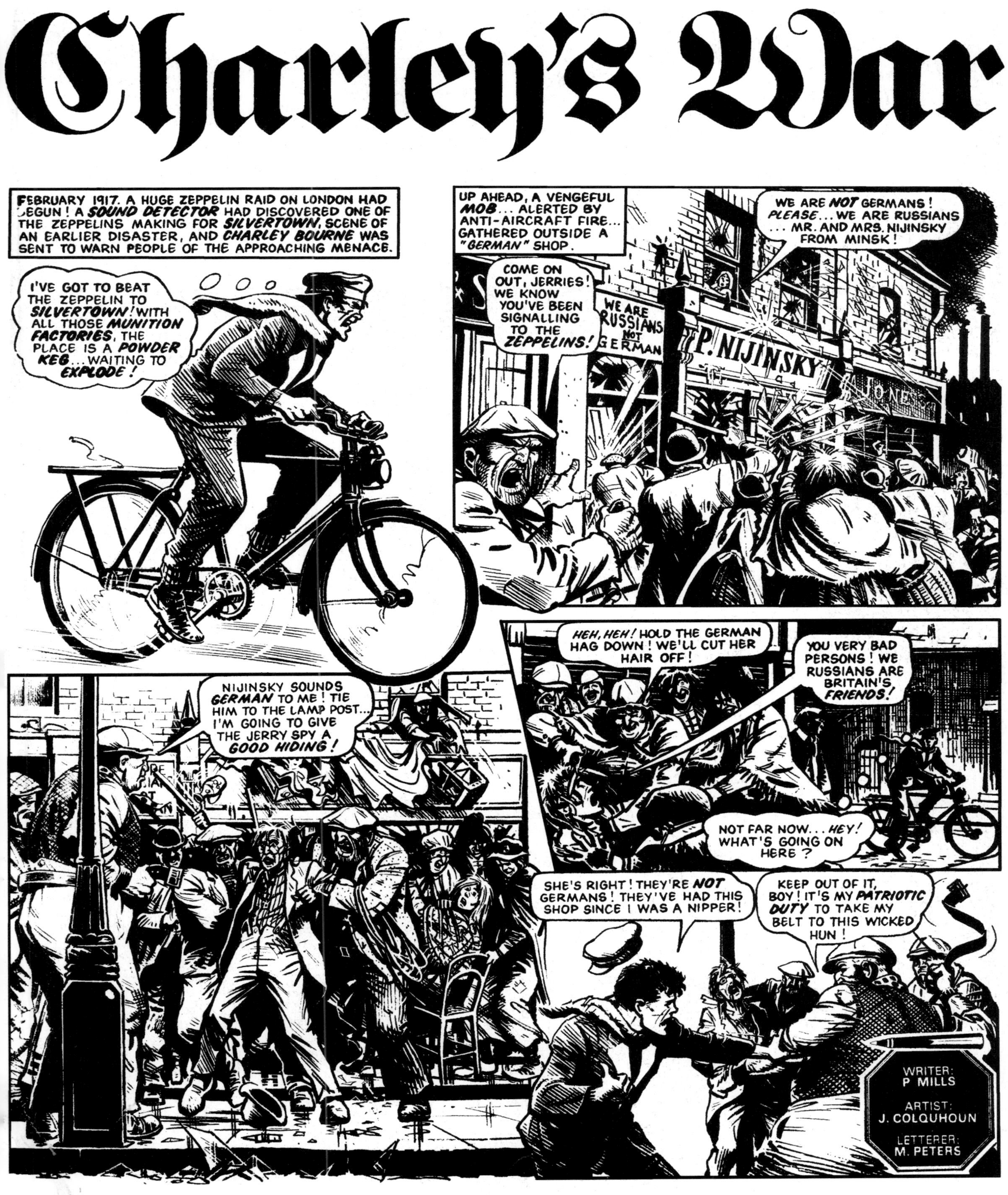
FEBRUARY 1917. A HUGE ZEPPELIN RAID ON LONDON HAD BEGUN! A SOUND DETECTOR HAD DISCOVERED ONE OF THE ZEPPELINS MAKING FOR SILVERTOWN, SCENE OF AN EARLIER DISASTER, AND CHARLEY BOURNE WAS SENT TO WARN PEOPLE OF THE APPROACHING MENACE.
I'VE GOT TO BEAT THE ZEPPELIN TO SILVERTOWN! WITH ALL THOSE MUNITION FACTORIES, THE PLACE IS A POWDER KEG... WAITING TO EXPLODE!
UP AHEAD, A VENGEFUL MOB... ALERTED BY ANTI-AIRCRAFT FIRE... GATHERED OUTSIDE A "GERMAN" SHOP.
COME ON OUT, JERRIES! WE KNOW YOU'VE BEEN SIGNALLING TO THE ZEPPELINS!
WE ARE RUSSIANS NOT GERMAN
WE ARE NOT GERMANS! PLEASE... WE ARE RUSSIANS ... MR. AND MRS. NIJINSKY FROM MINSK!
P. NIJINSKY
NIJINSKY SOUNDS GERMAN TO ME! TIE HIM TO THE LAMP POST... I'M GOING TO GIVE THE JERRY SPY A GOOD HIDING!
HEH, HEH! HOLD THE GERMAN HAG DOWN! WE'LL CUT HER HAIR OFF!
YOU VERY BAD PERSONS! WE RUSSIANS ARE BRITAIN'S FRIENDS!
NOT FAR NOW... HEY! WHAT'S GOING ON HERE?
SHE'S RIGHT! THEY'RE NOT GERMANS! THEY'VE HAD THIS SHOP SINCE I WAS A NIPPER!
KEEP OUT OF IT, BOY! IT'S MY PATRIOTIC DUTY TO TAKE MY BELT TO THIS WICKED HUN!
WRITER: P MILLS
ARTIST: J. COLQUHOUN
LETTERER: M. PETERS

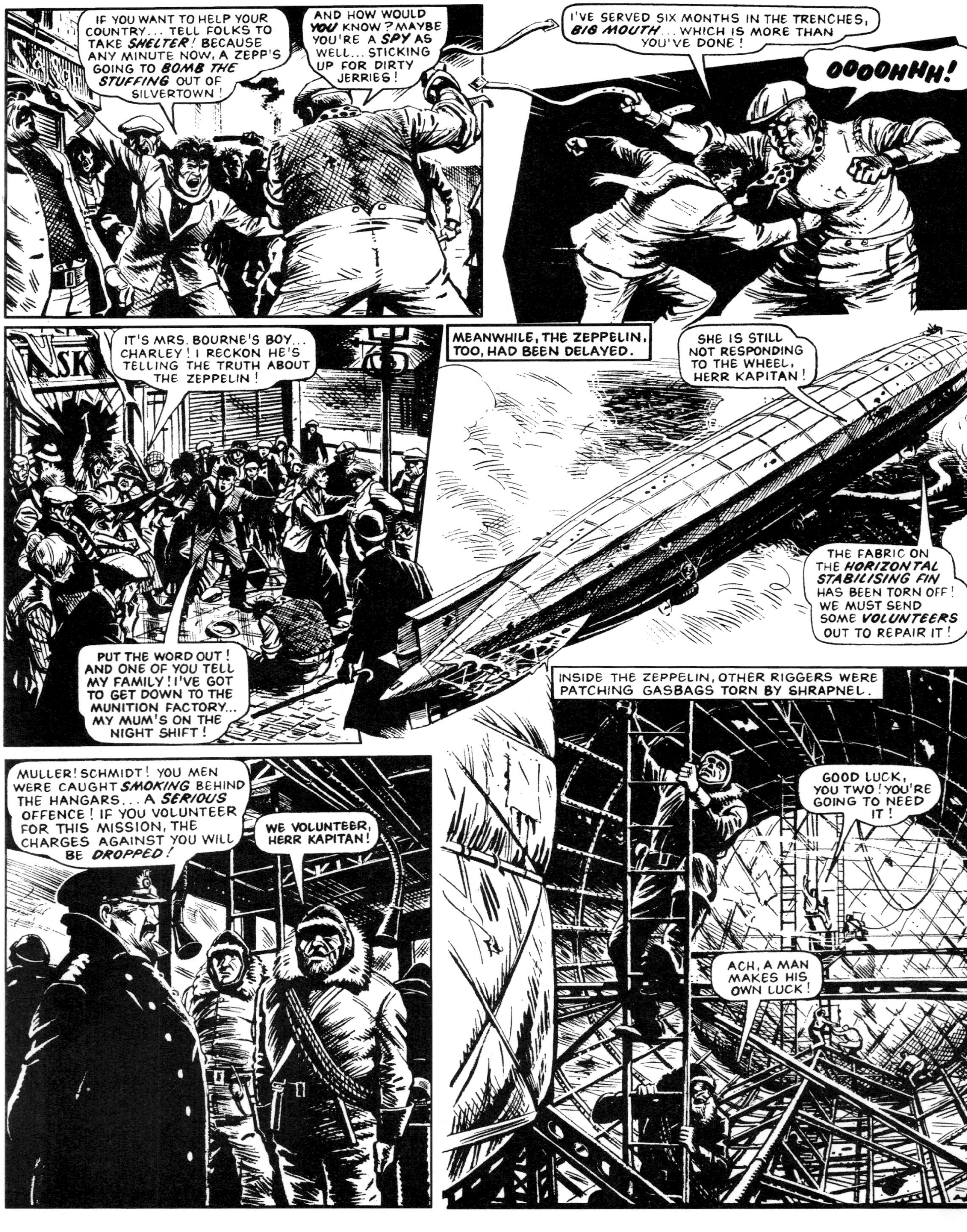
IF YOU WANT TO HELP YOUR COUNTRY... TELL FOLKS TO TAKE SHELTER! BECAUSE ANY MINUTE NOW, A ZEPP'S GOING TO BOMB THE STUFFING OUT OF SILVERTOWN!
AND HOW WOULD YOU KNOW? MAYBE YOU'RE A SPY AS WELL... STICKING UP FOR DIRTY JERRIES!
I'VE SERVED SIX MONTHS IN THE TRENCHES, BIG MOUTH... WHICH IS MORE THAN YOU'VE DONE!
OOOOHHH!
IT'S MRS. BOURNE'S BOY... CHARLEY! I RECKON HE'S TELLING THE TRUTH ABOUT THE ZEPPELIN!
PUT THE WORD OUT! AND ONE OF YOU TELL MY FAMILY! I'VE GOT TO GET DOWN TO THE MUNITION FACTORY... MY MUM'S ON THE NIGHT SHIFT!
MEANWHILE, THE ZEPPELIN, TOO, HAD BEEN DELAYED.
SHE IS STILL NOT RESPONDING TO THE WHEEL, HERR KAPITAN!
THE FABRIC ON THE HORIZONTAL STABILISING FIN HAS BEEN TORN OFF! WE MUST SEND SOME VOLUNTEERS OUT TO REPAIR IT!
MULLER! SCHMIDT! YOU MEN WERE CAUGHT SMOKING BEHIND THE HANGARS... A SERIOUS OFFENCE! IF YOU VOLUNTEER FOR THIS MISSION, THE CHARGES AGAINST YOU WILL BE DROPPED!
WE VOLUNTEER, HERR KAPITAN!
INSIDE THE ZEPPELIN, OTHER RIGGERS WERE PATCHING GASBAGS TORN BY SHRAPNEL.
GOOD LUCK, YOU TWO! YOU'RE GOING TO NEED IT!
ACH, A MAN MAKES HIS OWN LUCK!

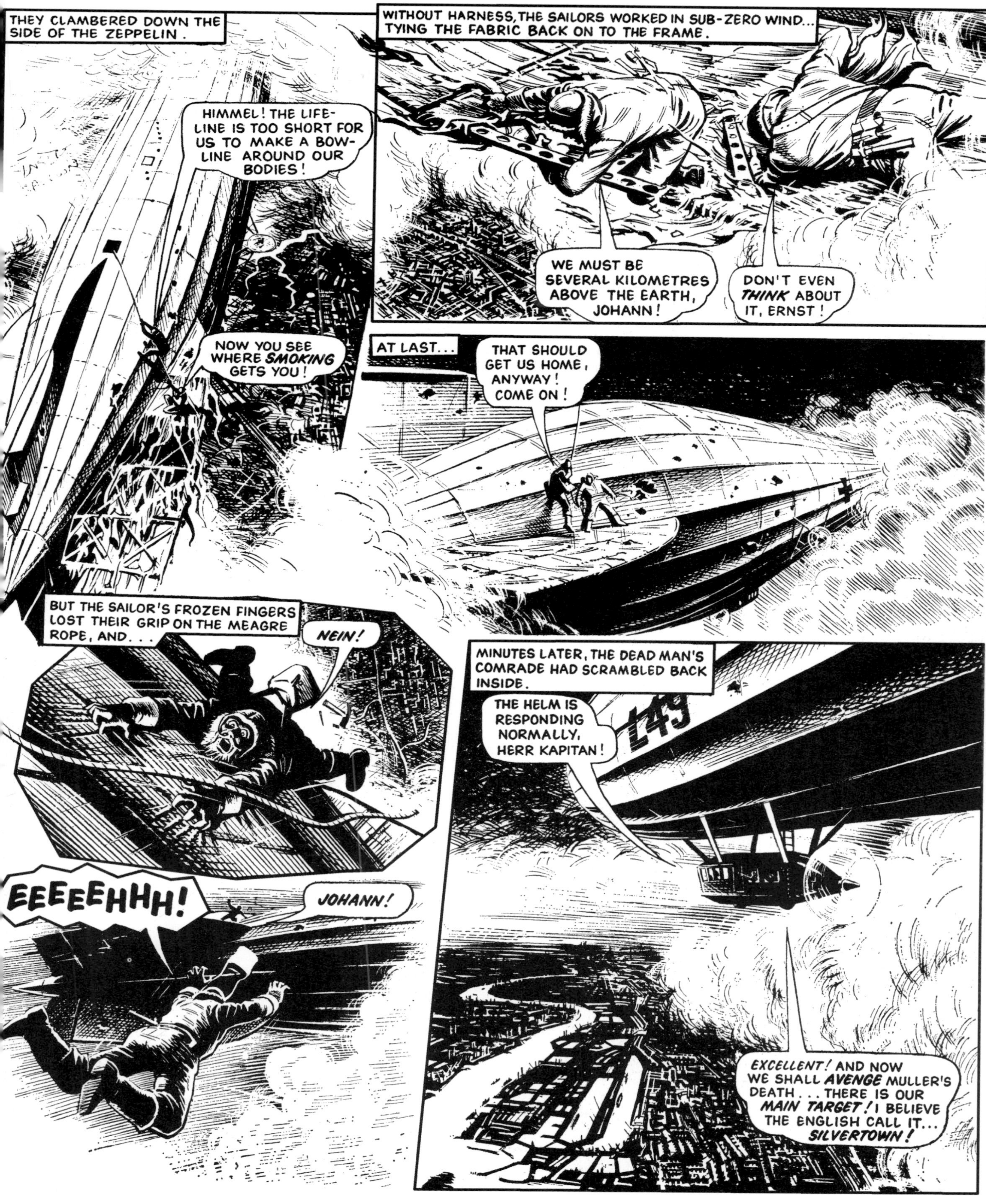
THEY CLAMBERED DOWN THE SIDE OF THE ZEPPELIN.
HIMMEL! THE LIFE-LINE IS TOO SHORT FOR US TO MAKE A BOW-LINE AROUND OUR BODIES!
NOW YOU SEE WHERE SMOKING GETS YOU!
WITHOUT HARNESS, THE SAILORS WORKED IN SUB-ZERO WIND... TYING THE FABRIC BACK ON TO THE FRAME.
WE MUST BE SEVERAL KILOMETRES ABOVE THE EARTH, JOHANN!
DON'T EVEN THINK ABOUT IT, ERNST!
AT LAST...
THAT SHOULD GET US HOME, ANYWAY! COME ON!
BUT THE SAILOR'S FROZEN FINGERS LOST THEIR GRIP ON THE MEAGRE ROPE, AND...
NEIN!
EEEEEHHH!
JOHANN!
MINUTES LATER, THE DEAD MAN'S COMRADE HAD SCRAMBLED BACK INSIDE.
THE HELM IS RESPONDING NORMALLY, HERR KAPITAN!
L49
EXCELLENT! AND NOW WE SHALL AVENGE MULLER'S DEATH... THERE IS OUR MAIN TARGET! I BELIEVE THE ENGLISH CALL IT... SILVERTOWN!

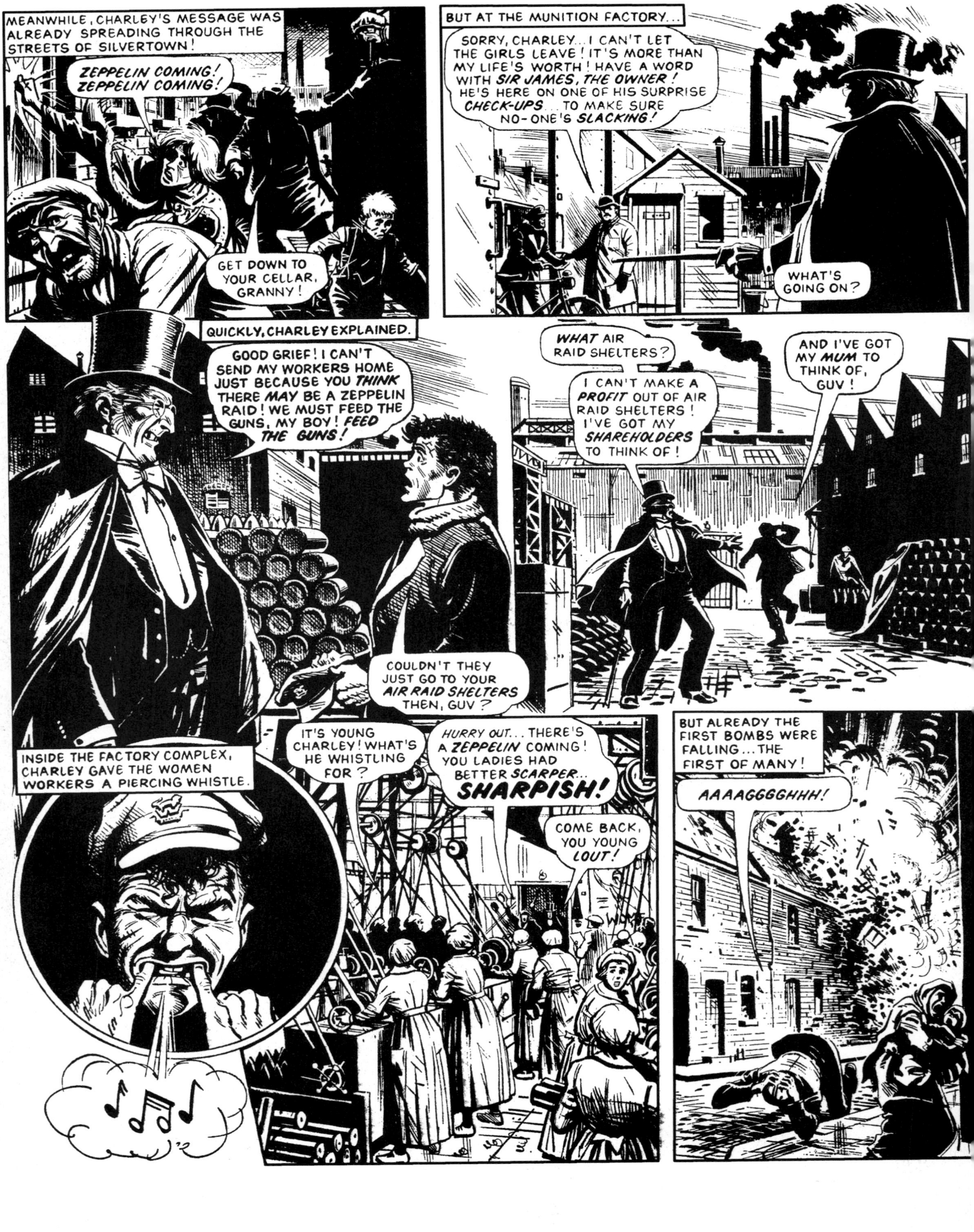
MEANWHILE, CHARLEY'S MESSAGE WAS ALREADY SPREADING THROUGH THE STREETS OF SILVERTOWN!
ZEPPELIN COMING! ZEPPELIN COMING!
GET DOWN TO YOUR CELLAR, GRANNY!
BUT AT THE MUNITION FACTORY...
SORRY, CHARLEY... I CAN'T LET THE GIRLS LEAVE! IT'S MORE THAN MY LIFE'S WORTH! HAVE A WORD WITH SIR JAMES, THE OWNER! HE'S HERE ON ONE OF HIS SURPRISE CHECK-UPS... TO MAKE SURE NO-ONE'S SLACKING!
WHAT'S GOING ON?
QUICKLY, CHARLEY EXPLAINED.
GOOD GRIEF! I CAN'T SEND MY WORKERS HOME JUST BECAUSE YOU THINK THERE MAY BE A ZEPPELIN RAID! WE MUST FEED THE GUNS, MY BOY! FEED THE GUNS!
COULDN'T THEY JUST GO TO YOUR AIR RAID SHELTERS THEN, GUV?
WHAT AIR RAID SHELTERS?
I CAN'T MAKE A PROFIT OUT OF AIR RAID SHELTERS! I'VE GOT MY SHAREHOLDERS TO THINK OF!
AND I'VE GOT MY MUM TO THINK OF, GUV!
INSIDE THE FACTORY COMPLEX, CHARLEY GAVE THE WOMEN WORKERS A PIERCING WHISTLE.
IT'S YOUNG CHARLEY! WHAT'S HE WHISTLING FOR?
HURRY OUT... THERE'S A ZEPPELIN COMING! YOU LADIES HAD BETTER SCARPER... SHARPISH!
COME BACK, YOU YOUNG LOUT!
BUT ALREADY THE FIRST BOMBS WERE FALLING... THE FIRST OF MANY!
AAAAGGGGHHH!

CHARLEY'S WAR

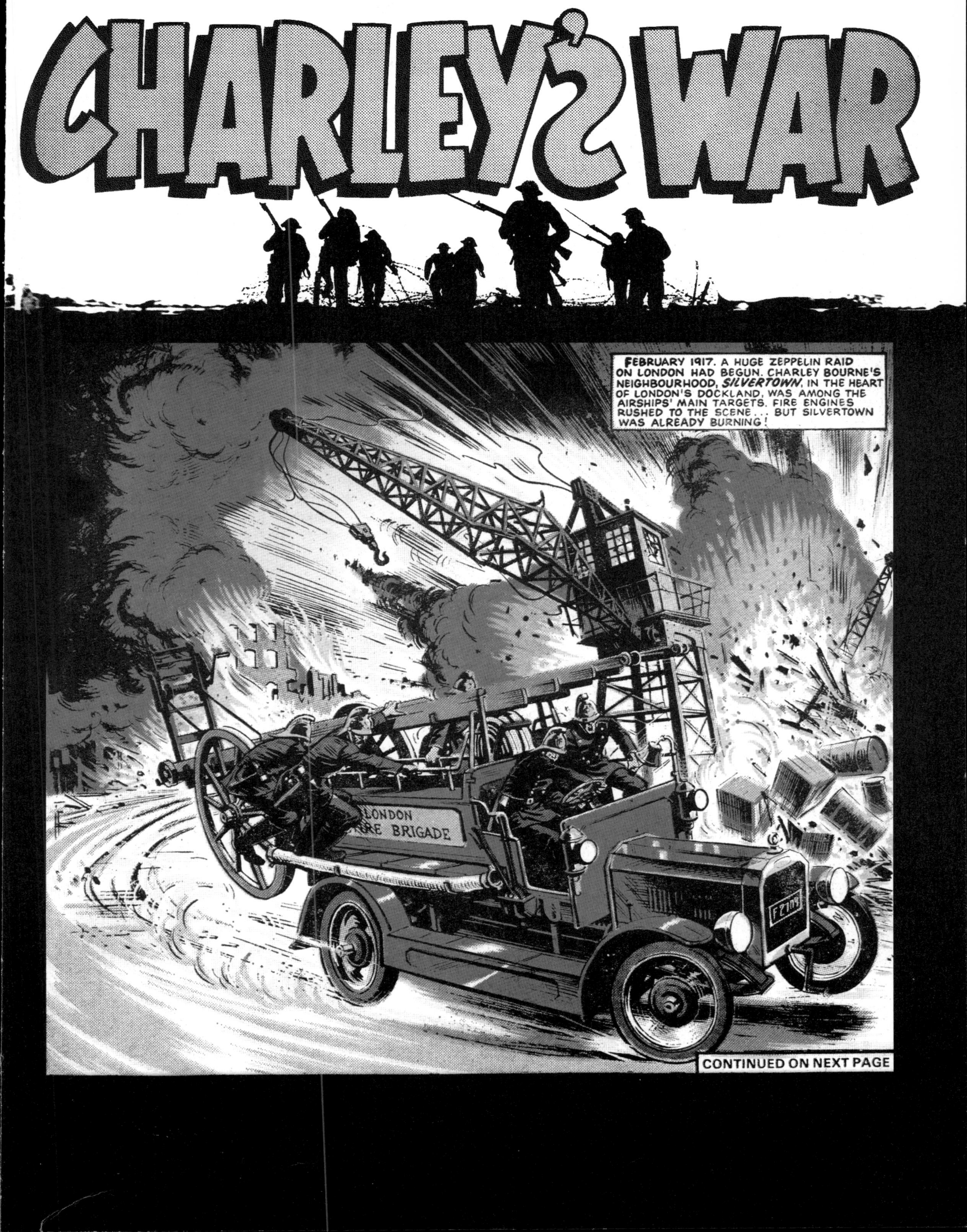
FEBRUARY 1917. A HUGE ZEPPELIN RAID ON LONDON HAD BEGUN. CHARLEY BOURNE'S NEIGHBOURHOOD, *SILVERTOWN*, IN THE HEART OF LONDON'S DOCKLAND, WAS AMONG THE AIRSHIPS' MAIN TARGETS. FIRE ENGINES RUSHED TO THE SCENE... BUT SILVERTOWN WAS ALREADY BURNING!
LONDON FIRE BRIGADE

CONTINUED ON NEXT PAGE

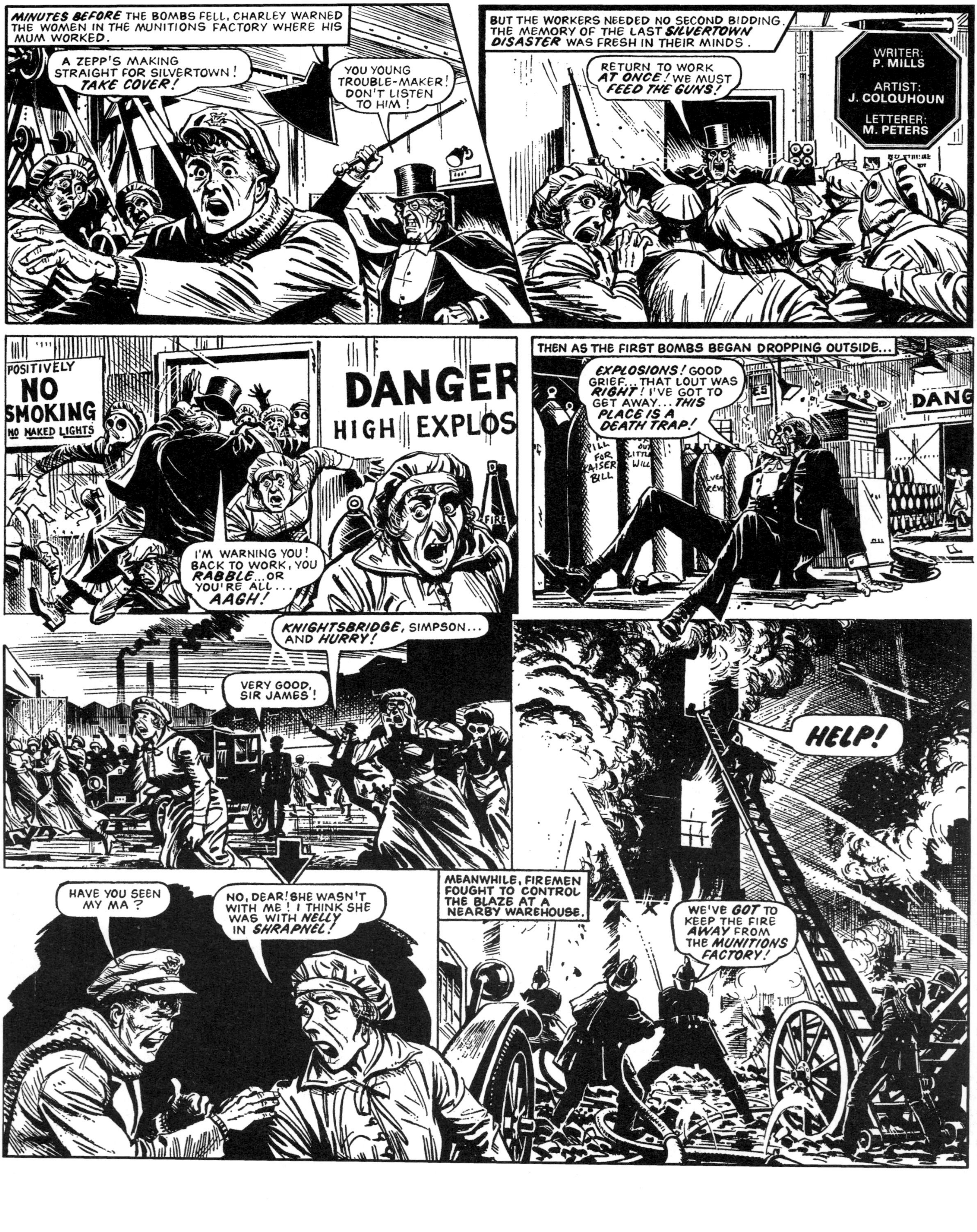
MINUTES BEFORE THE BOMBS FELL, CHARLEY WARNED THE WOMEN IN THE MUNITIONS FACTORY WHERE HIS MUM WORKED.
A ZEPP'S MAKING STRAIGHT FOR SILVERTOWN! TAKE COVER!
YOU YOUNG TROUBLE-MAKER! DON'T LISTEN TO HIM!
BUT THE WORKERS NEEDED NO SECOND BIDDING. THE MEMORY OF THE LAST SILVERTOWN DISASTER WAS FRESH IN THEIR MINDS.
WRITER: P. MILLS
ARTIST: J. COLQUHOUN
LETTERER: M. PETERS
RETURN TO WORK AT ONCE! WE MUST FEED THE GUNS!
POSITIVELY NO SMOKING NO NAKED LIGHTS
DANGER HIGH EXPLOS
I'M WARNING YOU! BACK TO WORK, YOU RABBLE...OR YOU'RE ALL... AAGH!
THEN AS THE FIRST BOMBS BEGAN DROPPING OUTSIDE...
EXPLOSIONS! GOOD GRIEF... THAT LOUT WAS RIGHT! I'VE GOT TO GET AWAY... THIS PLACE IS A DEATH TRAP!
DANG
KNIGHTSBRIDGE, SIMPSON... AND HURRY!
VERY GOOD, SIR JAMES!
HELP!
HAVE YOU SEEN MY MA?
NO, DEAR! SHE WASN'T WITH ME! I THINK SHE WAS WITH NELLY IN SHRAPNEL!
MEANWHILE, FIREMEN FOUGHT TO CONTROL THE BLAZE AT A NEARBY WAREHOUSE.
WE'VE GOT TO KEEP THE FIRE AWAY FROM THE MUNITIONS FACTORY!

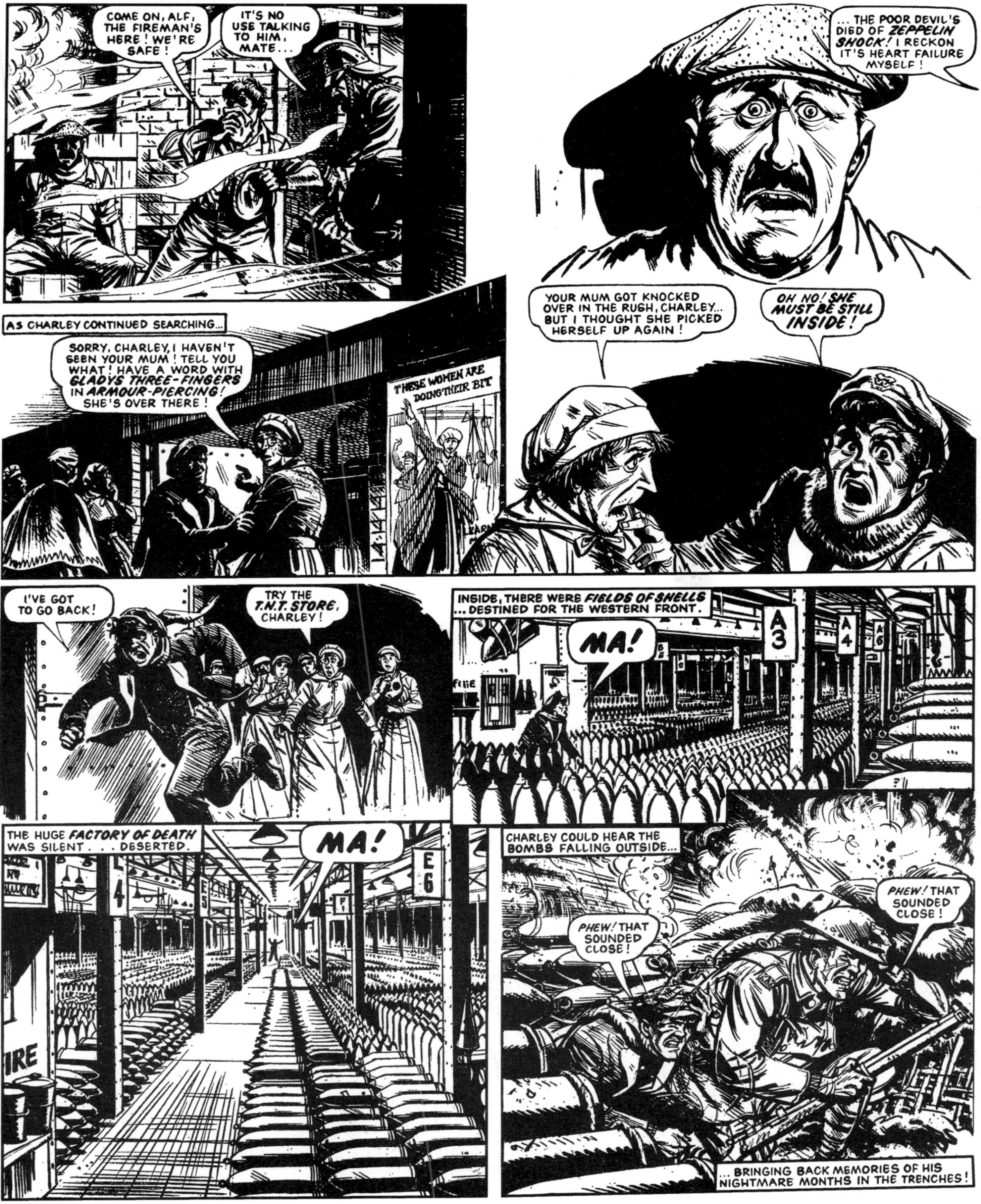
COME ON, ALF, THE FIREMAN'S HERE! WE'RE SAFE!
IT'S NO USE TALKING TO HIM, MATE...
... THE POOR DEVIL'S DIED OF ZEPPELIN SHOCK! I RECKON IT'S HEART FAILURE MYSELF!
AS CHARLEY CONTINUED SEARCHING...
SORRY, CHARLEY, I HAVEN'T SEEN YOUR MUM! TELL YOU WHAT! HAVE A WORD WITH GLADYS THREE-FINGERS IN ARMOUR-PIERCING! SHE'S OVER THERE!
THESE WOMEN ARE DOING THEIR BIT
YOUR MUM GOT KNOCKED OVER IN THE RUSH, CHARLEY... BUT I THOUGHT SHE PICKED HERSELF UP AGAIN!
OH NO! SHE MUST BE STILL INSIDE!
I'VE GOT TO GO BACK!
TRY THE T.N.T. STORE, CHARLEY!
INSIDE, THERE WERE FIELDS OF SHELLS ... DESTINED FOR THE WESTERN FRONT.
MA!
A3
A4
THE HUGE FACTORY OF DEATH WAS SILENT . . . DESERTED.
MA!
E6
CHARLEY COULD HEAR THE BOMBS FALLING OUTSIDE...
PHEW! THAT SOUNDED CLOSE!
PHEW! THAT SOUNDED CLOSE!
... BRINGING BACK MEMORIES OF HIS NIGHTMARE MONTHS IN THE TRENCHES!

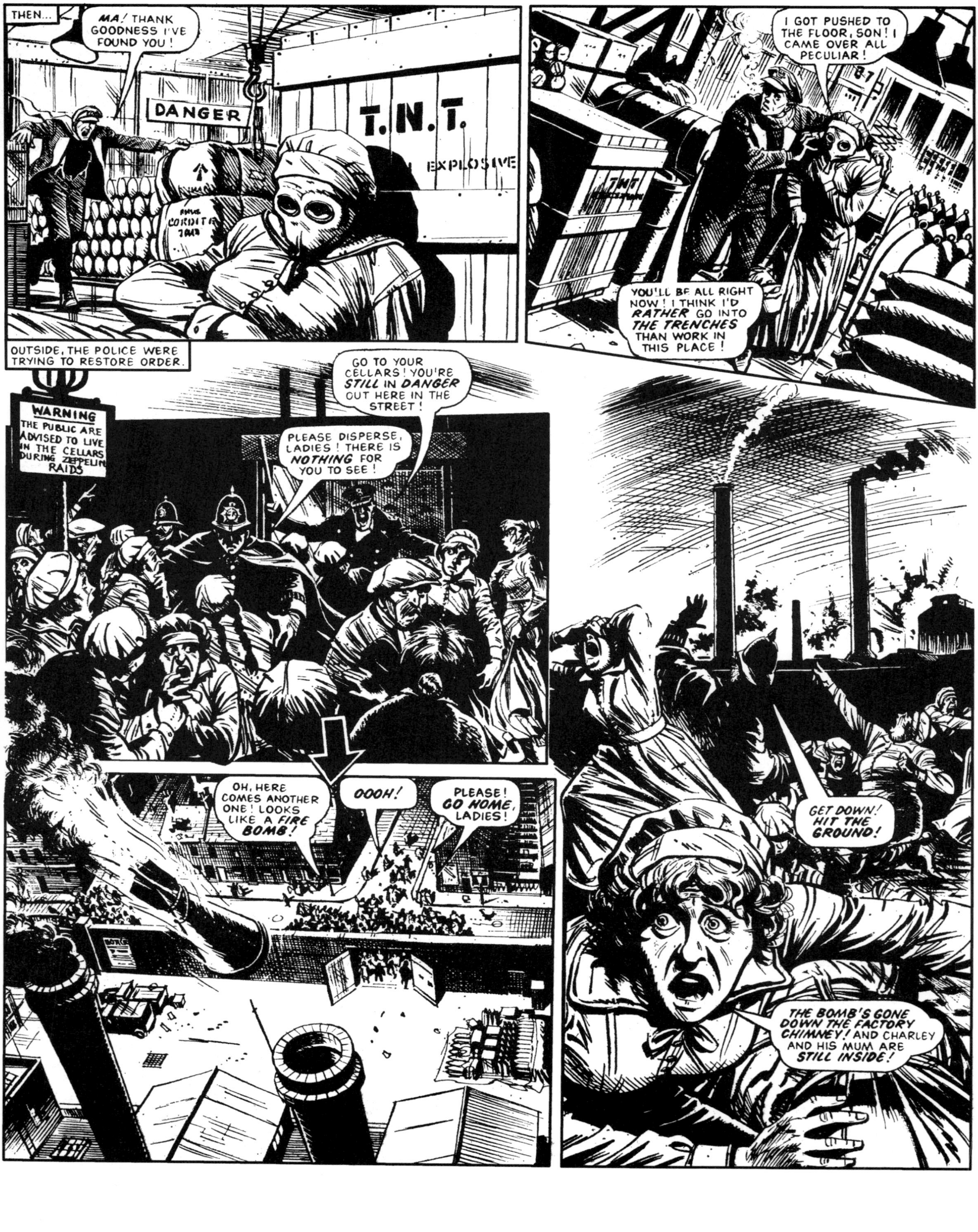
THEN...
MA! THANK GOODNESS I'VE FOUND YOU!
DANGER
T.N.T.
EXPLOSIVE
CORDITE
I GOT PUSHED TO THE FLOOR, SON! I CAME OVER ALL PECULIAR!
YOU'LL BE ALL RIGHT NOW! I THINK I'D RATHER GO INTO THE TRENCHES THAN WORK IN THIS PLACE!
OUTSIDE, THE POLICE WERE TRYING TO RESTORE ORDER.
WARNING THE PUBLIC ARE ADVISED TO LIVE IN THE CELLARS DURING ZEPPELIN RAIDS
GO TO YOUR CELLARS! YOU'RE STILL IN DANGER OUT HERE IN THE STREET!
PLEASE DISPERSE, LADIES! THERE IS NOTHING FOR YOU TO SEE!
OH, HERE COMES ANOTHER ONE! LOOKS LIKE A FIRE BOMB!
OOOH!
PLEASE! GO HOME, LADIES!
GET DOWN! HIT THE GROUND!
THE BOMB'S GONE DOWN THE FACTORY CHIMNEY! AND CHARLEY AND HIS MUM ARE STILL INSIDE!

STRIP COMMENTARY

by Pat Mills

MOMENTS LATER, THE TOMMIES BEGAN THEIR CRAZY, DESPERATE BREAK-OUT FROM "THE SCRUBS"...

COME ON, THE WESTSHIRES!

EPISODE ONE

The Donkey Men seem – like so many aspects of World War One – totally bizarre, yet they were authentic. I don't have the imagination to dream them up. Joe's artwork continues to bring the trench war totally alive. I'm often asked whether I'd consider doing something with *Charley's War* today – whether in comic strip, film or prose novel. Looking at these pages, it's hard to see how, because Joe's art is 50% of *Charley's War* and without his contribution, it would be an entirely different story.

EPISODE TWO

Although this battle with the Judgement Troopers is fictional, it is still a combination of a number of genuine separate action incidents. The heroism and non-stop action may seem a little *Ripping Yarns* for some and the serial has been criticised for showing such supposedly "unlikely" scenes. However, it is taken from a number of sources, including some upbeat and dramatic accounts of life in the trenches written and published during the Great War. One of the authors was Patrick MacGill, I recall. It's unlikely books that showed such "derring-do" would be reprinted today, because the accepted wisdom for our generation is that the conflict was unrelentingly boring, grim and nightmarish, with little room for more than just the very rare act of personal heroism. This has the unfortunate – and , I believe, entirely calculated – effect of diminishing the efforts of the individual. It makes the ordinary soldier (and we, the readers) seem powerless in the face of Armageddon.

EPISODE THREE

The conversation between the German Major and Colonel Zeiss, during which they discuss the inhumanity of poison gas and shrapnel, seems a little naïve now; yet it is worth remembering that the Germans saw the tank as an inhumane weapon of mass destruction. Today, we have been conditioned to accept it as an entirely legitimate weapon.

EPISODES FOUR TO FIVE

The humour in *Charley's War* has aged well, because we can all relate to its cynicism. Thus a soldier tells Charley to shut the door of a destroyed building: "You're letting the cold in." While I was writing the serial, I submitted a proposal for a TV comedy called *Over the Top* about World War One. Loosely based on *Charley's War*, it was an *Upstairs, Downstairs* in the trenches with an officer like Lieutenant Snell ringing a bell in his dug-out for his servant to bring him tea. It never got beyond proposal stage, but I was delighted to see – many years later – *Blackadder Goes Forth* bringing out the dark humour of the trenches. It's one of my favourite comedies. Today, cruel characters like Doctor "No" and the Officer who sends Charley and his mates back to the trenches would not be out of place in *League of Gentlemen* or *Little Britain*.

WHAT'S WRONG WITH YOU?

MY TEETH HAVE BEEN KNOCKED OUT BY SHRAPNEL, SIR.

WELL, WE DON'T WANT YOU TO BITE THE GERMANS. FIT FOR DUTY! NEXT!

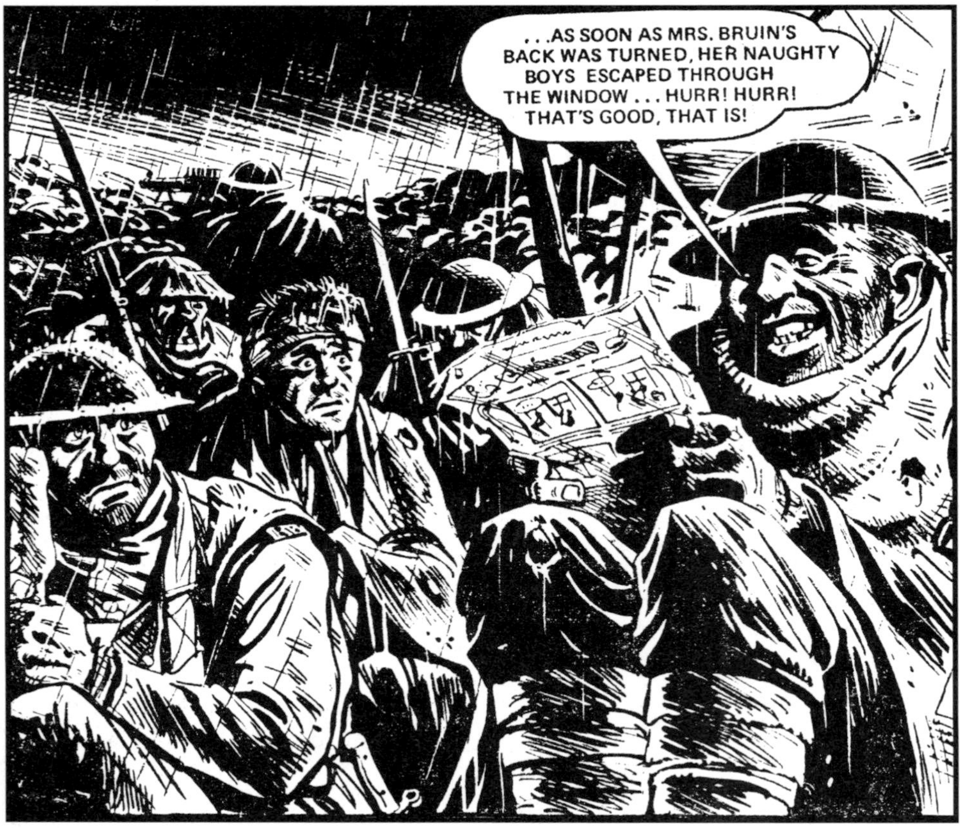
. . .AS SOON AS MRS. BRUIN'S BACK WAS TURNED, HER NAUGHTY BOYS ESCAPED THROUGH THE WINDOW . . . HURR! HURR! THAT'S GOOD, THAT IS!

EPISODE SIX

"Sandbag Pud" – what a wonderful idea! Only the British Tommy could dream that up.

EPISODES SEVEN TO EIGHT

The 'Queue of Death' sequence is very powerful and valid, although the Germans feel a bit arch for my taste today. If I was writing this now, I would still have them executing the Tommies – but in a less sadistic, even matter-of-fact way.

Editorial added that panel on page four: "The young soldier saw sorrow in his comrades' eyes, but also a grim resolve." I suppose they thought they had to further justify the soldiers' actions. It's unnecessary. Please ignore it.

EPISODE NINE

A brilliant opening pic from Joe. And the *Rainbow* comic is featured here! The look on Charley and co.'s faces as the soldier reads about Mrs. Bruin's naughty boys is sublime!

EPISODE TEN

The evil of the minds that dreamt up combining two gases so the Tommies would take off their masks is unspeakable. It was pointed out to me recently that the two-pronged gas attack is something echoed in modern terror tactics, whereby an initial bomb is then followed up with a second, activated a short time later, designed to maximise casualties and fatalities to the 'first responders' – police, fire, medical etc.

EPISODE ELEVEN

Champagne in the machine gun?!! I can hear some young establishment historian saying now, "Nonsense! That never happened." But, like the claim that the Tommies never brewed tea with the machine-gun's boiling water, he would be wrong.

EPISODE TWELVE

The character of Smith 70 was based on Doug Church, the art editor of *2000 AD*, who designed the visual look of the "galaxy's greatest comic".

EPISODE THIRTEEN

Editorial introduced this terrible *Charley's War* logo. How awful and inappropriate. It's like something out of a circus.

The Battle Police shoot deserters on the spot. This will possibly be disputed by a reader who wrote me a well-researched 'hate' letter a few months ago. He objected to the anti-war stance of the series and questioned the number of executions of deserters, challenging minor details for their authenticity. He particularly objected to a scene I showed – reprinted in Volume Two – where Tommies were tied by their wrists and feet to gun wheels during "Field Punishment Number One". He said they were only tied by their wrists. Therefore I was a liar and also a fascist whom the Kaiser would be proud of.

EPISODE FOURTEEN

Colonel Zeiss seems a bit arch today and his neo-Nazi characterisation clearly shows the benefit of hindsight. Despite that, he still works for me. I think he was a good villain.

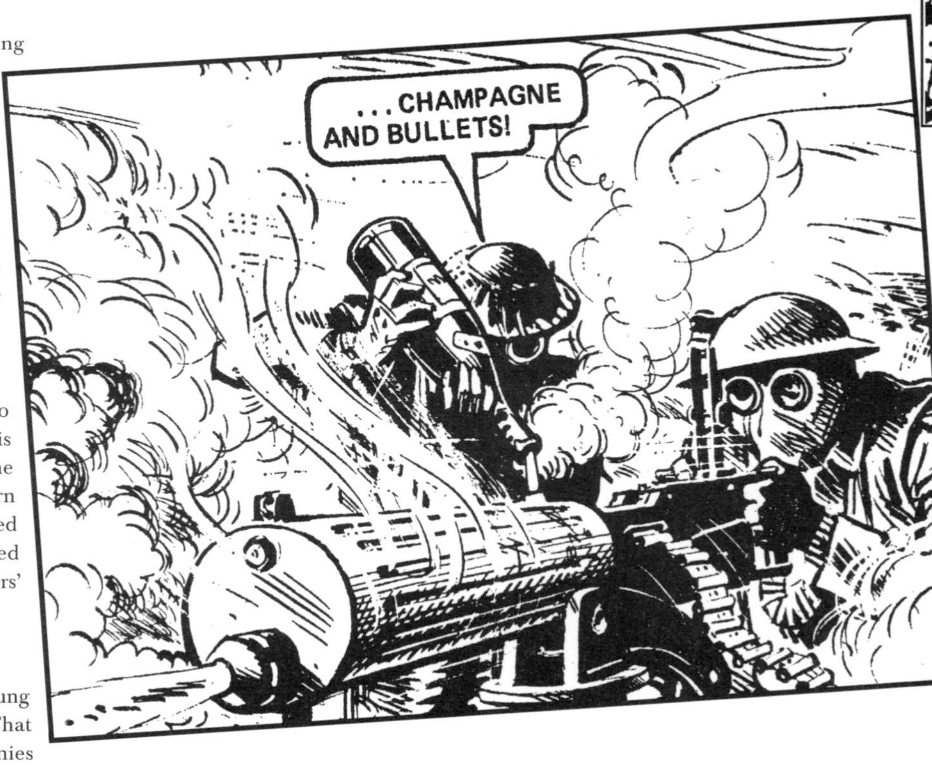
. . . CHAMPAGNE AND BULLETS!

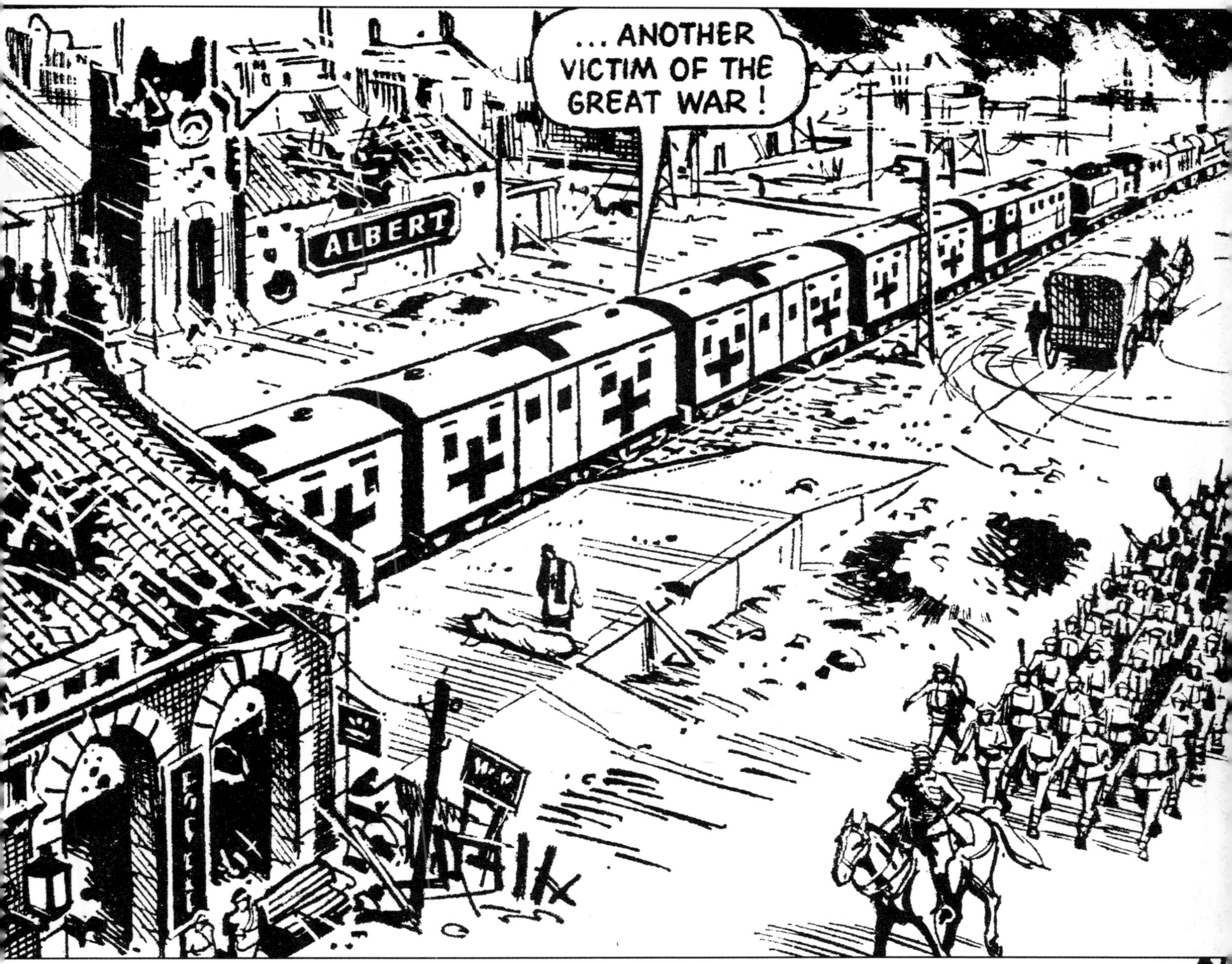

... ANOTHER VICTIM OF THE GREAT WAR!
ALBERT

EPISODE FIFTEEN

The final picture on the last page of this episode is worth lingering on. I'm 99% certain that the poignancy of this scene was created by Joe. I certainly don't recall writing it. It shows one train with wounded leaving in one direction, while fresh cannon fodder head off in the opposite direction. Left behind, on a platform positioned strategically between them, is a dead soldier going only to his grave. This is poetic and truly moving. The detail is astonishing and the movie-style down-shot is fabulous. Many a film director would envy it. And it's depicted in just a quarter of a page, too. This could explain why it has been overlooked as an iconic image. I'd like to see it much larger. Congratulations again, Joe. You remain my all-time favourite artist.

EPISODE SIXTEEN

By now *Charley's War* was so popular that editorial wanted it to appear on the cover every week, so they asked me to write the story in such a way as to generate strong cover images. Given the anti-war nature of the story, this was rather demanding and, inevitably, we would not always agree on what would make a good comic cover. So when editorial didn't like my ideas, they were relegated to ordinary-sized pictures in the story. This is what happened to my first abortive cover, which is seen here squashed into panel one. Based closely on a dramatic *Stern* magazine cover I found, it shows Charley drowning in mud in his hospital bed. I suspect editorial thought it too horrific or "lacking in action".

The ludicrous machine designed to cure post-traumatic stress disorder is taken from a reference I sent Joe. Even today PTSD is still not fully acknowledged or understood and its symptoms are often confused with conventional mental illness. Perhaps traumatic amnesia had something to do with why the soldiers declared in their song, "We'll never tell them." Many Tommies must have mercifully forgot the horrors of the trenches.

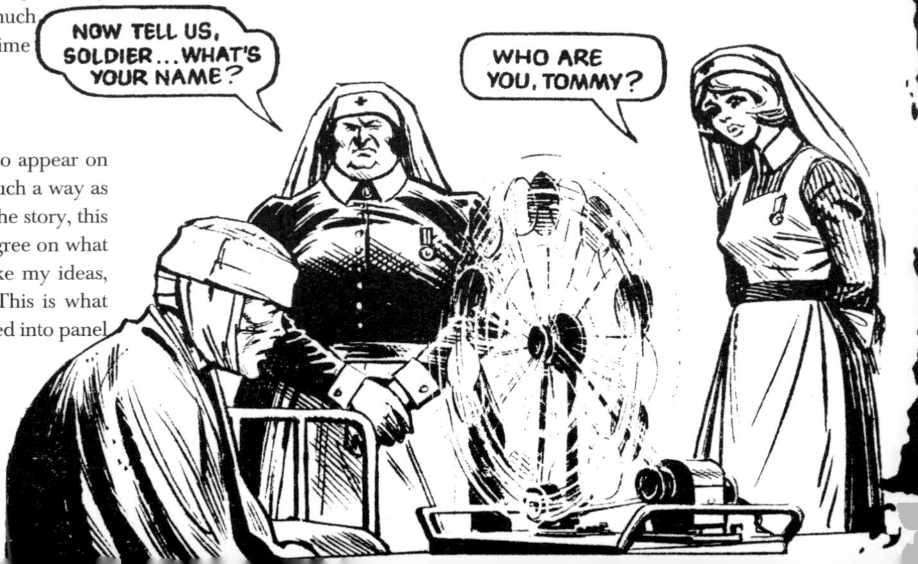

NOW TELL US, SOLDIER... WHAT'S YOUR NAME?
WHO ARE YOU, TOMMY?

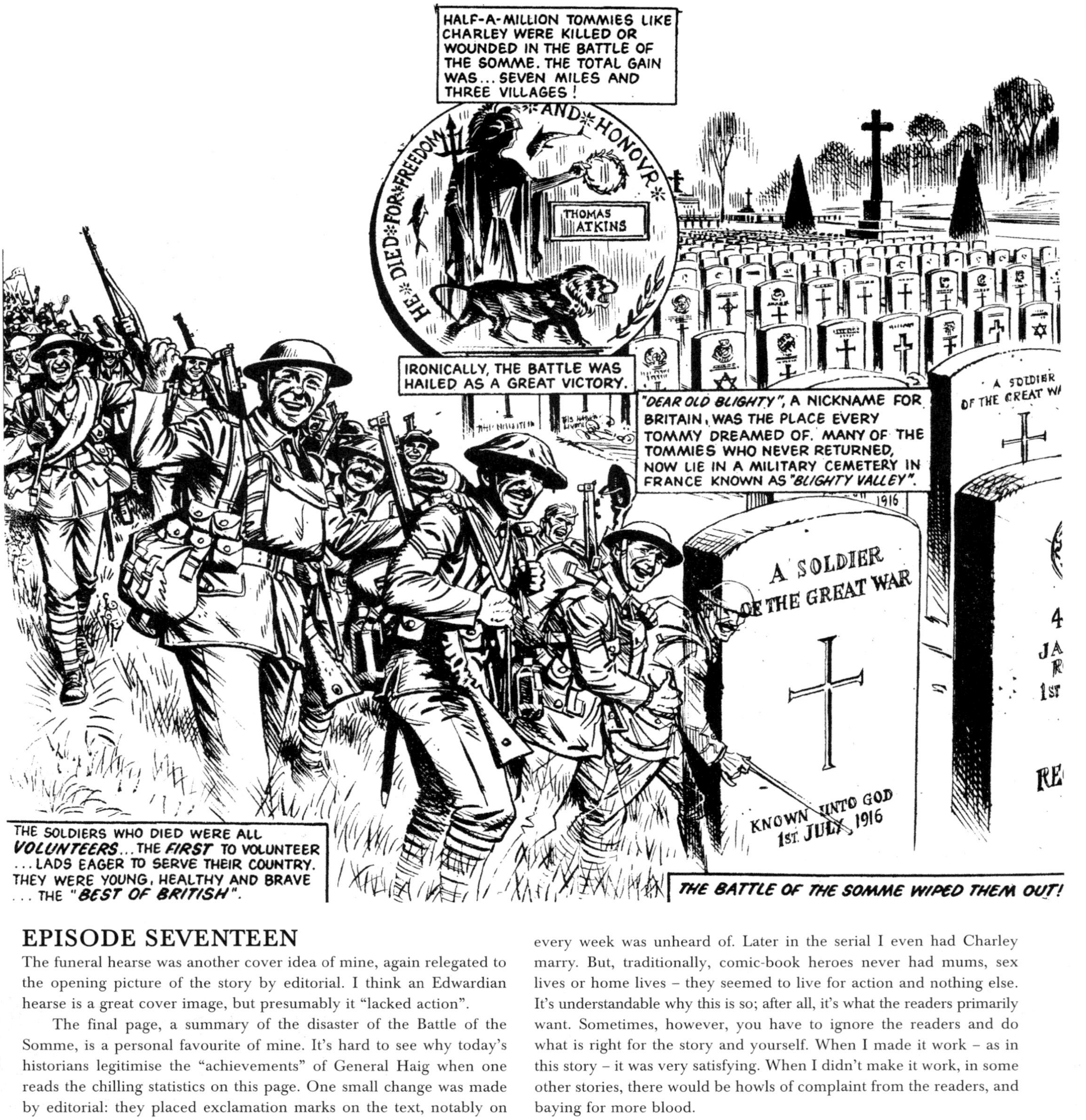
HALF-A-MILLION TOMMIES LIKE CHARLEY WERE KILLED OR WOUNDED IN THE BATTLE OF THE SOMME. THE TOTAL GAIN WAS... SEVEN MILES AND THREE VILLAGES!
HE DIED FOR FREEDOM AND HONOUR
THOMAS ATKINS
IRONICALLY, THE BATTLE WAS HAILED AS A GREAT VICTORY.
"DEAR OLD BLIGHTY", A NICKNAME FOR BRITAIN, WAS THE PLACE EVERY TOMMY DREAMED OF. MANY OF THE TOMMIES WHO NEVER RETURNED, NOW LIE IN A MILITARY CEMETERY IN FRANCE KNOWN AS "BLIGHTY VALLEY".
A SOLDIER OF THE GREAT WAR
A SOLDIER OF THE GREAT WAR
KNOWN UNTO GOD
1ST. JULY, 1916
THE SOLDIERS WHO DIED WERE ALL VOLUNTEERS... THE FIRST TO VOLUNTEER ...LADS EAGER TO SERVE THEIR COUNTRY. THEY WERE YOUNG, HEALTHY AND BRAVE ... THE "BEST OF BRITISH".
THE BATTLE OF THE SOMME WIPED THEM OUT!

EPISODE SEVENTEEN

The funeral hearse was another cover idea of mine, again relegated to the opening picture of the story by editorial. I think an Edwardian hearse is a great cover image, but presumably it "lacked action".

The final page, a summary of the disaster of the Battle of the Somme, is a personal favourite of mine. It's hard to see why today's historians legitimise the "achievements" of General Haig when one reads the chilling statistics on this page. One small change was made by editorial: they placed exclamation marks on the text, notably on "The Battle of the Somme wiped them out!", which seems so unnecessary. It would have been far more effective without an exclamation mark.

EPISODE EIGHTEEN

The need to start the stories on the front cover meant the stories would sometimes be rather jerky in order to devise a suitably powerful visual to begin each episode. This is a case in point. But at least it had action, which is why editorial approved it as a cover. The appalling, arch dialogue on the cover makes me cringe. It was added by editorial. It is really dreadful. Please ignore it.

This is where Charley's 'Home Front' story begins. It's worth stressing how risky this was as a concept. Until *Charley's War*, the idea of a hero having a home life and not being in front-line action against the enemy every week was unheard of. Later in the serial I even had Charley marry. But, traditionally, comic-book heroes never had mums, sex lives or home lives – they seemed to live for action and nothing else. It's understandable why this is so; after all, it's what the readers primarily want. Sometimes, however, you have to ignore the readers and do what is right for the story and yourself. When I made it work – as in this story – it was very satisfying. When I didn't make it work, in some other stories, there would be howls of complaint from the readers, and baying for more blood.

EPISODE NINETEEN

Again, there's a bit of a jerk between episodes here, because of the need for strong cover images. It's a pity, especially as my cover idea was turned down. This time I intended to show the Silvertown disaster as the cover; a truly apocalyptic event in the history of London. Editorial didn't think a scene of total desolation would make a good visual and relegated it to the story proper. I disagree; it just required more effort and design – street signs amidst the debris, the ruined interior of a terraced house, a discarded child's toy and so forth. But action covers are always "safer". This ongoing disparity of views emphasises what a maverick story *Charley's War* was in mainstream British comics. And still is.

Why is there that ludicrous Teutonic-styled logo on page one? How inappropriate.
The exquisitely drawn children singing "The Hymn of Hate" at the end of the episode seems the stuff of fantasy, but children would sing patriotic songs as their fathers went off to war in their Zeppelins. And I recall in the '70s, when the warships returned home from the Falklands, naval families greeted them singing Rod Stewart's "Sailing".

EPISODE TWENTY

A nice, safe, action cover here – editorial must have liked this one. The dialogue was added by them. Please ignore it. The Super Zeppelins may seem archaic now but they were the equivalent of the invisible Stealth bombers today. Zeppelins were known as the "Baby Killers"; an appropriate name for modern bombers, too. Then, as now, governments like to present their super weapons – planes, tanks, and missiles – as totally invulnerable, to terrorise and intimidate civilian populations. It reminds me of when the Serbs shot down a Stealth Bomber attacking Belgrade; they waved a banner for the CNN cameras saying, "We're sorry, America – we didn't know your planes were invisible."

EPISODE TWENTY-ONE

The opening picture was once again designed to be a cover, but clearly editorial thought it was too passive. Colchester is my home town so it's often featured in my stories.

The observation car and sound detectors featured in this episode put the "steampunk" fantasies of science fiction writers in the shade.

EPISODE TWENTY-TWO

Finally, a cover that both the writer and the editor liked! Although the colouring on it was fairly average, so it's just as well you are seeing it in black and white. This episode was reprinted recently in the *Judge Dredd Megazine*, just after the recent London Underground bombings.

It's chilling how at that time even the Underground wasn't safe. Often the Underground is presented in films as a welcoming "Spirit of the Blitz" shelter, but it was certainly not the intention of the authorities that it should be. During the Great War, people had to *force* their way down into the subway.

EPISODE TWENTY-THREE

I think Charley cycling on his bike must have been another cover that never happened. If so, editorial were absolutely right; it would have looked pretty flat. Now the next scene, with people rioting, would have made a strong cover, but there's no way I'd have got away with it. The ugly scenes of racism against Russians mistaken for Germans have their parallels in recent times. Then – as now – the popular press whipped up hatred against "the enemy within."

EPISODE TWENTY-FOUR

I went to great lengths to find the correct fire engine reference for the cover. In retrospect, this cover is too traditional for my taste and I wish I had thought of something more in keeping with the anti-war mood of the story. But it had action, so editorial were happy. Thankfully they didn't add any embarrassing dialogue from the firemen!

I particularly like the scene of Sir James scuttling off for Knightsbridge. The traditional propaganda image of the upper classes and the working classes all suffering together in wartime is open to question. No; the working classes suffered far more. As they lived around the munitions factories, they were a prime target and there is some evidence that wealthier parts of London were deliberately not bombed by the Germans. It is something I intended to explore in detail if I had ever written Charley into World War Two. I recall reading that in 1939 the authorities' first move – after the declaration of war – was not to make air-raid shelters for the East End, but to order an enormous quantity of coffins.

I sent Joe references of the factory of death and he has done an excellent job in depicting the fields of shells. Look at the letters on the sides of the posts – it gives you some idea of the vastness of the place. It must have been bigger than an airport car park. I think the scene where Charley runs through the empty factory shouting out "Ma!" would make a great cover. These "fields of shells" scenes really are classics and would benefit from enlarging or recreating by a suitable artist to fully appreciate their power.

The penultimate picture where a bomb is about to drop down a factory chimney is a masterpiece. The intricate detail of the streets below and the angle the bomb is falling are magnificent. A movie-maker could not have done better. We are left wondering… Is there is going to be a second Silvertown disaster? +

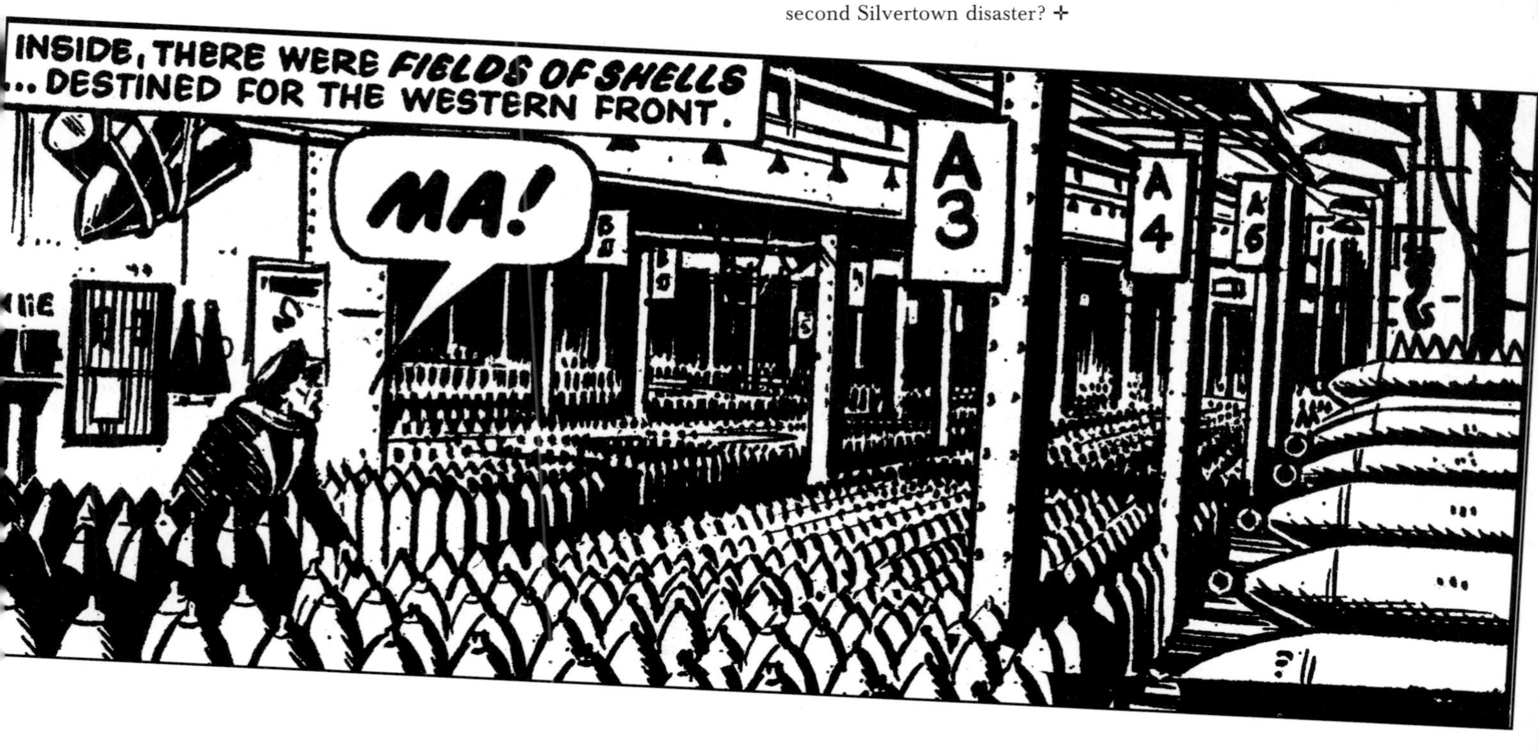
INSIDE, THERE WERE FIELDS OF SHELLS
... DESTINED FOR THE WESTERN FRONT.
MA!
A 3
A 4
A 6

ALSO AVAILABLE FROM TITAN BOOKS

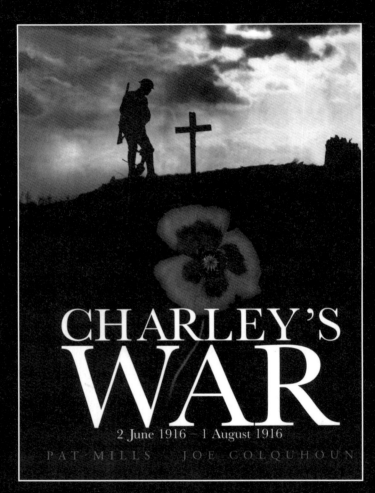

ISBN: 1 84023 627 2

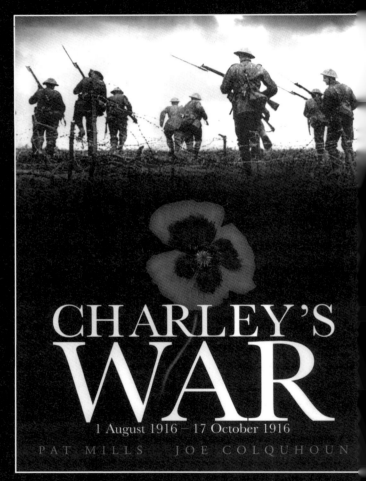

ISBN: 1 84023 929 8

COMING SOON
VOLUME 4

OCTOBER 2007

www.titanbooks.com

ACC. No: 02560030

ACC. No: 02560030